A Hare-Marked Moon

A Hare-Marked Moon

From Bhutan to Yorkshire:
The Story of an English Stupa

David Lascelles

Best wishes

David Willes

and from Manoj Joshi

U

unbound

Dec 2022

First published in 2021

Unbound
Level 1, Devonshire House, One Mayfair Place, London W1J 8AJ
www.unbound.com

Text design by Ellipsis, Glasgow

A CIP record for this book is available from the British Library

ISBN 978-1-78352-930-8 (hardback)
ISBN 978-1-78352-931-5 (ebook)

Printed in Great Britain by CPI Group (UK)

1 3 5 7 9 8 6 4 2

Homage to Tara!
Eyes like lightning instantaneous . . .
Resplendent as a thousand stars . . .
Joyous, radiant . . .
Holding in her hand the hare-marked moon.
From 'Praises to the Twenty-One Taras'[1]

Contents

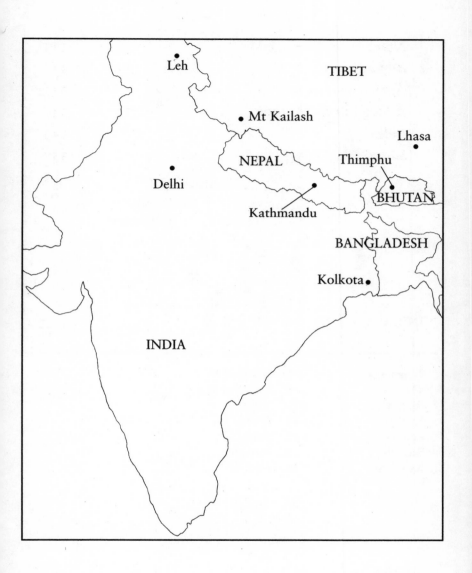

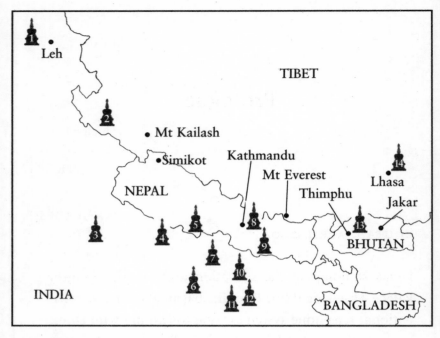

Prologue

I was standing in the reception area of the Gangtey Palace Hotel in Paro, Bhutan, battling with the international telephone system, trying to call my wife Diane back in England. Watching me with some amusement were four Bhutanese monks. We were due to fly early the next morning to Delhi and then on to England a couple of days later. The monks were coming to build a stupa, a Buddhist monument, in the grounds of my family's home, Harewood House in Yorkshire. For all of us it was a step into the unknown. None of the Bhutanese had ever been on an aeroplane before or travelled outside the Himalayan region; they had never driven on a motorway or seen the ocean. Two of them, including Lama Sonam, a master builder of stupas who was to supervise the project, spoke no English. I had no idea how they would react to a wholly unfamiliar environment, both physical and cultural: the language barrier, the weather, the food, the Yorkshire sense of humour.

I finally got through to Diane and we discussed arrangements: when we would be flying, how we would get to Yorkshire from the airport, who would be there when we arrived, and so on.

'How are you feeling?' she asked.

I thought for a moment. I knew that having the opportunity to be involved in building a stupa was seen as something very special by Buddhists. But what kind of a Buddhist was I? Was I a Buddhist at all? How was it all actually going to work when the Bhutanese reached England? I had no idea. It was a good question. How *was* I feeling?

'David? Are you still there?'

'Well,' I said, 'I think this is either the best or the stupidest thing I've ever done in my life.'

THE BUDDHA DIES: NORTH INDIA, c. 500 BCE

The monsoon was coming. The forests around the settlement of Kushinagar were thick with heat as the parched north Indian plains awaited the liberating, revivifying rains. The Buddha sat with his disciples under a tree by a stream on the outskirts of a small village, sheltering from the sun. He was eighty years old and had been on the road for more than fifty years, criss-crossing what are now the northern Indian states of Bihar and Uttar Pradesh on foot, living simply, teaching tirelessly. He was suffering from severe abdominal pains, brought on by the meal he had eaten the night before. His disciple Ananda was upset and angry with Cunda the blacksmith who had prepared the food that he could see was poisoning his teacher. Cunda was beside himself with remorse. The Buddha reassured them both that Cunda was not to blame. He knew his body was wearing out and the time of his death had come. The meal Cunda had prepared was, he said, one of the best he had ever eaten. Cunda should be happy that he had cooked the last meal that he, the Buddha, would eat on this earth.

The Buddha asked his disciples to make a bed for him on the forest floor between two trees. He lay on his right side, his head resting on his bent right arm, his left arm lying gently on his thigh, legs stretched out straight and relaxed. The Buddha and his disciples knew that he was dying. 'Birth is exhausted. The holy life has been lived out. What was to be done is done. There is no more of this to come,' he said.

Ananda begged the Buddha to let them find a more auspicious place in which to pass his final hours; not here in the middle of nowhere in what Ananda disparagingly called 'this little mud-walled town, this backwoods town, this branch township', but somewhere that was home to his many devoted followers, who would be only too willing to help look after him. The Buddha scolded Ananda gently. 'This was once the capital of a great kingdom,' he said. 'The streets were full of magnificent horses pulling carriages. Music filled the air. It was a beautiful place. We are in the right place.'

He asked Ananda if he or any of the other disciples had any questions to ask him, anything that was not clear from the teachings he had been giving them.

'Ask, my students, so that you may not regret it afterwards.'

The disciples were silent.

'Perhaps you do not ask because you are in awe of your teacher,' the Buddha suggested, teasing them.

The disciples still said nothing. Then Ananda spoke: 'I do believe there is not one of us with a doubt or a problem concerning what you have taught us.'

The Buddha smiled. 'It is the nature of everything that takes form that it will dissolve. Work out your own salvation with diligence.'

And so saying he died.

In the sweltering heat of the Ganges plain, cremation generally takes place quickly after death. This was no ordinary occasion, however. The Buddha's body was prepared for the funeral pyre in a way befitting a great prince: he was wrapped in cloth and covered in offerings of flowers and incense, before lying in state for a week. Word spread rapidly and his many followers gathered at Kushinagar: beggars, farmers, holy men, merchants and envoys from the rulers of the eight great kingdoms of the region.

Eight factions, all gathered in a state of considerable emotional distress in a remote spot in the Ganges plain, dripping with heat and humidity in the time just before the monsoon. Was there enough food, enough water for what must have quickly become a considerable gathering? Under these circumstances, it is not hard to imagine the situation becoming quite tense. First there was the build-up to the cremation and then the long wait for the flames of the funeral pyre to die down so they could collect the Buddha's relics from the ashes.*

This episode is often referred to as the 'War of the Relics', but one suspects it was more of an uneasy standoff between competing clans than some kind of confrontation involving soldiers and fighting. Like so many Buddhist tales, there is the literal meaning and there is the underlying metaphor. The fact that there was conflict at all does not reflect well on the participants, or their ability to put into practice what the Buddha had taught them. They were flawed human beings like any others, subject to the same emotions and tensions. But at least the episode has a satisfactorily balanced Buddhist conclusion.

The Mallas, the ruling clan of Kushinagar, the place where the Buddha died, initially assumed that they

---

* After the cremation of a great teacher or Buddhist master, pearl-like objects called *ringsel* in Tibetan (*sarirah* in Sanskrit) can often be found in the ashes. Scientific analysis has shown that they consist mainly of bone, compressed and crystallised by heat. It does not explain, however, why they are only found after the cremation of an enlightened being.

would be the sole guardians of his remains, that they alone would have the responsibility of building a repository for his ashes. What an opportunity this must have seemed, the chance to transform a sleepy backwater into an important place of pilgrimage, while at the same time paying suitable homage to the great teacher. Any such illusions were quickly dispelled by the arrival of representatives of the rulers of the neighbouring kingdoms where the Buddha had lived and taught. Each had their own ideas about what should happen to the ashes and the jewel-like relics that had been found in them. Though the Buddha's teaching stressed the sanctity of life, the virtues of tolerance and a gentle, pastoral, contemplative existence, this was a time of turbulent and often violent political uncertainty. Take Ajatashatru, for example, the young and dynamic ruler of Maghada, one of the most powerful kingdoms in the region. He had imprisoned his own father, Bimbisara – one of the Buddha's earliest and most steadfast supporters – and left him to die before repenting of his actions and taking teachings from the Buddha. Or Prasenajit, the hot-headed young King of Kosala, who, just a few years earlier, had responded to a perceived insult by the Sakyas, inhabitants of the small kingdom in north India where the Buddha himself was born, by massacring several thousand of them.

It was King Ajatashatru's representative who was the first to speak out: 'The Blessed One was a warrior; we too are warriors. We are most worthy of a share of the Blessed One's bones. We will build a monument to contain them and perform ceremonies in honour of them.'

Representatives of the other neighbouring kingdoms had equally strong views on why the Buddha's ashes should have their final resting place on their land and theirs alone. The Sakyas of Kapilavastu felt they had a special claim. Their kingdom was where the Buddha had been born and raised: 'He was the greatest of our blood; we too are worthy of a share. We too will build a monument and perform ceremonies.'

But the initial reaction of the Mallas of Kushinagar was to dig in their heels: 'We will not give up the bones of the Blessed One.'

Trouble was brewing. But what were the Buddha's closest followers – his personal attendant Ananda, his cousin Anuruddha, his son Rahul, Mahakassapa who actually lit the funeral pyre, and the rest – doing during all this? It does not seem that they intervened in the dispute, or tried to act as mediators. Were they too preoccupied with supervising the process of the cremation to notice the political tension? Or did they, as true followers of the Buddha's teachings, see it as inappropriate for them to become involved in what was developing into a sordid, materialistic dispute, one that might even turn violent? Perhaps they were simply overwhelmed by the situation.

One of the Buddha's followers did rise to the occasion, however – the Brahman Drona. Drona's most significant previous involvement is described in the Drona Sutra. This tells how he is walking down a road where the Buddha has recently travelled. In the dust he sees miraculous footprints, each step imprinted with a wheel with a thousand spokes. He follows the trail to where the Buddha sits in meditation under a tree. Filled with wonder by what he sees, Drona asks what sort of being he is:

'Are you a *deva* [the god of gods]?'

'No.'

'A *gandharva* [a celestial musician]?'

'No.'

'A *yakkha* [a deity to whom a sacrifice must be made]?'

'No.'

'A human being?'

'I am none of these,' the Buddha replies. 'I am simply awake.'

A wonderfully crisp answer, but Drona does not understand, so the Buddha gives him a more poetic explanation:

'Like a blue lotus, rising up, unsmeared by water, unsmeared am I by the world, and so, brahman, I'm awake.'[1]

Drona becomes a devoted follower and is with his teacher at the end. Faced with an escalating crisis, he takes a very practical approach. His is a classic Buddhist Middle Way: a compromise, but also politically astute. He begs the disputants to remember the teachings of the Buddha, to remember what he had taught them about forbearance:

'How can we allow a dispute about the remains of he who was the best of beings to become the cause of strife and wounds and war? Let us all unite in harmony and agree to make up eight parts. Let us divide up and distribute the Blessed One's bones fairly and let stupas be built in every land, so that in Buddha's light mankind may trust.'[2]

It seems that none of the representatives of the eight kingdoms was spoiling for a fight. They simply wanted what was fair, as they saw it, and so they quickly agreed to Drona's proposal. When the embers of the great funeral pyre had cooled, the ashes and relics were divided and each took away their share. Eight stupas were built to house them, each marking a place of significance in the Buddha's life.

The Sakyas of Kapilavastu built their stupa at Lumbini where the Buddha was born.

Another stupa was built at Bodhgaya where the Buddha achieved enlightenment.

The third stupa was built at Sarnath, where the Buddha gave his first teaching.

A fourth was at Jetavana Grove in Shravasti, where the Buddha would often teach during the rainy season.

A fifth was at Sankashya, where the Buddha is said to have descended from heaven where he was giving teachings to his late mother.

The sixth stupa was built by Ajatashatru, King of

Maghada, at Rajgir, where the Buddha and his followers were first given land.

The seventh was at Vaishali, the capital city of the Licchavis, the place where he informed his followers of his imminent death.

The eighth was at Kushinagar, the place of his death.

As the centuries passed, Buddhism spread across Asia, adapting its teachings to the culture of each country where it took root. In each country, too, the shape of the stupas they built to commemorate the Buddha and his followers underwent a change. In time, the teachings reached Tibet, high on its plateau behind the great wall of the Himalayas. There, eight different designs evolved, each linked to the eight places where the relics were housed.[*]

WHAT IS A STUPA?

In Sanskrit, the ancient language in which much of the literature of India's classical philosophy is written, 'stupa' has a literal meaning of 'heap' or 'pile'. At its simplest, a physical description would be: a pile of earth, a mound. It is likely that the word was originally used to describe some kind of burial mound, probably for a ruler or dignitary.

---

[*] There are many versions of the events surrounding the Buddha's death and its immediate aftermath. I've drawn on a whole range of them and put them into my own words.

Burial mounds are found across many cultures, not just in India or the Himalayas. There are chambered cairns in the Orkneys, long barrows in Oxfordshire, tumuli all across Eastern Europe, *kurgans* in the steppes of Russia and Ukraine, burial mounds in the North American plains, all of them variations on the same theme. North India was no exception. The Buddha talks to his disciple Ananda about the custom in his own culture of erecting a mound or a stone cairn at the crossroads to honour a great ruler. 'So should they treat the remains of an Awakened One,' he says – the remains of a spiritual leader as well as a temporal one in other words. On another occasion, the Buddha is sitting with a group of his students under the shade of a bodhi tree. One of them asks why a stupa is the shape it is. The Buddha takes the shawl from around his shoulders and folds it until it forms a square base. Then he takes his begging bowl and places it upside down on top of the square of material to make a dome. Finally, he takes the parasol he carries to protect himself from the blazing midday sun, opens it and balances it, handle down, on top of the bowl. The meagre possessions of a wandering holy man, expressing the essential shape of a stupa.

The basic form of the Himalayan stupa is quite simple: the base is a stylised cube made up of a series of stepped ledges; on top of that is a cow-bell-shaped dome; above that a cone-shaped spire made up of thirteen rings with a sheltering umbrella, topped by a half-moon and sun.

While researching and writing this book, I've heard them described as many things: as sculpture, as landmark, as place of worship, as place of pilgrimage, as mandala, as geomantic map-pin, as reliquary shrine. I've heard them compared to the pyramids of ancient Egypt. Someone even told me, very earnestly, that stupas were often used as landing beacons by visiting spacecraft. This was in the 1970s mind you.

A stupa in silhouette   The Harewood Stupa

The most poetic and also the most accurate description is that a stupa is a symbolic representation of the enlightened mind of the Buddha and a guide to the path to achieving it. When I set about commissioning the building of a stupa at Harewood, I had, without fully realising it at the time, also set about exploring that path.

The Buddhist concept of karma says that everything you do happens because of everything you have already done. A Buddhist might even argue that it is everything you have done not just in this life but in previous lifetimes as well. I don't intend to go back quite that far, but I am going to have to jump around a little in time and space to explore how the journey that led to the building of the Harewood Stupa came about.

It turned out to be a strange kind of journey, one with no clear beginning and with an ending that continues to be just out of reach. Every time you think you've got there, you realise you have a little further to go. It's like when you are walking in the hills with no particular destination in mind. I'll just climb this ridge: that looks like the top. Get there, enjoy the view and then head back home. When you arrive, you realise that it isn't the top at all, that there's another ridge beyond, a little higher than the one you just reached. Not too far, though, just one more ascent. But when you get there . . .

As they say in the Himalayas: if you want to see the mountain you're on, you have to climb the other mountain. And one of the things I kept on seeing, looking out from the mountain, was Harewood.

Harewood. A beautiful piece of English countryside, a green oasis nestled between the post-industrial energy of the conurbation of Leeds and the rugged romanticism of the Yorkshire Dales. 'A St Petersburg Palace on a Yorkshire hill', Simon Jenkins called Harewood House in his book *England's Thousand Best Houses*. It is where the Lascelles family, my family, have lived for more than 250 years.

Harewood House was commissioned by Edwin Lascelles (1712–95) and paid for with money his father Henry Lascelles had made in the West Indian sugar trade. This was a time when great fortunes were being made by many in Britain – the Church, the Royal Family, banks and finance houses, artistic and educational establishments as well as many individuals – on the backs of the enslaved Africans who were forcibly shipped to the Caribbean and the Americas to work the plantations that produced luxury goods for the European market: sugar, rum, cotton, tobacco.

Henry and Edwin bought the neighbouring estates of Harewood and Gawthorpe in the 1730s and building work started a little later. Henry didn't live to see it. A few years before the foundations for Harewood House were laid he took his own life, for reasons that are still not clear. Strangely, in a house full of portraits there isn't a single one of Henry, the man without whom none of it would have been possible. His name lives on, though: the eldest son of each subsequent Lascelles generation has Henry as one of his names. I'm David Henry George, but my eldest son is Benjamin George. There are no Henrys in the next generation.

Edwin employed the finest artists and craftsmen of the time for his ambitious and expensive new project.

The architect was John Carr of York. The fashionable young Scottish designer Robert Adam was responsible for the interiors, working with his frequent collaborator, the celebrated cabinetmaker Thomas Chippendale, born just up the road from Harewood in Otley. Joshua Reynolds painted the family portraits. Lancelot 'Capability' Brown designed the landscape. Much of Adam's and Chippendale's work is still in the rooms that they were originally made for and it is widely acknowledged as one of the finest country houses in England, with one of the best historic collections of furniture, paintings and porcelain.

The Victorian era brought many changes. There were thirteen children living there and extra rooms for them and their nannies and governesses were needed. The formidable Lady Louisa, wife of the 3rd Earl, employed Sir Charles Barry, best known as one of the architects of the Houses of Parliament in London, to make alterations. Below stairs the kitchens and servants' quarters were modernised and in some of the rooms above stairs Robert Adam's elegant designs done away with; an extra storey was added to both wings and, most dramatically, a formal terrace garden in the then very fashionable Italian style was interposed between the house and Capability Brown's landscape. Both world wars saw Harewood House used as a convalescent hospital and in the 1930s it became a royal household after the 6th Earl, my grandfather, married Princess Mary, the only daughter of King George V and Queen Mary.

The Lascelles have always been patrons of the arts. The house's builder, Edwin, set high standards with his original commissions. The oldest son of the 1st Earl, Edward, a man of fashion as his nickname 'Beau' suggests, invited two young, unknown artists, J. M. W. Turner and his friend and rival Thomas Girtin, to make watercolours of the new house. Beau also bought pieces of exquisite Sèvres china from the auction houses of revolutionary Paris. The 6th Earl, Harry, used an unexpected legacy to buy one of the finest English collections of Renaissance paintings assembled in the early twentieth century, many of them bought through agents while he was a serving soldier in the trenches of the First World War. The 7th Earl, my father, had a taste for twentieth-century art, including Jacob Epstein's monumental alabaster sculpture *Adam* – the first man in Christian mythology – which is the first thing a visitor sees when they come through the front door of the house. My wife Diane Howse is both an artist and a curator and she created the first designated space for contemporary art in any English country house. Harewood continues to have a lively and innovative programme of contemporary exhibitions alongside its historic collection.

Capability Brown's landscape is the broad sweep, the big picture, but woven into it are a variety of gardens. In front of the house is Barry's carefully controlled Italianate Terrace, with its geometric flowerbeds framed by clipped box hedges. Below it is the lush tropical growth of the Archery Border. The Lakeside Walk takes the visitor round to the Walled Garden, created a little before Harewood House was built, with vegetable plots, fruit orchards and greenhouses, gardening technology and techniques spanning four centuries, not all in good repair as this is written. On the way there is the Himalayan Garden, planted with rhododendrons, primulas and the whole range of Himalayan flora, a blaze of colour in the spring and summer, tranquil and sombre in the winter.

Embedded in this landscape and its gardens are buildings big and small. There is a historic ruin – Harewood Castle, built in the thirteenth century and abandoned some 300 years later. There is a church with fine alabaster tombs. There are working buildings built to support the wider estate as it has developed from the eighteenth century through to the present day: the Stables (now the Courtyard and the hub for day visitors with a café, shop, visitor centre and education suite), and Home Farm (converted to out-of-town offices and renamed Harewood Yard). There are follies like the mysteriously named Seven Eggs in the Pleasure Grounds near the house, where family and guests would walk and picnic in Victorian times.

In 1985 the Harewood House Trust was established, an educational charitable trust that now looks after the house, its contents and gardens for the public benefit. It is part of a group of major country houses known as

The Treasure Houses of England, and receives more than 200,000 visitors every year.

That, in a nutshell, 250 years in a couple of pages, is Harewood. Somewhere quintessentially English, an embodiment of much of what is generally held to be good and admirable in our national heritage.

That's one way of looking at it. But you could also say that Harewood represents privilege, inequality, patriarchy and – that particularly unpleasant characteristic of too many members of the English upper classes – a sense of entitlement. And it was built with money made as direct consequence of the slave trade. My ancestors owned enslaved people. They were far from unique in that, but it's a fact nonetheless. As the eldest son of the eldest son, sooner or later I was going to be expected to take responsibility for it all. How did that feel? What was I going to do about it? How was I going to navigate those dark historic currents? And what does bringing over a group of monks from the Himalayan Kingdom of Bhutan to build a stupa have to do with any of it? This book is an attempt to confront some of those questions.

Part One

First Journeys: Early Days

I was ten when I first went to India, accompanying my father and mother. In the early 1960s my father, George Lascelles, 7th Earl of Harewood, was for five years Artistic Director of the Edinburgh Festival and he was on a scouting mission. He had been invited to Japan to an event called 'The Tokyo East–West Music Encounter'. This involved Western ballet companies and orchestras visiting Japan, still a relatively rare occurrence in those days, as well as performances of Japanese theatre forms like Noh and Kabuki and by visiting dance troupes from India and Thailand. It is only recently I've tried to figure out why my parents took me with them. Maybe they thought travel would broaden my mind. Perhaps it was because their marriage was in trouble – they would separate and divorce a few years later – and my presence meant they were not solely in each other's company. I had no idea about any of this at the time.

The logistics of long-distance flying in those days – the BOAC Comet was de rigueur – meant a stopover in India, both on the way there and on the way back. This was a very grand affair: staying at the British High Commission and meeting the leading Indian artists and performers my father was interested in bringing to Edinburgh. We even had lunch with Prime Minister Jawaharlal Nehru himself. It was quite a few years before I realised that this was not the way most people travelled.

I was a prim little boy who fancied himself as a writer and I kept a journal, recording everything: from the people we met, the places we visited and the performances we saw, to who beat whom at the games of draughts or battleships I seemed to spend quite a lot of my time playing. Looking through an old typewritten copy of this diary I was amazed to find a rather wonky drawing I had made of the spire of a pagoda, which is the Japanese equivalent of a stupa, describing what it is made up of – 'heavenly elements', 'Buddha's umbrella' and so on. Not particularly accurate, but clearly I was interested enough to make such a drawing. It was an interest that didn't bear fruit for more than forty years. But it seems a seed had been quite unwittingly planted.

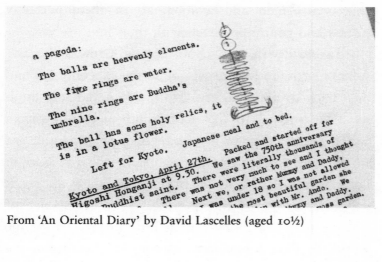

a pagoda:
The balls are heavenly elements.
The five rings are water.
The nine rings are Buddha's umbrella.
The ball has some holy relics, it is in a lotus flower.

Left for Kyoto. Japanese meal and to bed.

Kyoto and Tokyo, April 27th. Packed and started off for Higoshi Honganji at 9.30. We saw the 750th anniversary Buddhist saint. There were literally thousands of There was not very much to see and I thought Next we, or rather Mummy and Daddy, I was under 18 so I was not allowed the most beautiful garden she with Mr. Ando. We ... rgy and Daddy. ... moss garden.

From 'An Oriental Diary' by David Lascelles (aged 10½)

ON THE HIPPY TRAIL, 1969

Nobody called it a gap year in 1969. Years later, I tried to explain to one of my sons that the definition of a gap was that it came between something and something else – between leaving school and going to university, for instance – and was not some kind of open-ended holiday that lasted till you decided what you wanted to do with the rest of your life. My parents and I seem to have agreed quite readily to my spending some of my year off between school and university in India. I think they thought it would build on my earlier trip there with them, broaden my mind. I was mostly interested in hitting the hippy trail and seeing whether it was anything like my wildly romantic image of a sun-drenched beach world populated by beautiful and charismatic men and women, all of them perfectly stoned and getting in touch with their inner selves.

I travelled with two school friends, Drew Smith and Adam Curtis, and we drove round the subcontinent and then back overland to the UK in a battered VW minibus. We listened to the great south Indian musician Subbulakshmi sing in her hometown of Madurai, got stoned on the beach in Goa, watched elephants swim in Lake Periyar, slept in dodgy rat-infested hotels all over. It was a classic hippy trail experience, a real eye-opener for a naïve public schoolboy with little knowledge of the world. In Goa I remember sharing a chillum on the beach with a tall bearded Swiss hippy, the epitome of cool I thought, though I did wonder why he wore his shirt so tightly buttoned at the wrist. I soon found out. He was a morphine junky, hiding his track marks, not very cool at all when he was late for a fix. A few more romantic scales fell from my eyes. The highlight for me was the first time I saw the Himalayas: holed up on a houseboat in Kashmir, smoking a little opium, inviting folk musicians to come and play on the boat, buying food from the tradesmen in their brightly painted *shikaras* that scudded across Dal Lake and watching the giant shadows cast by the evening sun creep up the snow peaks on the far side of the valley. I thought then that Kashmir was the most beautiful place I had ever been to – and I still think that maybe it is.

We drove back overland, a journey that's quite impossible today. Across the India/Pakistan border, through Lahore and up to the Khyber Pass, with an overnight in Peshawar, one of the great border towns, dirty, dangerous, glamorous, romantic, somewhere you could find anything at a price if you knew the right place to go. If you didn't go to the right place, you just might not come back again. The Khyber Pass lived up to its reputation too, the road winding along the valley linking Pakistan and Afghanistan with grim rock faces looming above, perfect for the kind of ambush that had trapped so many armies in the past and would again in the future. But this was an unusually peaceful time in Afghanistan and Kabul was still a beautiful city, well watered, with broad tree-lined avenues, handsome buildings and travellers' cafés playing the Beatles' *White Album*, which had only been released a few weeks before I'd left home, so which I'd hardly heard. It made me feel quite homesick.

There was a problem on the border with Iran. There had been a rumour of a cholera outbreak in Afghanistan and the Iranians were not letting anybody in. People and vehicles piled up at the tiny border outpost – one hotel, one shop, not much sanitation. After a couple of days of this the border was suddenly opened, no explanation given, and we drove slowly in convoy across the couple of miles of no-man's-land. Nervous Iranian border guards with automatic weapons waved us towards a low concrete building where we had to open our passports, show our cholera certificates and join the queue: left for a booster shot, right for a rectal

swab. This was the moment I realised that my certifi-
cate, valid for just six months, had run out a few days
earlier. Booster jab for me. I was almost relieved. Then
we were all put into a quarantine camp, in tents,
behind wire, patrolled by more nervous Iranian soldiers
with guns. It was 20 July 1969 and someone had a
radio and we watched the moon as it rose, knowing
that for the first time, there were human beings on it.
The moon seemed to be sitting particularly low in the
sky that night. 'Fucking Americans have punctured it,'
somebody said.

Coming home was an anti-climax. Of course it was.
I had come back with what felt like a completely new
perspective on the world. At home, though, nothing
seemed to have changed at all, especially at Harewood.
Why should it? What did my little adventure matter
against its great and glorious history?

A few weeks later I started at Bristol University,
Special Drama, one of the very few such courses in the
country at that time. No such thing as Media Studies
in those days. Mine was not a glorious academic career.
I dropped out towards the end of my second year,
though I must say in my defence that I passed all the
exams that I took. I just didn't take all that many. 'I
hope you find what you're looking for, David,' one of
my course tutors said as I left, which puzzled me at the
time. But in a way she was right. There had been major
student riots in Paris the year before and a prolonged
sit-in at the Senate House in Bristol, too. We talked

about politics a lot, usually passionately, often ignorantly. 'I totally understand the Cultural Revolution!' somebody would say. 'Really?' someone else would respond. 'All that violence and killing? I thought you believed in peace and love.' 'It's the only way to free ourselves from the bondage of the past!' And so on. The absolute certainty of youth. And its ability to get it completely wrong.

I was still interested in theatre, but for me this meant the radical theatre of directors like Peter Brook, who was leaving the Royal Shakespeare Company to set up his own company in France, or travelling players like New York's The Living Theatre. And I loved the movies. I would watch everything, anywhere, anytime, several times a week: the French Nouvelle Vague, Akira Kurosawa's great Japanese samurai epics, the forensic documentaries on American institutions by Frederick Wiseman, as well as more mainstream stuff. I was obsessed with Lindsay Anderson's film *If*. It showed me that the attitudes and techniques of the film-makers I admired could be applied to something I thought I knew about and understood – the unfocused and indiscriminate rebelliousness of a public schoolboy. Perhaps I could make movies, too.

Where all this was going I don't think any of us had any idea. Though I'm not in touch with many of them now, people I was at university with have led varied lives, as you would expect. Mostly we haven't changed the world, or not as much as or in the way that we thought we would. If I did learn anything, it was that perhaps there was more than one way of looking at what was around me. That what I was told was true and what my own experiences showed were not necessarily the same thing. It was a while before that turned into anything substantial.

Second Journeys: A Seed Is Sown

We'd decided to go for a walk. A gentle stroll really, down the hill from Harewood House to the lake. The landscape at Harewood was shaped very much with walking in mind, an eighteenth-century creation by the most famous of all English landscape gardeners, Lancelot 'Capability' Brown. 'Nature abhors a straight line', Brown said and at Harewood there are winding paths and vistas and artfully placed plantations, so that wherever you walk there is something of interest: a view back to the house, a woodland stream, a hidden glade, a dramatic reveal. It all looks so natural, but it is all a carefully contrived artifice.

There were four of us that summer Sunday afternoon: Diane and me, Graham Coleman, an old friend from university, and Thupten Jinpa, a young Tibetan scholar. We were coming to the end of a culturally eclectic Harewood weekend. There had been the opening of an exhibition of contemporary art in Diane's Terrace Gallery in Harewood House itself and on Saturday night we were part of the audience for an outdoor performance by Tibetan masked dancers – the reason for Graham and Jinpa's visit. The dancers, dramatically lit by the flames of a huge bonfire, had performed a fire puja, a sacred ritual where the performers wear masks depicting fierce protective Tibetan Buddhist deities, dancing away the forces of ignorance and negativity, to a musical accompaniment of drums and cymbals and the boom and bray of Tibetan horns and trumpets.

The lake we were walking round is artificial, the centrepiece of Capability Brown's creation, formed by digging out and damming a stream, the Beck, to create a suitably impressive body of water when viewed from the grand mansion at the top of the hill. Our route took us along the narrow north-west arm of the lake known as the Channel, the water there deeper and darker than the rest. The path runs quite high above it, winding between dense bushes of rhododendrons and past a bank that a few weeks before had been thick with daffodils. Then it turns sharp left along the top of the dam and at the far end, about a hundred yards away, is a bridge where generations of my family have played Poohsticks and a thirty-foot-high waterfall that turns the lake back into the Beck again, to run straight and rocky for a couple of hundred yards before curving out of sight on its way towards the River Wharfe.

We stopped on the corner and looked back. The afternoon light was warm and low. Ducks and geese and the occasional grebe drifted across the murky stillness of the water. Trees and shrubs from Europe, the Americas and the Himalayas luxuriated in what seemed like perfect harmony. It all looked beautiful, perfectly natural: just the way Capability Brown would have wanted it.

We had been talking about how well the Lama Dance performance had worked the previous evening – surprisingly well, we all agreed, in what might have felt like an incongruous setting. I mentioned that Diane and I had talked a few times about the idea of having a Himalayan feature of some sort at Harewood to go with the Himalayan plants in the gardens. Graham and Jinpa were enthusiastic: a statue or a water-driven prayer wheel perhaps? Or a stupa?

We decided not to walk towards the little bridge but down some rugged stone steps that lead to the Rock Garden, nestled in the hollow behind the steep bank of the dam. There were rhododendrons down there, red, pink, purple and white, and azaleas and some straggly juniper trees clinging precariously to the rocky slope. It is a lovely spot, an area that feels secret, tucked away, apart from the world. A narrow path meanders through it and ends at a set of stepping-stones, which we teetered precariously across, looking back up at the cascade and listening to its watery roar. On the other side of the Beck everything was overgrown and unkempt, the grass waist-high and uncut, not a garden any more, just an area to pass through on your way back up to the path by the bridge that continued round the lake.

This would be a nice spot for a stupa, somebody said.

TIBET: A BUDDHIST TRILOGY, 1976–77

I've been fascinated by stupas ever since I first came into contact with Tibetan Buddhist culture in the 1970s.

Visiting Dharamsala, the Dalai Lama's residence-in-exile in northern India, for the first time in 1976 I would sit and watch Tibetans young and old, many of them only recently arrived from Tibet, muttering mantras and spinning rows of prayer wheels as they slowly circum-ambulated the stupa in the main square. I'd never heard a mantra or seen a stupa or a prayer wheel before. I wasn't even sure what 'circumambulate' meant.

Later on that same trip I went to Boudhanath (Boudha) in the Kathmandu Valley in Nepal for the first time. The Great Stupa there is an impressive structure whatever your religious beliefs – or lack of them, as was pretty much the case with me at that time. It is over 130 feet high, with a huge whitewashed dome that dominates the valley and towers over the circle of buildings that surround it. Boudha has been a significant place for both traders and pilgrims for many centuries, a key staging post between India, the home of Buddhism, and the high mountain plateau of Tibet. It is one of the most important places for Buddhists in the entire Himalayan region, a UNESCO World Heritage Site and one of Nepal's leading tourist attractions, the image you see on magazine covers and travel brochures.

It was not its fame or historical significance that struck me most, however. It was how this massive structure was a natural focus, both for the Tibetans and Nepalis living in the traditional wood and brick houses that encircled it and for the monks from the monasteries in the fields beyond. Every day they would gather, from before dawn to after dark, and circumambulate the stupa. Some had come specifically; others were simply on their way somewhere. Some would make offerings of flowers or incense; others would be deep in prayer, clicking the 108 beads on their *malas* (Buddhist rosaries) as they recited their mantras. But many people simply walked round it, some slowly and thoughtfully, others with a more purposeful stride, always in a clockwise direction. It seemed such a simple and non-doctrinaire way of engaging with your faith: matter-of-fact, relaxed, totally accessible, open to anyone. Although I knew very little about Buddhism at this point, I felt comfortable, at home even at Boudha, and found myself happily and only a little self-consciously joining the steady flow of people walking round, even venturing to spin the occasional prayer wheel. It was probably my first piece of Buddhist practice.

That evening, back at the hotel just off Freak Street, I drifted into sleep, still stoned on black Nepali hash. I dreamed I was in a broad flat shining place, perhaps a desert, perhaps a huge square. The light was very bright. The space I was standing in was full of little stupas. Some were new and clean and white. Some were dark with age, half-broken and tumbledown. At the far end of the field of stupas was an enormous white dome. I started to walk slowly towards it. However far I walked it never seemed to get any closer. I was aware of other people moving in the same direction, but could only catch glimpses of them as they flitted between the rows of little stupas. They seemed familiar. Were these people I knew? Friends or family perhaps? I couldn't be sure. One of them stopped and looked straight back at me. I realised I was looking at myself.

The next morning it was back to business. I was in Nepal on a recce for a documentary film, *Tibet: A Buddhist Trilogy*, travelling with Graham Coleman – the same Graham who was on the Harewood lake walk. We planned to shoot the film the following year in the Tibetan exile communities of India and Nepal. Graham was the writer and director. I was the producer and cameraman.

A year later, 1977, we were back and for nearly six months we drove round the subcontinent in a VW minibus full of film equipment. There were four of us: Graham and me, Robin Broadbank, the sound-record-ist, and Mike Warr, who was responsible for lighting, additional camerawork and still photography. Our journey took us the length and breadth of India.

We returned to Dharamsala, where I'd had my first encounter with stupas a year earlier, to film the Dalai Lama. He was a more easily accessible figure then, and much less travelled; his first visit to the USA was not until 1979. We filmed him in his private quarters, giving a teaching to selected monks on the Heart Sutra, one of Buddhism's best-loved and richest texts; we filmed him giving blessings to recently arrived refugees from Tibet; and we filmed him giving a public address on 10 March, the anniversary of the uprising in Lhasa in 1959 that triggered his flight into exile over the mountains to India.

We observed daily life, both lay and monastic, in the new Tibetan settlements in Bylakuppe and Mundgod in Karnataka in southern India, a hot and humid environment a million miles from the bleak majesty of the Tibetan plateau.

We travelled to the Indus Valley in the magnificent mountain landscape of Ladakh. The inhabitants of the village of Thiksey were ploughing, planting and irrigating their fields in the short growing season that their harsh mountain desert environment allowed them. In the monastery that stood on a rocky outcrop above the village, monks were receiving a teaching on impermanence and then went down to the village to perform the last rites for a homeless man, guiding his spirit through the intermediate state between death and re-birth as described in *The Tibetan Book of the Dead*.

And we recorded the preparations for and performance of a protective ritual at the Sakya Phulwary Monastery, a short walk from the Great Stupa at Boudha.

The stupa was just as impressive as I had remembered from our recce the year before, a massive white-washed structure built up like an enormous wedding cake in three layers of terraces, each terrace as wide as a street – wider than most streets in the vicinity in fact – and scattered with shrines and *chaityas*.* The very top terrace has 108 niches around its circumferences, each containing a statue of a deity. Above this is a huge dome, like the lid of a wok, white, but splashed with ochre yellow paint made of a mixture of mustard oil and turmeric in a design that outlines the petals of a lotus. At the base of the thirteen steps that make up the golden spire are the bright blue eyes of the Buddha, unblinking, all-seeing, full of a fierce compassion, facing each of the four cardinal directions. Below them a curtain of cloth, bands of blue, white, red, yellow and green, billows gently in the wind. At the very top of the gleaming spire, above the protective umbrella, sits a copper sun, crescent moon and eternal flame. This is the classic shape of the Nepalese stupa. You see many of them all across the Himalayas, but there are none to rival Boudha in scale or in majesty.

---

* Small shrines housing a stupa.

We spent an intense couple of weeks in the monastery at Boudha. We were filming the elaborate preparations for the protective ritual based on a text, *Dolma Yulduk* in Tibetan, which translates into English as 'The Tara Ritual of Expelling Obstacles'. The monks build an intricate three-dimensional cosmogram, a symbolic representation of the universe, densely populated with human figures, mansions, offerings and spirit-catching webs made out of coloured thread. During the course of the ritual performance all the negative and malevolent forces that threaten or obstruct us are invited into the cosmogram and transformed by the ritual invocation of the power of the female deity Tara, the Compassionate One, the Saviouress, the Mother of All Liberation, who holds in her hand the Hare-Marked Moon. Each performance of the ritual is about four hours long, seven of them over a week, and at the end the cosmogram, so painstakingly constructed by the monks just a week before, is carried out of the monastery in a dawn procession and ceremonially burned.

The filming had a certain rhythm to it, a routine. We were staying in rooms above a café just outside the ring of shops, restaurants and dwellings that encircled the Great Stupa. Today, more than forty years later, this road is clogged with traffic, thick with petrol fumes, badly surfaced, with pavements that are overcrowded, pot-holed and dusty. Electric wires are festooned round the telegraph poles in rat's nest tangles, hanging from the corner of buildings, looping precariously across the roadway. All very typical of the rapid and unregulated urban explosion that has swamped the Kathmandu Valley over the past thirty years. Even in 1977 it was busy. We were woken early one morning by a noise that sounded like the end of the world approaching. Stumbling to the window, we could see a row of men rolling huge empty metal oil drums down the road, to be used, we discovered later, as the supports for a makeshift stage at a wedding party. To describe the noise they made as thunderous would be an understatement.

Early every morning we would load up the VW van with our equipment and drive the short distance to the monastery, just the other side of the Great Stupa. It was pretty quiet at that hour. Some of the shops and cafés were just starting to open their shutters, set out their tables and sweep the area immediately outside, to the irritation of the local dogs trying to sleep peacefully in their dusty corners. It was these dogs that were to give me one of the scarier experiences of the trip.

The very last performance of the ritual was due to start very early in the morning, to finish at dawn, so it was agreed that we should set up our equipment and stay overnight in the monastery. Just before we were about to bed down I realised I had forgotten the charger for the camera battery. Running out of power on our final day would have been a disaster, so I decided to walk back the short distance to our rooms and collect it. Why not drive, someone suggested, but

I'd decided that the walk would do me good. It was only a few minutes. Mistake. Those dozy dogs, comatose in their self-defined patches during the day, were a very different proposition at night, fierce barking creatures with raised hackles and bared fangs, furious that a lone human should dare to invade their space. I shouted at them as they rushed at me, whirling the plug at the end of the battery lead at them in a pathetic gesture of self-defence. I jumped backwards towards the wall of the stupa, imagining at the very least getting some nasty bites that would require painful anti-rabies injections. I might even get savaged to death. Buddhists talk about dying in close proximity to a holy site guaranteeing a good re-birth, but this didn't feel very auspicious to me. Then I realised something: though they were running at me very aggressively, the dogs would always stop short, as if restrained by an invisible force field. Territory. It was all about territory. They were defending their patch and as long as I stuck close to the stupa wall, where I'd instinctively retreated, I was all right. Their territory was an area outside their home patch, very clearly defined to the dogs, invisible to me. The path round the stupa, close to the prayer wheels where humans walked as they made their circumambulations, was of no interest to them.

I arrived back at the monastery, a little shaken but in one piece. The others had heard the commotion, wondered what was going on, but hadn't made the connection to my ill-advised expedition. They thought it was hilarious. By that time I could see the funny side, just a bit. But I was glad I'd had the instinct to stick close to the stupa.

My different experiences at Boudhanath had only reinforced what everybody who lived there already knew and what I had also come to understand: this was a very powerful place. But where did that power come from?

THE LEGEND OF THE GREAT STUPA OF BOUDHANATH

Shamvara is starting to feel her age. She has worked hard all her life and built a successful business as a poultry keeper. She has four sons, each by a different father: her first son's father was a stablehand, the second a swineherd, the third a dog keeper and the fourth a poultryman. She has brought up her sons well and made sure they all received a good education. They are now respectable householders in their own right. What, she thinks, is she to do with the rest of her life? How can she use the wealth she has accumulated, more than she needs for herself, in a way that can benefit other people? So she makes a vow: 'I will build a Great Stupa, a receptacle for the Mind of all the Buddhas.'

But first, before building can begin, she must ask permission of the local ruler for land on which to build. She approaches him with great reverence and humility and makes her request. The king is impressed. Here is a self-made woman, someone who has risen from very humble beginnings, has raised four sons to become respectable householders and now wants to build a Great Stupa. 'This is truly astonishing,' he thinks. Before he grants her request, however, he makes one condition, a final test of her resolve. He will give her the land, he says, but no more than can be covered by the hide of a goat.

Shamvara has not become rich and successful by chance. She is clever and resourceful as well as hard-working. She takes the largest goat hide that she can find, cuts it thinly into a continuous circular strip and encloses a space that is large enough to contain the Great Stupa that she has dreamed of. Impressed by her ingenuity as well as by her devotion, the king agrees to give her the land on which the Great Stupa is to be built.

Construction begins. Working with her four sons and assisted by a donkey and an elephant, the foundations for the stupa are laid and brick walls built up to the third level. The rapid progress of the work arouses the jealousy of the rich and powerful from the local community, and a group of dignitaries petition the king:

'If a poor woman like this, a mere poultrywoman with four sons from different fathers, is allowed to construct such a Great Stupa, how much more will be expected of you the king – and of us, the wealthy men of your country? If you permit this construction, every one of us will be humiliated.'

But the king is adamant. He has given his permission. He will not change his mind. And so the Great Stupa has become known in Tibetan as *Jarungkhashor*, 'Permission once given cannot be taken back'.

Construction work continues, through the cold of the winter, the heat of the summer and the torrential downpours of the monsoon, day after day, week after week, month after month, four years of uninterrupted, back-breaking work, until the Great Stupa is completed up to the top of the dome. The hard labour has taken its toll on Shamvara. She is exhausted and realises that she will not live to see the end of her noble enterprise. She calls her four sons to her bedside and pleads with them to complete the work that they have begun together: 'You must finish it for me and consecrate it with great honour and reverence. Then you, my beloved sons, will have fulfilled the purpose of this life and the next by fulfilling my wishes.'

And with those words, she dies.

Her sons agree that they must carry on: 'We must repay her kindness to us and attain merit for her virtue.' So the work goes on, as relentless as before, for three more years, till the Great Stupa is finally complete. Then, sumptuous offerings are made and a ceremony of consecration takes place, attended by the Buddhas and bodhisattvas of the ten directions, by Manjushri, Vajrapani and Avolokiteshvara and many of the other deities of the Buddhist pantheon, both peaceful and wrathful.

> The earth shook three times. The boundless light of divine wisdom . . . eclipsed the sun and irradiated the night for five consecutive days.[1]

In his translation of the Legend of the Great Stupa, from which much of the above is taken, Keith Dowman puts the legend into context. He describes how Buddhist story-telling shapes history and geography into its own narrative:

> In Tibetan Buddhadarma-related literature, history is treated as an analogue to progress on the Bodhisattva Path [and] physical geography parallels and symbolizes the structure and topography of the mind.[2]

The Legend of the Great Stupa is far more than a charming tale of one woman's devotion and perseverance. It is a *terma*, a teaching that has been hidden away, to be rediscovered at a time when knowledge of Buddhism's ancient wisdoms has become weak. The legend is unusual in having two women at its heart: its protagonist, Shamvara, is a strong and independent-minded woman, and the *terma* is rediscovered in the temple of Samye Ling in Tibet by a nun. Shamvara is no ordinary mortal, however. She is Apurna, daughter of King Indra, who, as a punishment for stealing flowers from the garden of her father's heavenly kingdom, is re-born in Nepal as the daughter of simple country parents. Her dedication and generosity in constructing the Great Stupa allow her to attain Buddhahood and be released forever from the cycle of birth, death and re-birth.

After telling the story of Shamvara and her four sons, the Legend of the Great Stupa goes on to speak with power and passion about the innumerable benefits of making such a stupa; of how all those involved in its building will go on to become great rulers, wise ministers, devout practitioners and teachers of the Dharma; of how making offerings to it, circumambulating it or even just living in its vicinity will bring great merit. I was coming to understand that being involved with building a stupa is an important and powerful thing for a Buddhist, something that can change your life and influence everything in its vicinity.

The text also describes a time when all these benefits will be threatened, a time known in Buddhist teachings as the Kaliyuga, the age of decadence and corruption. These dark predictions, written many centuries ago, have been interpreted as foretelling the Chinese invasion of Tibet in 1950. The prophecies are often chillingly specific:

> From China, an army whose number will equal five measures of mustard seeds will invade Tibet and the clamor of terror will resound like thunder for many

years . . . One half of the Tibetan people will be slain
. . . the monks and priests murdered . . . the survivors
of this holocaust will escape to Sikkim, Bhutan, Nepal
and India as refugees. Those who remain . . . will be
massacred . . . by the barbarian iconoclasts.[3]

. . . there is fighting before the altar, the temples are
used as slaughterhouses . . . the scriptures, the images
of the Buddhas, the sacred icons, the scroll paintings
and the stupas will be desecrated, stolen and bartered
at the market place, their true worth forgotten.[4]

It foretells natural disasters, too:

No rains fall in season, but out of season the valleys
are flooded . . . Earthquakes bring sudden floods while
fire, storms and tornadoes destroy temples, stupas and
cities in an instant.[5]

Nepal has had its fair share of floods, storms and the
rest over the years and I was very aware of these prophecies when I was in Nepal in January 2016 to write the
bulk of this book. Just nine months earlier there had
been a major earthquake in the Kathmandu Valley. In
the immediate aftermath, after checking what had
happened to friends (no deaths, mercifully, but many left
homeless), I read how many historic buildings had
collapsed and started to scour websites to see what the
effect had been in Boudhanath. There was a crack in the

dome of the Great Stupa, superficial it was said, and some of the gold tiling on the spire had come loose. Nothing structural, it seemed. But further investigation showed the damage was far worse than had been originally thought. The quake had caused the spire to twist. There was a wide crack in the gold tiling, getting wider every day. It was unsafe, an accident waiting to happen. It would have to be dismantled and completely rebuilt. So what I saw when I arrived, looking across the rooftops from the balcony of the Hotel Tibet International, was just a dome, its whitewash faded and dirty, a ramp of bamboo scaffolding up one side, and a pole sticking out of the top with a small umbrella of striped cloth, forlorn and all out of scale, waving sadly in the breeze. Everything else, from the all-seeing eyes upwards, from where Shamvara's sons had started to build after the death of their mother in the legend, had gone.

I went to look closer. Some things hadn't changed. They still charged 250 rupees at the gate (I resented this at first, but realised that it was going to help the reconstruction – it wasn't about whether I got my money's worth), pigeons were still sunning themselves on the dome, devotees were still turning the prayer wheels as they made their circumambulations. Work had already started on the rebuilding. There were piles of new bricks on the lower platforms, being slowly passed up by hand towards the spire. One man was rendering the outer wall, where the rows of prayer wheels stand. It looked slow, but at least something was happening. Two to three years to completion, I was told.

But the atmosphere round the stupa was different: subdued, far fewer people (perhaps because of the time of year), and I was hustled twice as I circumambulated – serious hustles, one for medicine, one for food, genuine cases of hardship quite possibly, but that had never happened to me here before. Keith Dowman points out that when lightning destroyed the pinnacle of the Great Stupa during a storm in 1969, this coincided with the arrest of a man for dealing in stolen religious artefacts. He was the son of the abbot of one of the main monasteries at Boudhanath.[6] What accumulated karma had led to the latest damage, I wondered?

I was introduced to Khenpo Dorjee, a monk from a monastery next to the stupa, who was one of the group co-ordinating the restoration project. He explained that what I had thought was just a pole sticking out of the top of the dome was in fact a new *Sok-shing*.* It was replacing the existing one, which had been damaged and was anyway made up of three separate lengths of wood joined together, which was not correct. This three-piece *Sok-shing* had only been installed quite recently, he explained, after the 1969 lightning

---

* *Sok-shing*, usually translated as Life Tree, is a length of specially cut and prepared timber that runs through the centre of a stupa, its axis and its spine. I describe it and its function in more detail later.

strike damage. Khenpo Dorjee told me that the brand new *Sok-shing* had been very carefully prepared, painted in the proper way with golden mantras, blessed and consecrated along with a host of other artefacts – relics, holy texts and offerings. 'Much better than before,' he said. Because of the size of the Great Stupa, this *Sok-shing* just runs up the centre of the thirteen-ringed spire and the artefacts will be enclosed in plastic tubes and attached to it before it is bricked in, the bricks then painted gold. This will be a lengthy and costly process, though it need not, according to Khenpo Dorjee, be quite as lengthy or as costly as is being made out. 'If just we do it, we Buddhists,' he said, 'maybe five, six months. Not so expensive.' But the government is involved and so everything costs more. The more time, the more money will come in through donations and foreign aid. The more money comes in, the more there is to stick to the fingers of the many middlemen. I was indignant, but Khenpo Dorjee didn't seem too bothered. 'The most important thing is, we do properly.' Then, he said, something positive and beneficial and long-lasting will have come out of the natural disaster. Like the peacock, who kills poisonous snakes and consumes their venom, before opening his magnificent train and transforming himself into a thing of great beauty, bad energy will be transmuted into good and the Great Stupa will rise again, more splendid than ever. How long that will take remains to be seen.

GRAHAM AND JINPA

It was while we were making our documentary film *Tibet: A Buddhist Trilogy* that Graham and I met Thupten Jinpa – the fourth person on the Harewood lake walk. We filmed the annual Lama Dance at Zongkar Chode Monastery in Hunsur, Karnataka, south India, and Jinpa was playing the cymbals in the monastery orchestra. He was just nineteen and about to start his academic career at Ganden Shartse Monastery, where he regularly got top marks in his class as he worked towards his Geshe degree (the monastic equivalent of a university degree). Now, forty years later, no longer a monk and living in Canada, he is one of the most respected Tibetan scholars in the West, author of many books and translator of many more. But he is best known as the principal translator for the Dalai Lama when he visits English-speaking countries in the West. Jinpa has a unique combination of immaculate idiomatic English and a profound knowledge of Buddhist teachings, and his empathy with the Dalai Lama as he translates is wonderful to behold.

Graham and Jinpa have become close friends over the years, collaborating on various projects, most notably as co-editors of the first complete translation of *The Tibetan Book of the Dead*, one of the best-known works of Tibetan Buddhist literature in the West. And Graham, with a little help from me, went on to found the Orient Foundation.

The Orient Foundation for Culture and the Arts is a charity registered in both the UK and India. Four of the five people who made the *Trilogy* film are still involved with the charity: Graham is Chief Executive; Rob Broadbank, Pip Heywood, who edited the film, and I are trustees. Over the past thirty years or so the Foundation has both amassed the largest multimedia archive of Classical Indian and Tibetan Knowledge Resources in the world – 15,000 hours of material and rising – and developed methods for making this widely accessible. 'Creating, conserving and developing access to multimedia documentary resources' is how the Foundation's website describes it.[7]

Tibetan Buddhism has a huge body of literature, but its vitality depends on oral transmissions and commentaries on the root texts, knowledge passed on from teacher to student over many generations, a direct line from the Buddha himself and from the Indian and Tibetan teachers and scholars that followed. Communist China's occupation of Tibet in the 1950s and its brutal attempts to suppress Tibetan culture put all that in jeopardy. Many Tibetan teachers and practitioners had to flee their homeland and there was a very real danger that the continuity of centuries would be broken. Under Graham's leadership, the Orient Foundation has set out to help to preserve this ancient oral tradition, a huge collection, more and more of it generated by and all of it now administered by the monasteries themselves. It is priceless work, a vast digital archive helping to keep an ancient culture alive, and Graham has dedicated himself to it with extraordinary single-mindedness for most of his adult life.

So the walk round the lake at Harewood and our oh-so-casual conversation about stupas was no accident. It had its roots in a long, shared personal history. It was meant to be, though it didn't come to fruition till some years later.

Third Journeys: Bhutan and Back Again

It was early in the morning but already sunlight was pouring through the curtains of my room in the Pedling Hotel. I was in Thimphu, the capital of Bhutan. The city's gangs of street dogs had been quieter than usual that night and I'd slept pretty well. I peered down onto the patch of dusty wasteland below my window. The dogs which had sounded so ferocious during the night were now just a motley collection of mongrels sleeping quietly in the sun.

Beyond this tranquil scene stretched the corrugated tin roofs of Bhutan's capital city, the golden eaves of the distant Trashichhoe Dzong* catching the morning

---

* One of twenty-seven dzongs that are the centres of administrative and spiritual power throughout Bhutan, majestic architectural statements unique to the country. Trashichhoe Dzong has been the seat of Bhutan's government since 1968 and is where the state monk body is based every summer.

light. In the distance rose the wooded slopes of the valley, mist curling across them like dragon's breath, glimpses of the snow peaks showing above them against the dark blue Himalayan sky. It looked like it was going to be a perfect Bhutanese day – hot sun, cool breeze, the scent of pine trees in the air. Good omens all. And good omens were important because today was the day I was due to meet Lama Sonam Choephel. Stupaman. We couldn't resist the pun.

This was my second trip to Bhutan. Six months or so earlier Graham had suggested I visit to coincide with the conclusion of a project he had been running there since 2001, brokering an unlikely partnership between the Bhutanese government, Microsoft and European aid agencies to create a computer font that would enable Bhutanese to work on computers in their own language, Dzongkha. Bhutan was somewhere I had always wanted to go. For anyone whose young imagination had been captured by the Himalayas – as mine undoubtedly had – there was a wildly romantic allure about it. Overexcited travellers would describe it as a Shangri-La, the last remaining unspoiled place in the Himalayas. Hyperbole of course. I soon realised that Bhutan is as full of complications and contradictions as any other twenty-first-century country, certainly no Shangri-La, but it had been many years since I had been to the Himalayas. This would be the first time since our Harewood lakeside walk and speculations about a possible stupa site. A trip to Bhutan seemed like too good an opportunity to miss, a chance to try to reconnect with a part of the world that had always had a special place in my heart.

Soon after my arrival I was introduced to a young monk, Phub Dorji, one of the trainees on the computer project, a good English speaker and, like most Bhutanese, a sturdy walker. Many villages in Bhutan can only be reached on foot, across rugged mountain terrain, at altitude. Walking in the mountains is not a leisure activity in Bhutan, it's a fact of life. Early one morning, Phub Dorji and I climbed together up the steep track through the woods to the monastery at Phajoding, white dots on the hillside high above Thimphu.

Phub Dorji showed me round the sprawl of buildings that made up the monastery: monks' quarters, the kitchen block, retreat huts, shrine rooms dark with age, all very well looked after, with floors swept and altars properly tended.

'Do you know what this is?' he asked me, pointing to an object in a finely wrought metal stand that stood on a shelf by one of the altars.

I shook my head.

'It's a dragon's egg,' Phub Dorji said, very matter-of-fact. 'Would you like to hold it?'

He lifted it down from the shelf. It was surprisingly heavy, about the size of an ostrich egg, slightly pitted and a dark yellowy-brown in colour. I tapped it gently with a fingernail. Solid, not hollow.

'Baby dragon inside?' I asked.

'Have you seen a dragon's egg before?' Phub Dorji said.

I did once hear an old Tibetan lady describe seeing a dragon in a very remote and uninhabited part of northern Tibet. She was on a pilgrimage, she said, and had just reached the top of a high pass and there it was, coiled up like a huge snake, asleep on the barren plain far below. Disturbed by the presence of humans, it took to the air. It was of such a size, she said, that by the time the last coil of its body had left the ground, its head was already above the clouds. One flap of its great wings and it was gone.

The Bhutanese name for their country is *Druk Yul*, meaning 'the Land of the Thunder Dragon'. Their national flag features at its centre a dragon clutching a jewel in each of its claws. It is seen as a fierce but ultimately benign creature and master of all the elements; it can fly through the air, swim in water, walk on the earth and it breathes fire. In Buddhist art the dragon is often depicted in flight, 'bursting through the clouds of ignorance', and in its claw it holds a giant pearl, a symbol of wisdom and compassion.

On another occasion, Graham and I walked up to Tango Gompa, a teaching monastery not usually accessible to foreigners, where the young monks were refining their understanding of Buddhist philosophy in vigorous and animated debating sessions. I sat with Graham and his partner Dechen (they were due to marry in May the following year) by a brand new stupa just below the monastery. We ate oranges and biscuits and looked out across a thickly wooded valley, still blurred with mist in the morning light. The pine trees were the darkest of greens and their fragrance filled the air, the sky was that very particular Himalayan blue-black, the sun reflected off the golden roof of the monastery on the other side of the valley. It was hard to imagine being anywhere more beautiful or more serene.

We went to Bumthang, a long drive east from Thimphu over a series of passes: round one hairpin bend after another, glorious mountain views from the top, then a terrifying slalom down into the next valley – and then the next, and then the next one after that.

Bumthang is often described as Bhutan's cultural heartland. It is a set of connecting valleys and the name derives from the Dzongkha word *bumpa*, meaning 'an oval-shaped offering vase'. The name refers to the shape of the valley, broad and open, but also to its proliferation of sacred sites. Literally every few miles you come across something extraordinary. On the hillside above one monastery is a spring where the water runs cool in the summer and warm in the winter. At the back of a temple in the same monastery is a cave where the great Buddhist master Guru Rinpoche meditated, the outline of his body still visible, an indentation in the rock.*

Up a rough track at the far end of the valley is a pool in a mountain stream where a holy text was found, Mebhartso, 'the flaming lake'. Here, one of Bhutan's most revered lamas, Pema Lingpa (a *terton*, a finder of religious treasures, usually texts or holy objects left hidden by Guru Rinpoche to be discovered by later generations to keep the teachings alive), dived into the water holding a burning lamp. 'If I am mad, I will drown. But Guru Rinpoche tells me I will find religious treasure here,' he cried. Some minutes later he emerged, his lamp still alight, clutching a statue of the Buddha. The statue is now in a monastery nearby and is displayed on special days.[1]

In Bumthang it was not hard to understand the extraordinarily direct, almost physical bond with their faith that all Bhutanese seemed to share. It is there all around you, in the buildings you visit, the streams you cross, the hills that you climb, the very air that you breathe. And everywhere we went we saw stupas: in monastery courtyards, in the middle of villages, at the top of mountain passes.

---

* Guru Rinpoche (Padmasambhava in Sanskrit, which roughly translates as 'the Lotus-Born') is regarded by the Nyingma – the earliest school of Tibetan Buddhism – as their founder and is widely revered by them as the Second Buddha. He is one of the most important figures in the tradition, though the question of whether he is an actual historical figure, mythical or an amalgam of the two continues to be debated.

Graham and I recalled our conversations all those years ago about building a stupa at Harewood. Surely there must be someone here whom we could persuade to come to England and do just that. There was certainly no shortage of choice in Bhutan. There were very old stupas, lop-sided structures made out of roughly assembled stones, crudely whitewashed. There were brand new ones, cast out of concrete, sharp-edged and gleaming in the Himalayan sun. There were big ones and small ones, in a host of architectural styles. And they all had their own stories to tell.

DOCHU LA – THE PLACE OF THE 108 STUPAS

This is the busiest stretch of road in Bhutan. It snakes up from Thimphu through the pine forests, a few rhododendrons still glowing crimson in the trees, before starting the long and tortuous descent, a bend on average every nine seconds it is said, towards Punakha. Like many roads in Bhutan it is being resurfaced, two-lane blacktop all the way west to east within two years is the official line, but mostly it is still in pretty bad condition, untarmacked, slippery with red mud after the rain, with a steep drop down into the valley for long stretches. Just a day earlier a little Toyota taxi had plunged off the edge, killing the driver and all four passengers. A huddle of emergency vehicles and their operators were gathered at the site of the accident, peering down, working out how to winch what was left of the car back up.

In front of us was a slow-moving convoy of vehicles, at the head of which was a Toyota pick-up with a large bundle swathed in yellow cloth propped upright in the back: the body of a lama on its way to the cremation grounds in Punakha. Very auspicious to be following them, I was told. I hoped silently that our driver would continue to drive cautiously. Quite enough death for one short car journey already.

The pass we were climbing towards is called Dochu La. In wintertime when the skies are clear and the rain has gone, the views from here of the snow peaks that mark Bhutan's frontier with Tibet – at least seven of them well over 20,000 feet high – are spectacular. In spring and summer, as now, the pass is often shrouded in mist, clumps of prayer flags drift in and out of vision as they straggle up the hill and the clouds billow over them, and there is no view at all.

A large stupa marks the point where the road reaches the top of the pass. It is said to have been built by Drukpa Kunley, the Divine Madman, a wandering lama originally from Tibet, a tantric master with magical powers, renowned for his bawdy and irreverent teachings and for his outrageous sexual behaviour. He is a great favourite in Bhutan. His Iron Rod, his mighty penis, is immortalised all over by large wooden carvings that hang from the eaves of houses or by graphic drawings on their whitewashed walls, erect, hairy and ejaculating a great fountain of sperm. 'It has a head like an egg, a trunk like a fish and a root like a pig's snout!' exclaims the Lord Demon of Wodo, scourge of travellers over the passes between Bhutan and Tibet. Drukpa Kunley beats him over the head with it, subduing the demon so that he troubles weary travellers no more.

On another occasion Drukpa Kunley is confronted by a female demon known to feast on human flesh. She appears to him in the shape of a beautiful woman and they exchange pleasantries.

'Where have you come from?' he asks her politely.

'The mountain,' she replies.

'What brings you here?' he says.

'I have come for food and to find clothing for the winter,' she says.

'And what do you eat and what do you wear?' he asks innocently.

'I eat human flesh and wear human skin,' the demon snarls back.

'Then try this for size!' shouts Drukpa Kunley, unrolling his foreskin and enveloping her in it. 'May you be drenched by the summer rain and frozen by the winter snow.'[2]

Behind the old Drukpa Kunley stupa is a mound and covering it like a field of giant toadstools are 108 new stupas, built in the classic Bhutanese style: square with no dome, a whitewashed base with a broad red band about two-thirds of the way up, topped with a slanted roof of heavy slates and a small, gold-painted spire.

I had been up here several times before, most recently some years earlier when my daughter Emily and I had come to escort the stupa builders back to England. It looked very different then. Emily, Chen Chen Dorji (a Bhutanese friend who was to become a key figure in the stupa project) and I were on our way back from Punakha. We had been visiting the Dzong there. Twice a year, usually in November and May, the state monk body travels between the two great Dzongs in Thimphu and Punakha. Punakha, lower than Thimphu at 4,500 feet and correspondingly warmer, is the winter base and Thimphu the summer base. Until the 1960s, when Thimphu became the permanent capital, the entire government would migrate between the two.

It was early May when we were there and already large trucks, belching diesel fumes, brightly painted and with bumper slogans like 'If You Drink Don't Drive If You Drive Don't Drink' or 'Whisky Is Risky' or (my favourite) 'Better Be Late Than Be The Late', are trundling up the road from Punakha, laden with monks and their trunks. The Je Khenpo, Bhutan's senior monastic figure, would soon follow with his retinue and some of the holiest relics in the land.

I remembered this as a peaceful place, just a few picnickers or mountain gazers stopped at the roadside, but now it was a hive of activity. Hundreds of people swarmed over the mound where the stupas were under construction. It was surprisingly quiet in the still mountain mist, no shouting or hubbub of voices, just the steady percussive sound of stone and slate being worked by hand. At the foot of the slope, round the base of Drukpa Kunley's large square stupa, stones were piled high. A steady stream of volunteers gathered there to be loaded with large pieces of slate, the flatter pieces carried on their backs, the rounder ones in their arms, before staggering up the slope with them. There were men and women, young and old, all shapes and sizes, some of them almost invisible under their burdens, worker ants with a mission, because helping to build a stupa in however humble a capacity is seen as a highly meritorious act in Buddhist culture. And there were certainly a whole lot of people here gathering merit.

I couldn't resist the challenge and God knows I needed the merit, so I joined the queue. An old man with a mischievous twinkle loaded me up with a very large rock. I cradled it muddily in my arms and set off unsteadily up the slippery slope. Old ladies and young children bearing far heavier loads than mine skipped past me as I stumbled upwards. I was bathed in sweat and seriously out of breath (we were at 10,000 feet) by the time I deposited my load triumphantly at the top, my arms aching. Back down the slope Emily and Chen Chen were doubled up with laughter at my efforts.

Lunch break. Some families had brought their own picnics – Bhutanese-style with hot tiffin boxes full of rice and dal and chillies – but the majority of the workers sat in four long rows and waited patiently to be served rice and curry from large steaming buckets.

Everything was quiet and orderly. Was this what it looked like when the pyramids or Stonehenge were being built? No slaves or desert sands here, of course; this was a wholly voluntary workforce, but to see manual labour on such a scale and carried out with such focus and intensity is a rare sight in the twenty-first century. The whole project, started less than a year earlier, was sponsored by Ashi Dorji Wangmo, the eldest of the then King of Bhutan's four wives, all sisters. 'Is she especially religious?' I asked. 'The queens can be quite competitive,' was the enigmatic reply.

Now everyone stops here, tourist and Bhutanese alike, to walk round the stupas, take photographs, refresh themselves at the brand new teahouse with its gleaming Illy coffee machine and wonder at the mountain views, when you can see them.

The traffic makes its way round the road that circles the great mound. The Toyota pick-up with the yellow-wrapped body of the lama on board makes a slow motorised circumambulation, three times round in a clockwise direction, before continuing on its way down the winding descent to Punakha.

A STUPA? AT HAREWOOD? JUNE 2003

When I first broached the idea of building a stupa to people at Harewood the reaction was mixed. No hostility that I could detect, but a good deal of curiosity and a certain amount of puzzlement.

What is a stupa? people asked. And why do you want to have one here?

These were pretty obvious questions, but I found them curiously difficult to answer. Somehow, I hadn't moved on in my head from the 'wouldn't it be nice if' stage of the project to it being an approaching reality that would need planning, budgeting and some sort of reasonably coherent explanation about what we were embarking on. Just saying that it seemed like a really good idea clearly wasn't going to be enough. I sat down with everyone who would need to be involved with the project – the Trust Director, the Resident Agent, the Estate Manager, builders, gardeners, marketing and event managers – and tried to put my thoughts in order.

I described how gardens like the one at Harewood had always imported structures from different cultures all around the world. There are many examples of buildings based on designs from classical antiquity in the grounds of country houses across England: temples to Apollo or Venus or Dionysus, the whole pantheon of Greek and Roman gods and goddesses. Some houses have medieval follies, others Chinese teahouses or Japanese pagodas. At Harewood there is a small neo-classical structure in the woods near the house, known inexplicably as the Seven Eggs, and a little Himalayan-style shelter in the Rock Garden. There are drawings in the archives of a Temple of Venus in the woods, though no one knows for sure if it was ever built and, if so, exactly where. There were plenty of precedents, both here and elsewhere.

Next, I tried to find a way of explaining what a stupa was, based on what I had learned on my travels, far from comprehensive I knew. I felt wholly inadequate to this task, very aware of the gaps in my knowledge. Though I certainly knew more than the other people round the table, I wanted to be as clear and accurate as possible, without getting bogged down in jargon.

Stupas are symbols of the enlightened mind of the Buddha, of the concept of enlightenment and the way to achieve it, I said. You find them all across the Himalayas: Tibet, Nepal, Bhutan, Sikkim, Ladakh. They are religious monuments, but they are also accessible, somewhere people will gather, Buddhist or non-Buddhist.

The very first stupas were built as reliquary shrines to house the ashes of the Buddha himself, I continued, but they have grown to have many other purposes as well. They point upwards from samsara, the earthly realm in which we dwell, towards the heavens, towards nirvana, towards the possibility of release from the endless cycle of birth, death and re-birth in which we exist. I showed pictures of stupas and a drawn elevation on graph paper that I had been given.

But the outer form is only part of it, I went on to explain. Stupas are hollow structures, built up in a series of chambers, each of which contain religious objects, offerings and sometimes relics, too. It is what is inside a stupa that animates it, changes it from being an inert pile of stone into a living embodiment of the Buddha and his teachings, which is what Buddhists believe one to be. Someone described it to me like this: 'An empty stupa is a meaningless thing, like a bowl without water or a body without guts.' That is why we must bring over from Bhutan someone who has built stupas before and who can make sure it is all done properly, I said. Our own builders will do the construction work, but the monks from Bhutan – and they almost certainly would be monks – will be in charge of what goes inside.

There were concepts that I knew people might struggle with. Enlightenment? The endless cycle of birth, death and re-birth? The idea that just making something in the shape of a stupa was meaningless unless the right things were put inside it? I had already realised that building a stupa, at Harewood or anywhere else, was not like building a garden shed: agree a design, get some materials and a good builder and away we go. This would be much more than just a building project. I tried to explain what the process would be like, what the role of the Bhutanese would be and what our own builders would be expected to do. We discussed where the building materials might come from, what stone was available at Harewood from walls or barns that had fallen down and where any other stone, which would need to be cut to a precise size, might come from. A quarry in the Pennines was suggested. We talked about where the monks would stay and what domestic support might be required. They would probably want and need to be fairly self-sufficient.

The gardens would be open over the summer while the building was happening so we needed to agree a way of explaining what was going on to the general public. As an educational charitable trust, Harewood House had a remit to engage visitors with our cultural activities. This was going to be an interesting broadening of that scope.

Then there was the potentially tricky issue of planning permission. We took informal advice. The stupa wasn't really a building, our advisors agreed – it had no function, nobody was going to live or work in it. More of a sculpture then. Would that need planning permission? In a heritage landscape, technically, probably. But it was a grey area. Should we open Pandora's box and risk lengthy delays? In the end I decided we would just get on with it. What was the worst that could happen? If there was a fuss, we would apologise profusely, say we didn't realise permission was needed, and apply for it retrospectively. Were the planners really going to make us pull down a religious monument?

As we got into the practicalities, people at Harewood seemed to become more engaged with the project, a little bit excited even. There was still some scepticism, some doubt about what the relevance of all this was. But an idea had been born and was about to take its first steps out into the world. If anyone had any notion how it might turn out, that person should have been me. And I had no idea. I hoped, I guess, that I would discover the meaning of what we were doing in the actual doing of it. Though I was able to put up a reasonably confident front when talking to people about the project, actually I was riddled with doubts. Did everyone think I was crazy? Did I think I was crazy? I knew where it had all started, but not where it was going. It was a voyage into the unknown. But it was a voyage that it looked like we were going on together.

MEETING STUPAMAN: THIMPHU, BHUTAN, SUNDAY 11 MAY 2003

Six months had passed since my last visit and I was in Bhutan again. In the meantime Graham had been spreading the word about the Harewood Stupa project among his many Bhutanese contacts. Would the Art School, run by the formidable Lama Choki and his daughter Sonam, be the best place to start? I had written a couple of e-mails to Sonam trying to enlist her support. No reply. Not unusual: Bhutanese can be erratic correspondents, very much in the present, reluctant to engage in speculative exchanges with someone on the other side of the world who has an idea that may or may not turn into a reality.

Or should we make approaches through the Je Khenpo, the country's senior monastic figure? The

Orient Foundation had a good relationship with his office – the ubiquitous Phub Dorji worked there – they would be sure to know who had built what where and who might be interested in the kind of commission that was being proposed.

But we never got that far, because suddenly a chorus of Bhutanese voices all started to say the same thing: 'Sangay's dad, that's who you should talk to. Lama Sonam. He's your man.'

Sangay, Lama Sonam's daughter, is Dechen's best friend, from the same village in eastern Bhutan. Sangay worked at the Pedling Hotel, much the most efficient person in that charming but often lackadaisical establishment. And by a wonderful coincidence – if you believe in such things – it seemed that her father was one of Bhutan's most eminent builders of stupas. We were told that so far he had built more than a hundred. He had, for instance, made the one just below Tango Gompa, where we had eaten oranges in the sunshine and looked across the misty valley during my first visit.

We set off for Hongtso, the village where Lama Sonam lived, about half an hour's drive east of Thimphu, just where the road starts to climb up to Dochu La, the pass with the 108 stupas. We had telephoned to warn Lama Sonam that we were coming, but we weren't going straight to his house. First there was to be a brief visit to the monastery on the hill above the village because today was an auspicious day for more reasons than just the good weather. It was the anniversary of the death of

Ngawang Namgyal, the first Shabdrung, 'at whose feet one submits'. Ngawang Namgyal was a warrior monk from Tibet who is seen by all Bhutanese as the man who first unified their country in the seventeenth century, in effect the founder of the nation. Such was his importance in those early days that his death was covered up for nearly fifty years for fear of the political instability the news would create. His attendants told the world he was on a long solitary retreat, which I suppose was true in a way. So today was a public holiday, celebrated all over the country. Actually, the monastery was pretty quiet, though one of the King's wives passed us in a cloud of dust in her Land Cruiser as we walked up. She too was on her way to make offerings.

I stood by the small stupa outside the monastery – built by Lama Sonam, of course – and looked down onto the little hamlet of Hongtso. I'd been told there was a group of stupas somewhere in the village – one of each of the eight different kinds, a sort of showroom for Lama Sonam's prospective clients I guessed – and I quickly picked out the little cluster on the edge of the village, gleaming white in the pale sunlight.

I scanned the village with my binoculars. Which, I wondered, was Lama Sonam's house? On the side of the village closest to the monastery was quite a large building with a green corrugated roof. Was that it? He had recently been given a plot of land by the King in recognition of his life's work, and the house, though built in the traditional style, certainly looked new.

There was some kind of construction work going on right next to it, a square brick structure still only a few feet high. I could see squatting figures working the stones with their chisels, each stroke sounding sharp and loud in the still mountain air. It was a few moments before I realised what it was that they were building. Lama Sonam was making a stupa. In his own back yard. Right next to his house. Our visit was going to have the added bonus of enabling us to witness something I'd never seen before: a stupa under construction.

Lama Sonam came to greet us. He was a small man in his seventies, wiry and vigorous, bowlegged, with a weather-beaten face, eyes permanently narrowed against wind and sun, a wispy white beard and moustache, a shrewd and assessing smile. He was wearing a thread-bare maroon tunic, dusty and stained, a woollen hat in the same colour and no shoes. Introductions were made and he gestured to us to follow him into the house. He led us through the dark hallway and started to climb nimbly up the steep steps, half staircase, half ladder. I stopped at the bottom to remove my shoes. 'No, no, no! No need for that!' Lama Sonam laughed, grabbing my arm quite roughly. I stumbled up after him, one shoe dangling half-off. Very undignified.

We sat on low seats in a small, dark upper room, a large TV set in one corner, a calendar on the wall, but no other decoration. Tea was brought, with sweet McVitie's digestive biscuits and puffed rice. I was a little nervous. Would he agree to come to England? Would he need some persuading? If he thought it was all a stupid idea and wasn't interested, we had no Plan B to fall back on. I had scribbled some notes before setting off to remind myself of the key points of my pitch.

'So,' Lama Sonam said (speaking a combination of Dzongkha and the eastern Bhutanese language that is his native tongue), 'I hope you don't want me to start immediately because I've still got a few weeks' work before I finish this one.' He gestured through the little unglazed window at the structure outside. 'And then I've promised to build a really big one in Phuntsoling. But I could start after that.'

Graham and I looked at each other. Had we heard that right? If we had, then it wasn't going to be a question of 'whether' so much as 'when and how'. From what Lama Sonam had said, it seemed that he was keen and willing to come to England and build a stupa at Harewood without even a single word of persuasion from me or anyone else.

Why? Perhaps he'd heard of the work the Orient Foundation was doing. Perhaps he'd had a dream or made some kind of divination and based his decision on that. Perhaps Sangay had convinced him. Perhaps it was simply a case of a working builder, albeit of a rather specialist kind, seeing it as an interesting, prestigious and probably quite lucrative job. Who knows? Did it really matter? I smiled broadly and muttered something about how pleased I was that he was interested. Lama Sonam laughed, a wheezy chuckle as if someone had just told a risqué joke, a laugh which was to become very familiar.

We talked about where the stupa might be sited. I tried to explain a little about Harewood and got out a photoshop mock-up Diane had made, which showed how it might look in situ at the head of the lake – the place that Jinpa, Graham, Diane and I had first got excited about years earlier. Lama Sonam found this highly amusing, but wanted to know more. 'Where is it in relation to your house?' he asked. A stupa should be situated to the south and to the west of the building it is supposed to be relating to, he said. I assured him that it was. He nodded, satisfied it seemed. It looked like our chosen site would work, on paper at least.

How tall should it be? We debated. Graham favoured bigger, I favoured smaller. 'It should be a statement, not an apology!' Graham asserted. 'Yes, but it also needs to be in proportion to its surroundings!' I argued. We agreed eventually that between twenty and twenty-four feet was about right. The exact height would have to be decided sooner rather than later. Some of the preparatory work would be determined by the size of the stupa.

Should they come to England soon, at the end of the summer say, working through into the autumn (this was May already, remember)? I was cautious about this idea. There was quite a lot of preparatory work to be done: people at Harewood to be briefed, accommodation arranged, funding found. I suggested the idea of

Lama Sonam coming to Harewood on a recce over the summer, to make a definite decision on the site and the height and then coming back to build in the spring of 2004, when any overrun or postponement (almost inevitable I thought) would mean that the weather would be getting better not worse. The opposite would be the case with a summer start, running on into the autumn.

But the recce idea clearly wasn't going to be practical – two long journeys for someone over seventy who'd never flown before was not a good idea. Once in England, Lama Sonam was going to want to get on with it. He simply couldn't understand the idea of coming to England and not making the stupa.

We decided on a compromise: I would return to Bhutan in the autumn, with more photographs, maps and videos, which would help me give Lama Sonam a clearer idea of what was involved, what the site looked like and so on. I could also check on work in progress, because it quickly became clear that quite a lot of the components for the stupa would have to be made in Bhutan and shipped over to the UK. The materials and the craft skills would simply not be available in England. Construction work at Harewood would begin in spring 2004.

Lama Sonam had one final question, the most important one of all: did I want to do this properly? He was only interested in making a stupa in a wholly authentic way, as it would be done in Bhutan or Tibet or anywhere in the Himalayas. He had turned down an offer from Thailand recently because he wasn't convinced that the sponsors were sincere. I agreed of course that authentic, 'properly done', was the way it had to be. I only wished I was more certain about what 'properly done' would actually mean.

A week or so later, after Graham and Dechen's wedding, we were back in Hongtso. Once again, our timing was good: they were just starting to create the three-dimensional mandala for the first layer of the stupa outside Lama Sonam's house and were about to begin filling the chamber's hollow shell with statues, consecrated images and a variety of offerings.

Lama Sonam scuttled up the rickety bamboo ladder that was propped against the stupa, nimble as a mountain goat, not even using his hands. He beckoned to me and I lumbered after him. Soon, a small crowd of us were up there on the narrow ledge, Westerners and Bhutanese, looking down into a small chamber about four feet square and two feet deep, lined with bright red cotton cloth. Poking up through the centre was the end of what looked like a carved wooden plank, heavily coated in dark red varnish the colour of sealing wax. The four walls of the chamber had images of deities on them: photographs, postcards, photocopies. A bronze statue of Manjushri (a bodhisattva seen as the embodiment of wisdom and knowledge), about six inches high, stood on one side facing east.

One of Lama Sonam's assistants had followed us up the ladder with a tray of offerings: butter lamps, bowls of rice, painted conch shells, nuts, dried fruit, a Fanta bottle full of *chang* (Himalayan barley beer) and various *tormas*.* The assistant, Cheku, wrapped red cloth round his feet and over his mouth so as not to pollute the consecrated space and climbed down into the hollow to arrange everything. Lama Sonam stood on the narrow parapet and unrolled a very old-looking manuscript wrapped in an embroidered cloth, a diagram of the mandala, showing precisely where all the different objects and offerings should be placed. Although he wasn't doing any of the manual work himself, he was very clearly the man in charge.

'No, no!' he said, quite sharply, finger jabbing at his plan. 'Not that way! Put it over there. Yes – over there!' Cheku did what he was told.

More trays with more offerings came up the ladder and were passed down. Soon the entire floor area was filled; there was no room for Cheku to stand and he had to climb out again. He balanced precariously on the wall of the chamber, lying flat on his stomach to stretch down and place the final objects in their correct positions. Everything completed to Lama Sonam's satisfaction, a plastic sheet was placed over the mandala to protect it from the rain (the morning had turned showery) and then more of the red cotton.

---

* A Sanskrit word for a kind of offering cake, traditionally made from barley flour and butter, roughly cylindrical in shape and decorated with roundels of different colours. Designs vary depending on which deity the offering is being made to.

Later the chamber would be sealed, its contents never to be seen again, and the next section, the bell-shaped dome, the *bumpa*, would be built on top.

Synchronicity always seems to me to augur well. There had been a fair amount of it recently: the Sangay/Lama Sonam family connection first and foremost; a stupa actually being built at the time of our first meeting; our second meeting coinciding with the filling of the chamber. There was a long way to go, but the signs, so far, were good.

There were still practicalities to agree. By the time I returned to Bhutan in a few months, preparatory work would already be under way and it would be too late for anyone to change their mind. Some decisions needed to be made now, but first we needed to agree some basics.

How long would it take to build?

Lama Sonam reckoned at least one month of actual building, but there were many things that would need to be prepared first. He thought he would need two assistants to come to England and work with him through the actual building process.

What were these preparations and where would they take place?

The list was long. There were the *tsa-tsas*,* probably several thousand of them, very important. And we

---

* Small relief images of a deity or religious artefact (such as a stupa), traditionally made of baked clay or plaster, the image created using a mould or stamp.

would have to find and buy different jewels, depending on what kind of stupa we were going to make. We discussed this and agreed it should be an Enlightenment Stupa, designed to commemorate the Buddha's enlightenment. That was a big decision made.

Then there was the top part of the structure: the thirteen-ringed spire and the umbrella, sun, moon and jewel tip that sat on top of it. These should be made out of copper, and that would be expensive. We agreed that the thirteen rings could be looked at separately, made of a different material perhaps and then painted. The decorative surround for the niche where the statue of the Buddha would sit would need to be copper, too, so also expensive, or gold – even more expensive. We agreed on copper. All this work could only be done in Bhutan.

We talked about the *Sok-shing*, the Life Tree, a specially cut and prepared length of wood that runs through the centre of the stupa, linking the chambers; its central axis, its spine, both literally and metaphorically. This is what had been poking up through the floor of the chamber we had watched being filled earlier. Only certain types of wood would do. What kind of wood, I wondered? Could we find it at Harewood – there are lots of trees there? No – it must be cut in a special way and carefully prepared, with mantras painted on it, and that again could only happen in Bhutan.

We were getting somewhere, but the costs were rising and the logistics were not getting any simpler.

Materials for everything that needed to be made or sourced locally would cost in the region of £10,000. Labour would be on top, though in Bhutan that would be quite cheap. But anything made here would have to be packed up, put in a container and shipped to England: perfectly feasible, but another cost, and the time it would take to get it there would have to be factored into our schedule. This was starting to be like a film budgeting exercise: look for the best deals, but never lose sight of the creative aims; tight budget control, high production values. 'Doing it properly', the guiding principle of the whole project, was not just about how much you spent, but about making sure that the money you did spend was on the right things.

It wasn't going to be easy – far more expensive and rather more complicated than I'd imagined, but the Harewood Stupa project was now well and truly under way.

THE ENLIGHTENMENT STUPA

We had agreed with Lama Sonam that we were going to build an Enlightenment Stupa. I knew what the shape of that was and I knew that it related to the place where the Buddha achieved enlightenment, Bodhgaya in the north Indian state of Bihar. The Enlightenment Stupa was one of eight different shapes, different design variations, according to the Tibetan

Buddhist tradition. Each of them related to a place that was important in the Buddha's life and each of them was situated in one of the eight most powerful states in the region in his lifetime, as agreed at the time of his death and cremation.

The Eight Great Stupas

1. Heaped Lotuses
2. Enlightenment
3. Many Doors
4. Miracles
5. Descent from Heaven
6. Reconciliation
7. Victory over Death
8. Parinirvana

The Lotus Stupa (sometimes called the Stupa of Heaped Lotuses) was built by the Sakyas at Lumbini, the place of the Buddha's birth.

The Enlightenment Stupa was in Bodhgaya, the place he achieved enlightenment.

The Stupa of Many Doors was built in Sarnath, where he gave his first teaching, shortly after he achieved enlightenment.

The Miracle Stupa (or Stupa of Great Miracles) was in Shravasti, where the Buddha always based himself during the rainy season.

The Descent from Heaven (or God Realm) Stupa was in Sankashya.

The Reconciliation Stupa was in Rajgir.

The Complete Victory (or Victory over Death) Stupa is in another place where the Buddha liked to base himself, Vaishali, and it is where he gave his last teaching.

The Nirvana (or Parinirvana) Stupa is in Kushinagar, where he died.

I realised that sooner or later I would have to visit these sites, which were now part of an increasingly popular Buddhist pilgrimage route. The story of the evolution of the Himalayan stupa has close links with the life story of the Buddha. Going on the pilgrim's trail would surely show me more about how and why they came to be and the significance of the different places, the sites of the original eight Relic Stupas, where the ashes and relics of the Buddha were housed.

But that research would have to come later. First there was a lot of work to do to prepare for Lama Sonam and his team's journey to England the following year.

PUTTING UP PRAYER FLAGS: HAREWOOD, 12 JUNE 2003

Before leaving Bhutan, I'd been given some very specific instructions by Lama Sonam. We had to mark out where the stupa was going to be – the place at the head of Harewood Lake – by putting up prayer flags.

Phub Dorji came to my room the night before my departure with a small bundle: three lengths of prayer flags, which had been consecrated by the lama who had presided over Graham and Dechen's wedding ceremony. I remembered half noticing them on the altar, along with numerous other gifts and offerings, and wondering idly what they were for. Now I knew.

'You must put them up June twelve. Auspicious day,' Phub Dorji said. 'In morning early – before eight. Not eat – drink only. One tea is OK.'

We had returned to a spell of classic English summer weather: days of glorious sunshine, followed by days of torrential downpours. As a result the gardens at Harewood were looking particularly lush and green. But today, prayer flag day, 12 June, it did not look like the weather was going to be good. Heavy showers were forecast.

Trevor Nicholson, Head Gardener at Harewood, was already there when we arrived, good and early, as Phub Dorji had insisted. He had brought a ladder and some bamboo sticks. These seemed a little flimsy to support the flags, so he rushed off to get a saw to cut some sturdier lengths of wood to size. He cut three eight-foot lengths and then he and I dug holes and planted them firmly in the ground in a triangle. We attached the flags to the top of the poles, lit some incense, circumambulated and we were done. It was about 8.15.

That was pretty effortless, Graham said. Trevor, sweating heavily from his exertions, gave him an old-fashioned look.

And the weather was perfect: bright and clear, sunlight filtering through the rhododendron leaves, a swan cruising through the early morning mist rising from the lake. It felt like an auspicious beginning.

Back home, having breakfast, we talked about whether we still thought that we had chosen the best, the most appropriate place. The texts on stupa building all say that the ground must be 'good' – not rocky, clogged with thorns or in a place infested with insects. It should be somewhere where 'many beings are going and coming' – by a thoroughfare of some sort, but not obstructing it. The main thing that all the texts emphasise is that it 'should be seen', in a public place, not tucked away for someone's private enjoyment. Particularly when the Himalayan Garden was complete and the new paths laid, this site, chosen quite casually some years before, seemed to meet all these requirements.

I felt sure that we had chosen the right location. The first steps had been taken, 'done properly' as Lama Sonam had insisted. Maybe it was going to work out well, not be an embarrassment, to me or anyone else involved in the project.

BACK TO BHUTAN: JANUARY 2004

I was back in Lama Sonam's house in Hongtso. He and his team had been hard at work in the intervening months.

He showed me the *Sok-shing*, the Life Tree, the central axis of the stupa, whose base would sit on a crossbar in its second chamber and whose tip would penetrate the fifth chamber, the dome or *bumpa*. Selecting the right tree and preparing it properly are both very important.

Firstly, the tree had to be the right kind and from an auspicious place. Lama Sonam had chosen a mountain juniper from the wooded slopes above Wangdi in central Bhutan, a place strongly associated with Guru Rinpoche. Secondly, the tree should be felled the day after the new moon by a man all of whose siblings are still alive. Thirdly, the trunk of the tree must be dead straight, with no branches coming out of the section to be used. Finally, the eastern face of the tree should be clearly marked, so that the *Sok-shing* would face in the same direction when positioned inside the stupa. Then the tree would be ready to be prepared. Apparently this technique is quite often used in house building in the Himalayas. Planks cut from the east side of a tree would be used to build the east side of a house and so on, the principle being that the natural grain of the wood would make it more weather resistant.

I was looking at a length of wood, dead straight, about ten feet long and planed square, tapering from about two inches square at the thick end to about one and a half at the thin. It had been painted bright red and was covered with hundreds of mantras, delicately picked out in gold leaf. Every couple of feet was a simple mandala, no more than some coloured concentric circles. More mantras would be painted at the centre of each of them in England once the *Sok-shing* was ready to be put into place. The length of the *Sok-shing* determined the size of the stupa, so it looked as if we would have a twenty-seven-foot stupa at Harewood – a little higher than I'd imagined but probably about right. Either way not something to worry about.

Next to the *Sok-shing* was a great pile of mantras, all bundled up, tightly rolled and wrapped in yellow muslin. The largest bundle was about a foot long, the shortest only a few inches. The mantras relate to many different deities, but mainly the Buddha, Guru Rinpoche and Manjushri, I was told. Later, in England, the bundles would all be wrapped round the *Sok-shing* before it was put into the stupa. Next to them was a row of sealed jars, some made of glass and some of pottery, containing a range of offerings, each with a particular property: long life, prosperity, averting evil spirits, removing obstructions, and so on – all the beneficial effects the building of a stupa was supposed to have. There was a range of other objects, too: a tiny and minutely detailed mandala on a red wooden block, some mysterious jars that no one would tell me much about, bags of incense, four wooden *phurbas* (ritual daggers) and a fine statue of the Buddha, about twelve inches high and brought from India. Lama Sonam told me there was more in storage in Thimphu, ready to be shipped.

Next, he showed me the *tsa-tsas* – or, rather, a single *tsa-tsa*, as the others had already been packed into large cans, the kind you keep cooking oil in, ready to go to the shippers for transportation to England. Each was a couple of inches high, a kind of simplified, small-scale stupa. Ours were roughly equal numbers of yellow, blue, red, green and white, colour coded to match the different mantras inside. The protective umbrella that sits above the thirteen-ringed spire was represented by a little scrap of cloth, stuck to the top of each one. Every stupa is packed with thousands of *tsa-tsas*, multiplying the benefits the same number of times. Lama Sonam told me that 4,500 of them had been made for the Harewood Stupa, all of them consecrated. They were quite fragile and had been carefully packed in their tins, though I was a little concerned to discover that the packing that had been used, traditional in Bhutan apparently, was armfuls of twigs and leaves from various Himalayan shrubs and other plants. What would UK Customs think of that, I wondered?

I showed Lama Sonam a photograph of Harewood House in the snow, taken just a few days before I'd left for Bhutan. He seemed very taken with it, insisted on keeping it, a picture of his sponsor for this exciting new project. I tried to explain to him it probably wouldn't be snowing when he came to England in the spring. As I left he was showing it enthusiastically to his family. He seemed to be becoming genuinely excited at the prospect of coming to England.

A couple of days later I was sitting in Chen Chen Dorji's office in Thimphu, waiting for Lama Sonam. As the project developed, Chen Chen had become an increasingly key figure. He was a burly countryman from Haa in the west of Bhutan, funny, bawdy and direct. With a different accent he might have been a Yorkshireman. He was to co-ordinate everything at his end and act as banker for the project – our Bhutanese production manager. I got him to draw up lists of what was needed, to buy or to get made, where it was going to come from, what it would cost and to make sure he got receipts for everything.

Lama Sonam arrived, a little late, accompanied by a shabbily dressed young man with a fresh cut on his nose and one very bloodshot eye – one of his assistants I assumed. He looked like he might have had a rough night. They were both hot and sweaty, barely visible behind the large copper ornaments they were carrying. Lama Sonam had the sun and crescent moon that would sit on the very top of the stupa and the young man was holding the parasol that would sit between them and the thirteen-ringed spire. The craftsmanship was impressive. Five crocodile heads surrounded by swirling clouds glared out from the parasol, mantras above each one: OM AH HRI TRAM HUM.

'They look great!' I enthused – very much the right thing to say, as it turned out that the scruffy young man was the coppersmith who had made them: Jampa Yeshe, coppersmith by Royal Appointment, one of the best around, Chen Chen assured me. We drove up to his workshop in Mothitang, Thimphu's poshest suburb, full of minor palaces, aid agencies and homes for expatriate bankers. Jampa Yeshe's workshop was none of these. It was little more than a shack leaning up against one of the smarter places, with dogs, cats and chickens scratching in the dust and sexually explicit graffiti on the wall. Inside, there was barely enough space for all of us. A tiny forge spat sparks and an assistant crouched in a corner, working on another commission. A welding spark had given Jampa Yeshe the cut on his nose and his bloodshot eye – no room for health and safety precautions in this workshop. He showed us the start of his work on the *Bumpa*

Gokhem, the Vase Gate or frame for the niche where the Buddha statue I'd seen earlier would sit. Fine work, executed in the most basic of environments.

We went to see the shipping agents. Everything would be put in a container in Thimphu, they explained, driven over 500 miles by road down to Kolkata, the nearest Indian port, then put on a boat to England. The journey would take a couple of months – probably. It had been agreed that April would be the best time for Lama Sonam and his team to get to England, the start of spring and – in theory anyway – better weather and a good time to be working in the open air in Yorkshire. That meant that we didn't have all that much time. Chen Chen and I went through the list of what we had already:

Mantra bundles (small, medium and large size):	12,100 ngultrum*	(£173)
Buddha statue:	6,000 ngultrum	(£86)
Gold paint for *Sok-shing* calligraphy:	8,600 ngultrum	(£123)
Phurbas (wooden × 4):	8,400 ngultrum	(£120)
Sealed offerings jars (and contents):	7,500 ngultrum	(£107)
Tsa-tsas (4,500):	12,000 ngultrum	(£171)

---

* Bhutanese unit of currency, tied one to one to the Indian rupee. In 2004 £1 = 70 ngultrum.

Painting of *tsa-tsas*:	560 ngultrum	(£8)
Twigs for packing:	2,800 ngultrum	(£40)
Sun, crescent moon and other copper work:	25,000 ngultrum	(£357)
More *tsa-tsas*:	600 ngultrum	(£9)
More twigs for more *tsa-tsas*:	200 ngultrum	(£3)

Chen Chen told me he would have to go to Nepal to get more statues; the quality of the work there was better than Bhutan, he said, a reluctant admission from a patriotic Bhutanese. We went shopping in Thimphu's lively market for offerings to go into the first chamber at the bottom of the stupa, which needed to contain the things that surround us in this, the world of samsara: clothing (a *gho* and a *kira*, traditional Bhutanese male and female outfits), musical instruments (cymbals, long monastic horns and so on) as well as a variety of ritual objects and offerings.

The day before I left, Lama Sonam surprised me by saying he didn't think it was a good idea for his daughter Sangay to accompany him. I had assumed she would be his cook and housekeeper and would look after him. She and Dechen, who would be in England with Graham, could spend some time together, too. But Lama Sonam said he preferred to have two of his usual assistants, who would be competent domestically, and who could also help him with making the stupa, performing the various ceremonies (pujas) and so on. I was disappointed for Sangay, but I could see the logic.

Time now to return to England and make sure everything was in place for their arrival. I would be back again quite soon, in April, to meet the team, whose make-up had not yet been finally decided, and bring them back to England. I thought I might need help with this and talked to my daughter Emily. An experienced film production co-coordinator, used to moving film crews and movie stars round the world, a cat-herder extraordinaire, she was excited by the idea of visiting Bhutan to help with travel arrangements, visas and the challenge of chaperoning a group of people with no experience of modern travel whatsoever all the way to England. The real adventure was about to begin.

FILLING IN FORMS: THIMPHU, MAY 2004

A few months had passed and Emily and I were back in Bhutan. We had arranged to meet Lama Sonam under the clock tower in Upper Market in Thimphu at 11 a.m. We had been delayed in the Lower Market, forgetting that today, Saturday, was when it was at its busiest. Unlike my last visit when we'd been buying things to go in the stupa, this time we'd mostly been shopping for food: dried mushrooms, asparagus, a bunch of delicate fiddle-head ferns, as well as bananas,

Indian mangoes and some delicious wild strawberries. Emily even bought some *churpi*, the small, rock-hard cubes of cheese that taste like the scrapings from inside a trekker's sock, a Bhutanese country favourite that most foreigners try just the once. Emily was no different. She tried it just the once.

We were running a little late and Lama Sonam and his two assistants were sitting patiently on a bench as we drove up. It was the first time I'd seen all four of the building team together and the first time I'd met Kesang, Lama Sonam's son. There had been some debate about whether he would be a suitable member of the party. He had, I was told, an unreliable reputation, liked a drink. Always hard to tell fact from rumour in these situations in Bhutan, but Lama Sonam had made an impassioned plea, saying how he would need Kesang's personal as well as professional support, swearing he would be no trouble, threatening not to come himself if he didn't have Kesang to look after him. I had exchanged a few animated e-mails and phone calls with Graham and Chen Chen about it before Emily and I flew out. In the end we agreed that Lama Sonam must have the support around him that he wanted. Kesang was on the team. What I hadn't realised till this meeting was that he was a monk. He was very attentive to his father, trying hard to make a good impression.

So here we all were:

Lama Sonam Choephel, wizened and wispy bearded, in a slightly cleaner *gho* than usual, the effect spoiled by the extremely scruffy pair of pyjama trousers in garish tartan that he was wearing underneath.

Cheku, his chief assistant, a monk I'd met when I was in Bhutan before: small, quiet, with enormous buck teeth. He was the man I'd seen putting all the offerings into the stupa in Hongtso under Lama Sonam's strict supervision a year earlier.

Kesang Choephel, quite tall, with a big broad face and speaking far better English than I'd expected. It also turned out that he'd already been abroad – to Thailand, Taiwan and Hong Kong, all of which should help the practical aspects of the trip.

And Phub Dorji, of course. I thought he was uncharacteristically subdued when Emily and I arrived in Bhutan, particularly at supper the first evening. Maybe he was just tired, but we wondered whether he was perhaps more apprehensive about it all than he liked to let on. But this morning he was more his usual self: chatty, informative and attentive, his excitement about the trip starting to bubble up.

There was a purpose to our meeting. We had to fill in the UK Visa Application Forms. Phub Dorji pointed at a small tent that had been erected in the square, selling lottery tickets to help fund the rebuilding of a monastery. It had a plastic table and five chairs, a perfect impromptu office. We commandeered it for the price of a fistful of lottery tickets and got down to business.

They had all brought passport photographs as requested, though Kesang had only brought one and Cheku's must have been at least ten years old. Lama Sonam was clearly keen to get his questions in first. The first one, inevitably, was about the weather and we tried to explain the vagaries of the English summer – predictable only in its unpredictability, never the same two days running, but probably no snow. We had a couple of practical issues, too. If any of them liked butter tea, we would have to bring some bricks of black tea with us because it was impossible to buy in England. Nobody did. Did anybody chew paan? That, too, was unobtainable in England and probably illegal to import. No again. Sighs of relief – I'd been a bit worried about that one.

'What about *churpi*?' Lama Sonam asked (the hard cheese cubes Emily had just tried and disliked in the market). Er, no, not available in the UK. Emily and I looked at each other. I knew what she was thinking. There was no way we were going to get that through Customs officially and it was the kind of thing, even sealed in plastic bags, that would send any sniffer dogs demented. This wasn't the moment for a showdown, however, so we moved swiftly on. Something for another day.

We started to go through the visa form with them: 'Do you have a criminal record?' 'Are you a terrorist?' 'Are you a war criminal?' all of which they thought quite amusing. Then, just when I thought we were on to the more straightforward section, it started to get unexpectedly complicated.

'Date of birth?'

Lama Sonam looked puzzled, thought for a bit and said: 'Wood Monkey Year.'

My turn to look puzzled.

'Seventy-seven year old,' Phub Dorji interposed, trying to be helpful.

'What day and month?'

More puzzlement. Clearly Lama Sonam had no idea.

Emily suggested we wait and see what it said on his passport and put the same thing on the form.

When we got the passport a little later, Lama Sonam's date of birth was given as 1 January 1927. The Bhutanese passport office had clearly had the same problem as us – no idea of the actual day. But we had a date, even if it was almost certainly made up. I later discovered that, if their passports and other documents are to be believed, an awful lot of Bhutanese seem to have been born on 1 January.

We moved on.

'Marital status?'

Giggles from the monks. But Lama Sonam has been married at least twice, which we thought was probably too complicated to go into, especially as Bhutanese men, if divorced, don't necessarily expect to have any contact with their previous family, or even support them. When asked about children, Lama Sonam didn't even mention his daughter Sangay, for instance, who had been our original contact with him. So, for simplicity's sake, we decided just to put down what he told us, which was the details of his present marriage and offspring: two adult sons including Kesang and an eleven-year-old daughter.

'Mother and father names?'

A husky cackle from Lama Sonam.

'Since long time passed away!' he laughed wheezily.

He simply didn't understand why we should be interested in the details of someone who had died some time ago (Phub Dorji reacted in the same way). But we got some names down in the appropriate boxes. We knew we had to obey the cardinal rule of successful dealing with bureaucracy: answer all the questions in a way that the official reading it can understand while staying as close to the truth as possible.

Next came the tricky bit: employment history and details of income. How do you apply criteria designed for tourists, students or asylum seekers to three monks and a freelance stupa builder? Monks have no income and are supported by the state or by their local communities; Lama Sonam had always lived from one project to another, relying on the generosity of sponsors or patrons. He had been successful enough to support a family and build a new house, but he had never had what could be described as a regular income. We tried to concoct a form of words that reflected the real situation, again in a way that an official in the High

Commission in New Delhi could understand. Hopefully the fact that I was taking responsibility for them in the UK and that they had return tickets would outweigh any incomprehension about how they actually supported themselves in Bhutan.

Soon we were done and went our separate ways, with an appointment to meet on Monday morning to gather all the documentation together. It wasn't so long now till we would all be leaving for England.

ENGLAND BOUND: PARO TO YORKSHIRE, MAY 2004

The travelling party had assembled at the Gangtey Palace Hotel in Paro: Emily and me, Lama Sonam, his son Kesang, his assistant Cheku and Phub Dorji. We were flying to England the next day. We drank tea in the garden with its beautiful view across the valley to Paro Dzong, well-kept fields sprouting green and fresh. The Bhutanese were all looking very smart. Lama Sonam wore a brand new *gho*, bright red tracksuit bottoms and a rather nifty hat. He liked hats. Cheku's head was freshly shaved.

Everyone was packed and ready to go, though the contents of my suitcase were unusual, to put it mildly. Inside were the large copper sun and crescent moon which would sit on the top of the stupa, a pair of cymbals, two *thangkas*,* a pair of thigh-bone trumpets (actually made out of wood), a *gho* and a *kira* and a statue of the Buddha. For some reason, none of these had made it into the shipping container. They were going to take some explaining to UK Customs if they decided to look in my case. My own clothes were all stuffed into a cheap Chinese-made holdall, bought at the market the day before. The Bhutanese had, as instructed by Emily, packed anything that could be construed as a weapon into their stowable suitcases, including several large knives and a considerable quantity of chilli powder, and were taking anything valuable with them as hand luggage. Taking Emily at her word, Lama Sonam insisted on carrying a three-foot wooden maquette of a stupa with him onto the plane, which he held on his lap for most of the journey. Thursday 20 May was an auspicious day to begin a journey, the Bhutanese especially reassured because it was the very same day that the monk body was making its annual transmigration from Punakha to Thimphu for the summer. This was lucky, because the tickets had been booked some time before and changing the date of our flight would have disrupted everything, auspicious or inauspicious.

We posed for a group photograph outside the hotel. Everyone seemed relaxed enough, though I suspected

* A type of Tibetan Buddhist painting depicting a religious subject and mounted on a brocade surround that can be rolled up and put away when not on display.

there were nerves below the surface and not just among the Bhutanese. I had an almost totally sleepless night, partly brought on by a bizarre conversation with Chen Chen about not generating too much publicity about the project because the monks didn't really have official permission to go to England and might get into trouble when they got home if Bhutanese officialdom got to hear about it. I mulled this over, wondering why it hadn't come up before. I started to speculate about the problems we were bound to have with visas for our fellow travellers, either getting them in Delhi or being allowed in with them at Heathrow. Then I worried about the strange contents of my suitcase being confiscated by UK Customs, before concluding that this was the most insane and ridiculous project I'd ever undertaken and – it was after 3 a.m. by now and we were due to leave at 5.30 – deciding that the best thing would be to call it all off now and save us all inevitable embarrassment and humiliation. What was the point? It was all going to be a disaster. I started to compose in my head how I was going to tell everybody. It would be disappointing, of course, but really it was the only sensible thing to do . . .

I was woken by someone knocking on my door. It was 5.15, just time to splash my face with water, have a cup of tea (powdered milk and water boiled with ginger and a tea bag – I thought at that moment that it was the most delicious drink imaginable) and stumble into my clothes before we set off for the airport.

With Emily as group leader and me bringing up the rear, we queued our way through the tedious round of airport procedures: check-in, airport tax, X-rays, Customs, Immigration, security checks. This was the first time Lama Sonam had been on a plane and there were many things he seemed to enjoy about the process. He was entertained by the suitcases disappearing off on the conveyor belt, giggled when the metal box he carried round his waist set off the metal detectors and at Delhi Airport was reduced to helpless laughter by the sight of a man pushing a huge snake of trolleys across the baggage collection hall. The last straw, on the way out of Delhi, came as I was undergoing the customary frisking after my metal hip set the metal-detector bells ringing. I looked up and there was the whole party, Emily and the four Bhutanese, doubled up with laughter at the spectacle. Not very Buddhist to mock the afflicted, I told them grumpily.

On the flight we had made sure Lama Sonam got a window seat, but unfortunately the wonderful views of the high Himalayas on the flight from Paro to Delhi were mostly obscured by cloud. The plane seemed to be half full of monks – a good omen surely – one of them a tall and handsome young Bhutanese on his way to complete his master's in philosophy at the University of Colorado, the first Bhutanese monk to get a foreign degree, he told me. He spoke excellent English and not only knew Phub Dorji (of course) but had helped sponsor the eating-oranges-and-biscuits stupa below

Tango Gompa, the first one built by Lama Sonam I had ever seen. We explained our project to him. 'You have the best man here,' he said reassuringly.

Delhi was hellishly hot and humid and noisy and smelly and polluted. The Bhutanese were looking slightly shell-shocked by the time we reached the offices of Clear Path Tours in Connaught Place, right in the middle of New Delhi. Clear Path ('Specialist in Buddhist Pilgrimage') is run by Tenzin Chogyal, a diminutive but extremely energetic Tibetan monk and an old friend of Jinpa's. His business enterprises include film consultancy, organising Tibetan cultural groups going to the West and creating children's books of Buddhist folk tales, as well as the travel company, all conducted with considerable entrepreneurial panache and a wonderful generosity of spirit.

We'd arranged for the Bhutanese to stay at Tenzin's offices, thinking relatively familiar surroundings would be more important than a comfortable but unfamiliar modern hotel environment. This was a success. They were happy to be around Tibetans and by the time we met for supper that evening everybody was in good spirits again. Tenzin and Lama Sonam in particular were getting on splendidly. Lama Sonam had spent time in Tibet when he was younger, serving his apprenticeship as a stupa builder. So when Tenzin showed him stills from the set of the 1997 movie *Seven Years in Tibet*, on which Tenzin had been a consultant, Lama Sonam chuckled with delighted recognition at the pictures of the actors playing Lhasa aristocrats in their elaborate costumes, hairstyles and headdresses. Because, of course, the period of the film, mid- to late 1940s, was when he was there, so this was exactly how he remembered Tibet. Living History. Life and Art imitating each other.

Suppertime. A range of curries and a pile of fresh chapattis arrived on the table. 'Oh I like these,' said Lama Sonam. 'I remember once I was in an Indian army camp. They kept bringing more. We had a bet and I ate sixty of them.'

Visa collecting at the High Commission was achieved in record time – two-and-a-half-hour turnaround, slightly to Tenzin's chagrin. He had clearly spent long and frustrating hours there on many occasions in the past.

Then the flight to England, leaving India as always at a time of maximum inconvenience – 11.30 p.m. check-in for a 2 a.m. flight – and arriving at Heathrow at 7 a.m. UK time. There were long queues at the airport. 'Like sheep and goats,' said Lama Sonam. He was quickly getting the hang of air travel.

Emily and I would check on the monks from time to time during the flight. Lama Sonam was mostly asleep and Kesang was surfing the movie channels, but Phub Dorji and Cheku seemed to be transfixed by the world map with the little graphic of the plane inching very, very slowly across Central Asia. Every time we went back to see them they still seemed to be watching it. Clearly they thought it was the most interesting thing on.

There were no problems, miraculously, when we got to Heathrow, either at Immigration or Customs: no awkward questions, embarrassing suitcase checks or strip searches. The luggage even appeared quite quickly and, far faster than I'd expected, we were through. My fears of a hostile and bureaucratic introduction to the UK for the Bhutanese were completely unfounded. The automatic doors out of the Arrivals Hall slid open and the look on the faces of the Bhutanese as they felt the bright sunny cool of a perfect early English summer's morning was a joy to see.

'Like Bhutan, not like Delhi!' Phub Dorji said delightedly.

Emily and I were home. The Bhutanese had been safely delivered.

The Fourth Journey: The Harewood Stupa

APPROVING THE SITE: HAREWOOD, MAY 2004

It was a long drive from Heathrow to Yorkshire. Lama Sonam prayed loudly in the back seat of the minibus for the entire journey, wide awake even after the long flight. Cheku, Phub Dorji and Kesang dozed intermittently, their faces pressed against the windows, or stared silently as the landscape and the motorway traffic flashed by. They seemed a little overwhelmed by it all.

It was lunchtime before we arrived at the converted stables in the heart of the Harewood Estate that was to be home for the Bhutanese for the next few months. It is an attractive stone and wood building that belies its less than glamorous name – The Hovels. There are two large airy rooms downstairs with floor-to-ceiling windows, a small kitchen and a shower room upstairs. The monks all seemed relieved to be in the countryside again and amazed at how green everything was. A reception committee was waiting: Diane and our two Weimaraners (Smudge and Momo); Christopher Ussher, Resident Agent at Harewood, with his wife Sarah and their nine-year-old daughter Daisy; my PA Brenda Grant and her husband Dennis. Old friends Judi Alston and Andy Campbell, who had both been in Bhutan for Graham and Dechen's wedding, were there, too, to film the arrival. Christopher, an ex-Gurkha officer and fluent Nepali speaker, had arranged for a young soldier from nearby Catterick Barracks, Corporal Dawa, to come and act as cook for a couple of days and to show the new arrivals the ropes: dishwasher, supermarket, the domestic necessities.

Corporal Dawa had prepared a Bhutan-friendly lunch of rice, beef curry, dal and vegetables. The Bhutanese started to relax, clearly touched by the warm reception and both surprised and amused at finding people they could talk to in Nepali. Whatever it was Christopher was saying to them, they obviously thought it very funny. I was ready for an afternoon snooze, tired out by a long and sleepless journey. Lama Sonam had other ideas. He wanted to see the stupa site as soon as possible. This promised to be interesting. Would he find our chosen spot at the head of the lake suitable? It wouldn't be a total disaster if he didn't, though agreeing an alternative could prove tricky.

We made our way through the little white gate in the stone wall that surrounds the lakeside gardens. The greenery was dense and overgrown, and we pushed our way past thickets of rhododendrons, laburnum, wisteria and magnolia all in full May blossom. It felt like entering a magic garden. We arrived at the clearing where Trevor, Graham, Dechen and I had put up the prayer flags a year before. Lama Sonam got his compass out. I knew that the stupa was supposed to be to the west and to the south of the building to which it is relating – in this case Harewood House, to which, of course, the whole Capability Brown landscape is oriented. That was what Lama Sonam was checking now. He gestured at the buildings visible a couple of hundred yards away through the trees.

I tried to reassure him. 'They're just farm buildings, not Harewood House, not the Big House,' I said.

Lama Sonam peered at his compass again, tapping it vigorously with a grimy fingernail. 'Big House which way?' he asked.

You can't see the house from here. It is only half a mile away or so at the top of the hill, but the steep slope and the trees in full summer foliage make it invisible. I pointed as accurately as I could in roughly the right direction. Lama Sonam nodded and looked again, rather dubiously, at his compass. Clearly he wasn't entirely convinced.

I realised there was only one way we could see the house and the head of the lake at the same time. 'We'll have to go out in the boat,' I said.

The *Capability* is a rather elegant electric boat,

decked out to give tourists a ride on the lake during the summer. It was moored nearby and ready to go. General eagerness and hilarity greeted this idea, particularly from Smudge who immediately dived into the water and started swimming after a swan. We all climbed rather tentatively on board – boating isn't really a Bhutanese pastime – but they seemed happy enough, enjoying the novelty as the *Capability* glided silently out onto the water. Smudge dripped over everybody and seemed eager to plunge back in and resume her foolhardy pursuit of the disdainful swan. Lama Sonam cupped the compass in his left hand, rather officiously I thought. He was dead serious, concentrated. He was going to make sure this was right. The other Bhutanese were less concerned and gazed around them, exclaiming at the richness of vegetation and wildlife.

'Like Paradise!' Phub Dorji said.

It was a glorious May afternoon. We drifted gently along, passing more rhododendrons in full blossom, a pair of mallards with eight fluffy ducklings scooting along behind, a grebe squatting on a nest among the reeds, a row of herons crouched on an overhanging willow branch. Harewood House swung into view, the rich green of the South Front that stretches up to Charles Barry's Terrace dotted with black St Kilda sheep, Canada geese and a pair of storks, escaped from the Bird Garden. Harewood could not have been looking better or more enticingly luxuriant. My only concern was that the Bhutanese would think England was always like this.

We stopped the boat in the middle of the lake. I pointed towards the house and then back towards where we had just come from. A smile crept over Lama Sonam's face and he nodded vigorously. No need for a compass now. Yes, it was fine; the stupa's positioning was as it should be. We could go ahead as planned. I breathed a sigh of relief.

Next step was to consecrate the site: to ask permission, if you like, of the land we were about to dig up and build upon. Monday was deemed to be an auspicious day, the day after tomorrow – Lama Sonam certainly wasn't hanging about. But first the right things needed to be gathered so that the necessary ceremonies could be performed properly. I tried to get Phub Dorji to help me draw up a list, but he was so excited that it was difficult to get him to concentrate. Some of the things the Bhutanese had with them, part of the bizarre contents of their suitcases. Others would be easy to find – a table to use as a temporary altar, a rug for the monks to sit on. We could buy flour and ghee for *tormas*, rice and dried fruit for offerings in a supermarket in Leeds. I had a consecrated Buddha statue at home.

There had to be plenty of wood and foliage to burn – the most important offering of all for this particular puja – and it needed to be the right kind of wood, something Himalayan, not any old firewood. Next day, Lama Sonam headed off into the trees with Trevor and

Phub Dorji. I could hear sounds of hacking and sawing. Some of the trees that are common in Bhutan are quite rare in the UK, something that Trevor knew, of course, but Lama Sonam in full flow is not an easy man to stop and I hoped we weren't going to create too much environmental havoc getting him what he wanted.

The foragers emerged from the trees dragging shrubbery and piled it up more or less where the stupa was going to go, ready for the puja. Mission accomplished, Trevor was keen to show the Bhutanese round the Himalayan Garden. It was hard to say which was stronger – their delight at recognising one plant or tree after another (blue poppies, Bhutanese pine: 'The Thimphu, not the Punakha kind,' Phub Dorji informed us) or Trevor's pleasure at seeing their pleasure.

We agreed to reconvene at eleven o'clock on Monday morning to consecrate the site. This would be marked with the performance of a puja by the monks, a sacred ritual involving the reciting of prayers, the playing of music and the making of offerings. There would be a similar performance at the completion of each stage of the building work. Each puja would be different depending on the occasion, but the structure of each one remained essentially the same.

First, the monks would generate the motivation within themselves to act with the intention of seeking enlightenment, not just for their own sake but for the benefit of others. The principle of acting on behalf of others is at the heart of Vajrayana Buddhist practice,

Vajrayana being the form of Buddhism that was first introduced to Tibet from India in the seventh century and has been the main tradition there ever since.

Offerings are made both to the Buddhas and to the deities appropriate to the particular puja. For the consecration of the stupa site, these would include the deities who look after the land and who might be disturbed by the building work that was about to begin. Later on, at the completion of each chamber, offerings would be made to the deity or deities residing within that chamber: Manjushri,* Tara,† Amitabha‡ and so on.

Then the monks generate in their minds the awakened qualities of the Buddhas, so that they themselves become, for the duration of the puja at least, an embodiment of those awakened qualities. Once building had begun, the Buddhas thus invoked would be invited to enter into the physical form of the stupa and the monks would extol the luminous qualities of the Buddhas that are now resident within it.

Finally, any merit accumulated by the proper performance of the puja is dedicated to the welfare of all sentient beings.

---

* The embodiment of the knowledge and wisdom of all the Buddhas, traditionally depicted with a sword in his right hand and a text in his left hand.

† A much-loved meditation deity, embodying the feminine quality of active compassion.

‡ Also spelled Amitayus, and called Tsepakme in Bhutan, a deity connected with long life, sometimes known as the Buddha of Boundless Light.

A small crowd had gathered by the agreed time, though Lama Sonam, with typically erratic Bhutanese time keeping, was already going strong. He and Cheku sat cross-legged on a rug facing the improvised altar, *tormas* and bowls of offerings arranged in front of the Buddha statue. Lama Sonam had a white and purple shawl draped over his customary grubby dark red *gho*, reading glasses perched precariously on his nose. In his right hand he held a small double-headed drum, which he rattled by rapidly rotating his wrist; in his left hand was a hand-bell.

Bursts of drumming and bell ringing punctuated his chanting. Cheku was by his side, totally focused on what he was doing, the master's trusted and invaluable assistant. Phub Dorji was busy and practical and in the thick of things, keeping the offering fire stoked, joining in the chanting from time to time, improvising a shade to stop the flour and butter *tormas* melting in the hot sun. Kesang skittered round the edges, helping where he could, not always seeming certain what he was supposed to be doing. The smoke billowed thick and white from the burnt offerings, blowing, as smoke always does in the open air, wherever you are sitting, straight into the faces of the spectators.

My father and stepmother Patricia arrived a little after eleven in the electric golf buggy they used to get around Harewood now they were less mobile. It was their first encounter with the Bhutanese and I wondered what they would make of it all. Mildly supportive was how I would have described their attitude to the project so far, curious rather than overly enthusiastic. They both had travelled quite widely in the subcontinent and had a strong affection for it, especially Indian classical music, dance, art and architecture. My father loved the virtuosity of the great performers (he'd passed some of that love down to me) and the wild, rich, operatic quality of the mythology and imagery of Hindu culture that had inspired it. But Buddhism was another matter. Not as varied. Not as colourful. A little austere for his tastes perhaps. I remember once looking with him at a statue of the Buddha, sitting serenely in a meditation posture. A beautiful image. 'A bit of a boring fellow, don't you think,' he said, trying to wind me up, with some success. He liked to prod people to see what sort of reaction he would get. 'You've never seen paintings of tantric deities on the walls of a Tibetan temple, though, have you?' I thought, but didn't say. I probably should have done. But I very rarely argued with my father, even when I didn't agree with him.

Lama Sonam broke off his chanting to greet them and, to my father's considerable surprise (and mine), he and the other monks all produced white prayer scarves, *kadas*, from inside their robes and draped them round his and Patricia's necks. We teased Lama Sonam afterwards that he had only done it because he was jealous that not only was my dad older than him, but he also had a far bigger and whiter beard – both true, but the honour was sincerely offered and gracefully received. By noon they had finished. Christopher, who, like the Harewood Stupa project, was born in a Year of the Sheep, broke the earth with a trowel and was honoured with another *kada*. Phub Dorji and Kesang enclosed the site with a length of coloured threads, twisted together, passed round poles in the four corners and strung with seeds which Lama Sonam had brought with him in his suitcase.

A project was born. Everything was now ready for work to begin.

LAMA IAN: HAREWOOD, MAY 2004

Lama Sonam unrolled his diagram of the stupa, an elevation drawn on squared paper. It wasn't the same as the sketch he had shown me in Hongtso; it was bigger and there seemed to be more detail. This was to be the blueprint. Or so I thought.

Ian Copeland looked sceptical, not a good sign as his involvement was crucial to the success of the project. Ian is the Estate Manager at Harewood, a builder by trade, and he was to be the link between the monks and the Yorkshire craftsmen and labourers who woud under-take the construction work. Ian comes from north-east England but has lived and worked much of his life in Skipton in the Yorkshire Dales. This was a Hongtso/Skipton co-production and Ian was the key to it.

'I thought you said the proportions were important,' Ian said.

'They are,' I said. Lama Sonam and the others nodded in agreement.

'But this drawing isn't accurate,' Ian said. 'Look – the squares aren't even all the same size.'

He was right. The grid was hand-drawn and on closer examination the stupa was more than a little lop-sided.

'What I need is a scale drawing. You understand? Scale drawing?' Ian said.

Phub Dorji, official translator, looked concerned.

'Scale drawing!' Ian repeated a little louder. 'One square, one unit. A unit can be one inch, one foot, one metre, anything. You make the drawing. I'll build it. But if the drawing isn't accurate, then . . .' He made a dramatic mime of a building collapsing.

The Bhutanese all laughed – a little nervously.

We realised we could calculate the exact size of the stupa from the one component we already had – the crescent moon and sun I had carried back from Bhutan in my suitcase. This was four units high on the drawing and measured sixteen inches high in reality. Easy calculation: one unit equals four inches. We looked at the drawing again and counted the squares across the bottom. Thirty-two of them. Thirty-two times four inches equals 128 inches, which is ten feet eight inches. The base was going to be ten feet eight inches wide.

Now it was Lama Sonam's turn to look sceptical. He either didn't trust or didn't understand the calculation.

'We must get some proper graph paper,' someone suggested.

'I've got an idea,' Ian said. 'Just give me a minute.' And he dashed out.

The Bhutanese were looking apprehensive. Phub Dorji told me that Lama Sonam was worried in case we thought he'd made a mistake or didn't really know what he was doing and would not make a good stupa. I tried to be reassuring.

'Nobody has any doubt at all about Lama Sonam's knowledge of stupas and how to make them,' I said. 'But to build one here in England is different from in Bhutan. All the knowledge is in his head and we must have the information in a form that everybody here can understand, too. That means on a piece of paper that people here can refer to when they are working. You will not have to do any of the physical work. The workmen here will do all that, from your plans and designs. What you must do is supervise and make sure the work is right – that and perform the rituals and pujas of course.'

It turned out that when Lama Sonam was younger, he used to do almost all the construction work himself: masonry, carpentry, painting and so on, as well as the planning and drawing and all the rituals. I think he hadn't till this moment realised (though he had been told) how much of the physical labour was going to be taken off his shoulders by Yorkshire builders and by modern machinery. He looked pleased, if still a little uncertain about how this system would actually work in practice.

Ian reappeared with two lengths of timber about twelve feet long.

'This is the height of the square base of the stupa,' he said, referring to Lama Sonam's drawing and then marking a point some eight and a half feet up the timber. 'On this piece of wood you mark each part of the base – first step one unit, second step one unit, broad plinth four units and so on. Then we will have a scale model on paper and full-size measurements on here.'

When I came back a few hours later, work was in full swing. Lama Sonam loved the graph paper and he and Cheku had already started on the technical drawings – not just for the Harewood Stupa but of all the eight kinds for future reference. The length of wood had been marked out as discussed. Lama Sonam had created a wooden rule for himself, with the basic four-inch unit and multiples thereof marked up on it. Christopher appeared with a set of drawing instruments to replace their improvised compass of string, drawing pin and pencil. There was a proper compass, dividers, a protractor and so on, all in a smart leather case rather like one I remembered having at school.

It seemed like a mutually acceptable working method was evolving, both sides trying their best to accommodate the other. Ian was often frustrated by Lama Sonam's refusal to believe in mathematics and his rather approximate approach to measuring. The Bhutanese in turn were initially a little taken aback by Ian's forthright and remorselessly practical approach to every problem. But they made each other laugh and a genuine rapport was developing.

'I'm trying to make them understand mathematics,' Ian said. 'I don't mind really if they don't get it – at the moment they think I'm a genius!'

And before long the Bhutanese had their own nickname for him. 'Ian, he is always action,' Phub Dorji said. 'You must do like this, you must do like that. But he is good man, so now we call him Lama Ian Action.'

The problem with measurements rumbled on through the whole project. The fact was that Lama Sonam simply wasn't very good at measuring. He seemed to be working on the opposite of the old builder's principle of 'measure twice, cut once'. He certainly knew the principles, no question about that, but when it came to actually measuring something or laying it out he could not be relied on. I'd be fairly sure that, in Bhutan, he'd have simply adjusted as he went along, either physically doing the building himself or sitting by the people who were and that as a result it would all work out fine in the end. On the other hand, there are some fairly wonky stupas in Bhutan (none built by Lama Sonam, I'm sure!). And sometimes they do fall down. The Harewood Stupa, on the other hand, has a thousand-year guarantee, inside and out. Both Lama Sonam and Lama Ian had staked their professional reputations on it and that was good enough for me.

SOME GEOMETRY

The confusion about the diagram had really brought home how important the technical side of the building process was going to be. I loved the simplicity of the basic components of the stupa – the cube, the sphere and the cone – and how these had evolved into its sophisticated and harmonious sculptural form. But I was also coming to realise there was far more to it than that. There was a point where basic mathematical geometry evolved into something far more complex – sacred geometry, the symbolic meaning of shapes and forms. This is fundamental to all Tibetan Buddhist visual art: building a stupa, ensuring the correct proportions when drawing a deity or knowing how to create what is perhaps the most spectacular manifestation of Tibetan religious art – the sand mandala. More about sand mandalas later.

Let's start with the simplest form of all: a single point, a mark on a piece of paper. A point has no inside or outside, no top, no bottom, no side. A point has no dimension. It is simply a point.

•

Draw a second point and make a line between it and the first point. The first point can be described as passive, the second as active. By drawing a line between them you have entered the second dimension.

You want to make a square. Swivel the line to a position vertically above the passive point and then do the same above the active point. Draw a line between the two new points. You want to enter the third dimension? Simply lift the square vertically to the same height as its four sides. You have a cube.

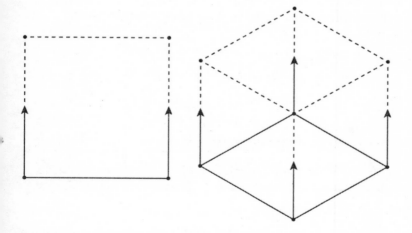

You want to make a circle. Simply rotate the active point round the passive one. Then spin the circle on its axis and you have described the shape of a sphere.

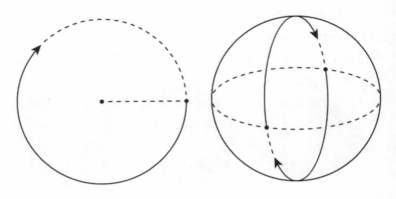

An equilateral triangle is next. Fold your original line upwards from both the passive and the active point to ninety degrees then inwards till the two lines meet equidistant to the original position of both points. To enter the third dimension, you must find a point above and equidistant to the three corners of the triangle and draw three lines up to it. You have a tetrahedron.[1]

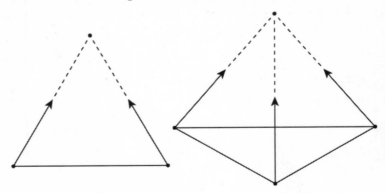

The cube, the sphere and the tetrahedron are the fundamental geometrical components of all three-dimensional objects, both natural and man-made. And if you place the tetrahedron on top of the sphere on top of the cube you have the building blocks of the Himalayan stupa.

Buddhist teachings are full of lists – the Four Noble Truths, the Eight-fold Noble Path and so on – but they seem to be particularly keen on lists of five, for reasons nobody has ever really explained to me. Five fingers or five senses perhaps? The number five comes up again and again when describing what makes a stupa.

So, following the rule of five, let's add two more to the three basic geometric shapes we have already described: an inverted hemisphere (like the Buddha's upturned begging bowl) and a jewel-drop (like a teardrop or a stylised flame).

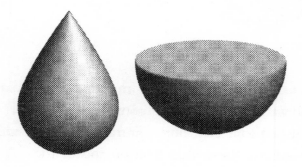

Place the two new shapes on top of the cube, the sphere and the tetrahedron and you have the five geometrical components of a stupa.

Each of these five shapes has an element, a colour and a cardinal direction associated with it.

The first four elements – Earth, Water, Fire and Air – we are familiar with. The fifth, Space, is the element that both encloses and is enclosed by everything: it is above everything, below everything, surrounding everything and within everything. In depictions of landscape in traditional Tibetan paintings the element Earth is represented by rocks and mountains and fields, Water by rivers and lakes and waterfalls, Fire by flames, Air by cloud formations and Space by clear sky and rainbows.[2]

Similarly, the five colours roughly correspond to the scientific description of the visible spectrum, the colours produced when white light is dispersed by a prism.

To the four cardinal directions with which we are all familiar, Buddhist teaching adds a fifth: Centre. This is because a stupa is also a three-dimensional mandala, something that is visually very clear when viewed from above. The heart of the mandala, the centre of the stupa, becomes the fifth direction. Mandala translates literally as 'circle' and all mandalas grow outwards from a central circle. It can also be defined as a sacred space expressed as a simple outline (see the drawing overleaf), as an elaborate sculpture or painting, as a built structure like a stupa, even as a landscape. When I attended a week-long Dzogchen ceremony on Holy Island (the one off the island of Arran, not Lindisfarne in Northumberland), the whole island was consecrated as a mandala, therefore a safe and sacred place, for the duration. A mandala is sometimes described as a cosmogram or a stylised representation of the world, but it is more accurate to say that it is a symbolic map of the nature of mind.

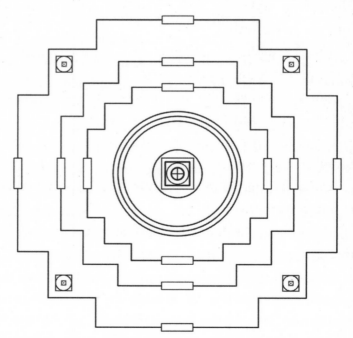

An aerial view of the Great Stupa at Boudha and a simplified outline of the Dharmadatu mandala

Let's add a final set of five: the five Jina Buddhas. These are not historical Buddhas like Buddha Sakyamuni, who lived and taught in this world. Rather, they represent the different qualities of the Buddha, the deeper meaning of his teachings. They are sometimes known as the Five Wisdom Buddhas, or the Five Victorious Buddhas, and they have their own mandala, the Diamond World Mandala. Each Jina Buddha has its own mudra* and sets of attributes. Each Jina Buddha is associated with a particular colour and a particular cardinal direction, and in larger stupas of the Himalayan style you will often find their statues set into the outer wall:

Amoghasiddhi, the Buddha of Unfailing Success, is green and is found to the north.

Ratnasambhava, the Jewel-Born, is yellow and is found to the south.

Vairocana, the Illuminator, the Sun, is white and is found to the east.

Amitabha, the Buddha of Boundless Light, is red and is found to the west.

Akshobhya, the Immovable, is blue and is found to the centre.

---

* A symbolic hand gesture, made as an offering or act of homage to a deity.

Shape	Element	Colour	Direction	Jina Buddha
Cube	Earth	Yellow	South	Ratnasambhava
Sphere	Water	White	East	Vairocana
Tetrahedron	Fire	Red	West	Amitabha
Hemisphere	Air	Green	North	Amoghasiddhi
Jewel	Space	Blue	Centre	Akshobhya

The shapes that make up a stupa, at first sight quite simple, are starting to grow into something more complex. There is an easily understood visual progression here: the cube has slimmed down into the elegantly tiered square base, the sphere stylised into the bell-like dome and the cone into the ringed spire. Buddhist iconography and symbolism are now built into the design too.

In some Buddhist countries, the words used to name parts of the body – the seat, the torso, the crown and so on – and the names of the parts of the stupa are the same. In others, the words for 'stupa' and for 'Buddha' are identical. Some scholars argue that in Buddhist art the image of the Buddha and the image of the stupa are interchangeable.

In the drawing overleaf, devised by the artist Robert Beer, the Buddha sits in full meditation posture: cross-legged, settled, comfortable. The niche containing the Buddha statue is centred on his heart. The sun and moon and jewel tip on top of the thirteen-ringed spire form the characteristic top-knot on top of his head. In the theoretical grid on which this striking image is based there is a direct correlation between the artist's

The five building blocks

Enlightenment Stupa silhouette

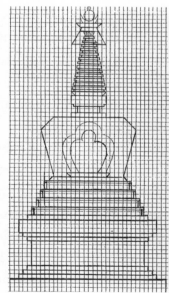

Lama Sonam's grid

The Harewood stupa

grid describing the idealised proportions of a seated Buddha and the grid laying down the proportions of an Enlightenment Stupa.[3] I think it was only at the moment I saw this diagram that I fully understood that what we were building, once complete, was a representation of the Buddha himself.

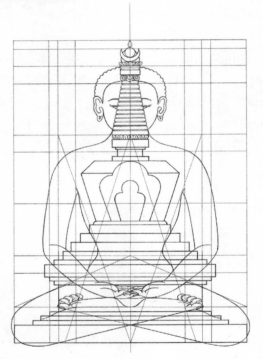

THE SHIPMENT ARRIVES: HAREWOOD, MONDAY, 21 JUNE 2004

The shipment from Bhutan arrived at last, more than four weeks after the monks. This was frustrating, because I'd thought I had started the process when I was in Bhutan some six months earlier. First there were delays when Chen Chen had problems getting a flight to Nepal to buy the statues that were an important part of the shipment, then more delays while the exact composition of the building team travelling to the UK was decided, then even more delays for reasons I never made out. The idea of taking the ideal arrival date and then working back six weeks to find when the shipment should leave didn't seem to have occurred to anybody. In the end nothing really happened till early May. Then everything was packed into boxes and sent off by truck overland from Thimphu to Kolkata, loaded into a container, put onto a boat, then – for reasons we never discovered – taken off the boat again at Colombo in Sri Lanka and onto another one bound for the English port of Felixstowe, due to dock on 15 June.

It was then that we realised the Bhutanese shippers had made a mistake. They had checked the delivery address – The Estate Office, Harewood, near Leeds; they knew the shipment was going to somewhere there was a large country house, had looked up Leeds on the internet, found Leeds Castle, assumed that was where the shipment was headed and were very pleased with themselves for having arranged shipment to a port that they believed to be quite close to its final destination. Unfortunately for this plan, Leeds Castle is in Kent and has nothing to do with the city of Leeds, which is more than 200 miles away in Yorkshire. I hadn't the heart to tell them of their error, which in the end only added a few days to the schedule.

The delay had not been too costly. The time had flown by: acclimatisation time for the monks, then a period of drawing and planning and logistics, getting the Bhutanese design team and the UK building team speaking the same operational language and used to the idea of working from detailed and accurate designs that everybody was agreed on.

There had been an interesting debate about what the finish would be. Lama Sonam had assumed it would be whitewashed, like almost every stupa in Bhutan. I was equally clear that it had to be made of local stone, a combination of stone found on the Harewood Estate and stone from a quarry in the Pennines that would be specially cut when measurements needed to be precise. It was important that the stupa looked as if it was part of the garden landscape in which it sat, not something alien that had been flown in from outside, and the local sandstone is very attractive: warm and robust, very Yorkshire. It was to be an authentic Himalayan stupa, made exactly as one would be in Bhutan or Nepal or Tibet, but it should be built out of local materials. Lama Sonam was impressed when we showed him the quality of the stonework in the walls and buildings at Harewood. There is no tradition of stonemasonry in Bhutan and whitewashing often covers up some pretty rough-and-ready work. The clincher came when we took him to see York Minster, one of the greatest examples of the stonemason's craft anywhere in the world. 'The successors of these great craftsmen will be the men who build the stupa at Harewood,' I announced dramatically if not entirely accurately. But Lama Sonam was already sold on the idea. Natural local stone it would be.

Today was the day the shipment was finally due to arrive at Harewood. It was a bright morning. We had been lucky with the weather so far on this project – storms were due later, but it was sunny for now. The UK agents had been tracking the shipment conscientiously since it left Colombo. We received daily reports: on schedule, two days late, back on schedule and so on. Despite the constant updates we were all getting a little nervous. Phub Dorji told me that Lama Sonam asked him every morning when the shipment would arrive.

'Soon,' Phub Dorji would say. 'Tomorrow.'

Lama Sonam would sigh and shake his head gloomily: 'Lost at sea.'

In the end it arrived at Felixstowe a day later than expected, not bad for such a long journey. Customs was the next hurdle. My PA Brenda had been very thorough with the paperwork. Everything had to have an individual coding, not only what it was ('A bead necklace' or 'A wooden religious statue') but exactly what each item was made of, right down to what kind of wood or what kind of stone. Often I had no idea and in several cases I hadn't even seen the object in question, in which case I just made it up. The important thing was to get something down on the form that was as accurate as we could make it. So a bead necklace was described as 'Coral and semi-precious stones: value £33.33'. (I had asked the agent in Bhutan to mark everything down to around a third of its value to lessen the chance of being charged import duty, a request that he had taken rather more literally than intended.) The fear was that Customs would open the boxes and find all kinds of things they weren't expecting or wouldn't understand: tin cans full of plant material, statues full of rolled-up bits of paper with mantras printed on them, jars full of butter and so on. They could have had a field day. But our luck held, as it had when travelling with the monks and their strange hand baggage, and the shipment was cleared within twenty-four hours.

The truck with the container was due at Harewood on Monday morning. At 7.15 I got a phone call.

'The truck's at the office. Security are going to escort it down to The Hovels. Is that OK?'

I jumped in the car and hurried down. Christopher intercepted me en route.

'The driver's being difficult. Says he won't go down as far as The Hovels, the branches are too low and will scratch his precious truck. So I've told him he'll have to unload by my office.'

Lama Sonam was particularly impressed by the size of the truck, which was indeed pristine and, we discovered, on its first run. No wonder the driver didn't want to scratch it. He explained the procedure: once cleared, the container had been sealed by Customs, so we would need some powerful bolt cutters to break the seal. From the moment the seal was broken responsibility for the load transferred from the shipper to the receiver. This was a symbolic moment, the end of a long journey, so clearly the breaking of the seal was an action that demanded a theatrical gesture. Ian appeared with some massive and very rusty bolt cutters, almost too heavy for me to lift. I brandished them clumsily like some kind of giant medieval weapon, then, with a heave and a snip, it was done. Everyone clapped. A forklift truck of rather different age and pedigree to the container lorry arrived from a neighbouring farm, plastered with mud and pig shit and very smelly. There were six wooden crates inside the container and the forklift lifted them out one by one while we stood round drinking sweet tea in the sunshine.

'I wonder if they've put an old Bhutanese lady in one of the crates for me,' said Lama Sonam, wistfully.

With a farewell blast of his air-horn, the container driver was gone. We loaded the crates back onto a trailer, attached it to a tractor, and all set off for The Hovels.

'This stuff has come seven thousand miles,' Christopher said. 'For God's sake don't let's drop it now!'

The unpacking began. It was strangely emotional to see all these things, bought all those months ago in Thimphu market or made at Lama Sonam's workshop in Hongtso, emerging from their cases into the

Yorkshire sunshine. Now *all* the ingredients were here. It felt like a major turning point.

'Isn't it great when a plan comes together?' I said.

'This is no time to be quoting *The A-Team*,' said Ian.

The *tsa-tsas* took up most space, three of the six crates, but, then, they are one of the most important ingredients of the stupa. Brenda thought they looked like fairy cakes. Miraculously, only three had broken in transit. They had already been consecrated when they were made, but now they had to be blessed all over again before being put into the stupa – a lot of work, with cases to be unpacked, candles to be lit, incense burned and prayers offered up. Another crate contained the statues. The first to be unwrapped was the big Buddha statue I had seen already in Lama Sonam's house in Hongtso. This would go in the niche in the domed part of the stupa. The other, smaller statues I had not seen before. Chen Chen had bought them in Nepal and they were already en route by the time I was back in Bhutan in May. They were very fine, elegantly cast in copper and bronze, with delicate features and hands. No time to get attached to them, though – a good Buddhist lesson here – as they wouldn't be visible for very long. Three of them would go into the three chambers inside the stupa: first Tara (active compassion), then Manjushri (wisdom) and finally Amitabha (long life). The three smallest ones – the Buddha, Chenresig (Avalokiteshvara in Sanskrit), Guru Rinpoche – would be attached to the *Sok-shing*.

Other cases contained all the other items we knew we were not going to be able to get or make in England: sealed pots of offerings; Bhutanese clothes and ornaments; a full set of monastic musical instruments (drums, bells, cymbals and horns); a sword, bow and arrow; several dozen rolls of mantras printed on paper and bound in yellow muslin.

The *Sok-shing* was individually packed in a long, thin case. The monks unwrapped it very carefully from the layers of fabric in which it had travelled. It looked much the same as it had when I'd seen it in Lama Sonam's workshop in January, with one important addition: its broad base had been carved into the shape of a *dorje*, the thunderbolt that clears away the clouds of delusion, and the narrow top was shaped like a stupa. Within a few days the elaborate process of preparing the *Sok-shing*, re-empowering and dressing it like a living thing, had begun.

First the monks wrapped it top to toe in several layers of yellow muslin. Then forty-two small paper packets were placed on the upper surface, the east face, which had been carefully marked when the juniper tree was cut down on the hillside above Wangdi all those months ago. The packets were then bound tightly to it with coloured thread. Each one contained a holy relic of one sort or another, described in writing on the outside of each packet. One packet, for example, contained medicines given to me by a Bhutanese friend, Genzing Dorji, owner of the Gangtey Palace Hotel, which she had had specially consecrated. Another had been brought from Bhutan by Phub Dorji and contained relics of the 69th Je Khenpo, a tiny pinch of ashes from his cremation. Then, the three small bronze and copper statues, of the Buddha, Chenresig and Guru Rinpoche, were heavily swaddled in cotton wool and yellow cloth before being secured with more coloured thread.

In the photograph above Lama Sonam was in The Hovels wrapping holy texts. They would be lashed to the ever-expanding cylinder of the *Sok-shing*, which lies on the chairs on the left of the picture. In the background are some of the other artefacts, which were to end up inside the stupa.

Lama Sonam continued to prepare the bundles of rolled-up mantras, sticking the smaller ones end to end to make long cylinders about eighteen inches long and binding two or three cylinders together. These, along with the larger rolls, were packed round the outside of the tree, between and round the three statues, looking like sticks of cartoon dynamite tied to a ship's mast, then all lashed on as tightly as possible, Phub Dorji pulling at the thread till his fingers blistered and bled. Then four lengths of coloured cloth were cut to the same length as the *Sok-shing* and wrapped round everything, relics, statues and mantras, before being tied tight with more thread and stitched at either end. More and more fabric was added until the *Sok-shing* had become a cylinder of dense cloth, about a foot in diameter, several times its original weight and with no hint of all the things underneath. It looked like a giant doner kebab wrapped in Christmas paper. The only part of the once slender and delicately painted length of wood that you could now see was the stupa carved at one end and the *dorje* at the other end. Finally, everything was sealed with a kind of resin, oxblood in colour and made, Lama Sonam said, from insects that you found in the kind of juniper tree that the *Sok-shing* was made from. This didn't sound very likely to me: Buddhists would not want to kill thousands of insects, especially for this purpose, but I couldn't get a satisfactory answer from Lama Sonam or any of the other monks. 'From insect,' was all they would say.

This mysterious substance had come all the way from Bhutan in irregular, lumpy blocks. Now the monks were smashing these blocks up, pulverising them and boiling the powder in water to make a thick, sticky, toxic-looking paste. This was then painted all over the wrapped *Sok-shing*, forming a seal that protects the tree and everything attached to it from the elements. Lama Sonam told a story about a 600-year-old stupa he was once asked to repair and reconsecrate. When he broke through the resin sealing the *Sok-shing*, all the objects inside still looked brand new.

The powdered insects – or whatever they were – bubbled away dangerously in a cauldron in the yard outside The Hovels. We asked Lama Sonam if there was an alternative substance we could use, something easier to handle and apply – and safer – than the resin. Ian suggested some kind of plastic coating. 'How long would that last?' Lama Sonam asked. 'I don't know – maybe a hundred years,' Ian replied. 'Not long enough,' said Lama Sonam. So, traditional resin it was.*

Now the *Sok-shing* was ready to take its place at the heart of the stupa. But first, the First Chamber in the base of the stupa had to be filled with worldly goods, some brought from Bhutan, but with some interesting local additions.

---

* I later discovered that the substance was indeed 'from insects', but not from dead ones. It was a resinous secretion, very like lac, the substance used to make varnish, shellac and sealing wax, also traditionally used as a red dye. So we could say, truthfully, that no insects were killed in coating the *Sok-shing*.

THE FIRST CHAMBER: HAREWOOD, JUNE 2004

The foundation of the stupa contains the First Chamber. This chamber is quite large, around four feet square and three feet deep, lined first with plywood, then with red cotton cloth attached to the walls and floor. It is the base of the stupa, representing samsara, the world we all live in, and so it is full of a whole range of worldly goods.

The first thing that went into the chamber was a mandala made of a pair of crossed *dorjes*, cut out of tin, painted and placed exactly in the centre of the square, pointing in the four cardinal directions. Rice was thrown onto it as an offering.

Next it was the turn of all the things that we surround ourselves with in our busy lives. First were the tools, mostly agricultural as befits a country like Bhutan with a predominantly rural population: there was a model of a plough and yoke, a spade, a hammer, a saw, a sickle, a screwdriver, an axe, a pair of scissors – and a couple of modern Western additions: an old mobile phone (without battery, we didn't want any inappropriate ringtones sounding off during the build) and an old camera, a representative tool of my trade, film-making.

Next were the musical instruments, the full monastic orchestra: a thigh-bone trumpet or *kanglin* (this one actually made out of wood, one of the things I'd been nervous about having in my luggage coming back from

Bhutan); a pair of long horns (*ragdung*) concertinaed down to their shortest length; a pair of *gyaling*, large reed instruments like the Celtic shawm or the Indian *shehnai*; two pairs of cymbals, both thick and thin (*sil nyan* and *bub*), which are played by the chant leaders in monastic ceremonies; a large drum usually mounted in a frame, but sometimes on a stick (*choenga*); a *dradu*, a small double-headed hand-drum; a bell (*drilbu*); and a *dorje*. After the musical instruments came the weapons: from Bhutan a bow and arrow and a sword in a sheath, from the UK a decommissioned hand-gun.

Everyone had been encouraged to contribute something of their own to go into this chamber. They brought a range of ornaments: my sister-in-law Andrea brought a crystal, Brenda gave a brooch, Emily a locket and her husband Matt a stone. Various ornamental beads and a clasp and locket for a *kira* had come from Bhutan. Diane contributed a more poetic collection. There were two of her own photographs: one of smoke, and the other an aerial shot of her land art project in the Harewood Walled Garden, Spiral Meadow. There was also a poem by our friend Thomas A. Clark and two sprigs, one of English herbs and the other of oak, the most English of trees.

Then the first batch of *tsa-tsas* was placed along the east and west wall. On top of them went *tselma namsum*, flat clay tablets, triangular in shape with an impression on them of the three deities whose images would also be placed into the next chambers of the stupa: at the apex of the triangle was Tsepakme (long life), bottom left Tamdrim (a wrathful form of Chenresig), bottom right Tara.

Each of the four corners was marked with the three kinds of victory banners: *gyaltsen* (a pleated umbrella shape), *chubur* (an umbrella shape made up of triangular pieces of fabric) and *darchang* (a flat banner), followed by the four wooden *phurbas* I had been shown in Lama Sonam's workshop. Small photocopied images of the Eight Auspicious Symbols (*tashi zegay*) were placed along the west wall. Inside the stacked rows of *tsa-tsas* and *tselma namsum*, Lama Sonam lined up nine different kinds of traditional Tibetan herbal medicines. They had been in the mysterious jam jars whose contents I did not understand when I was shown them in Bhutan.

Next in towards the centre were various offerings: water, flowers, incense, candles, wine, rice, with two butter lamps at either end – heat and light, food and drink, the essentials of life. Then three different kinds of offering jar were carefully placed on the crossed *dorjes* in the centre, eleven of them in total. The first kind, *lu bum* (*bum* means jar), was for the water-dwelling spirits; the second, *khachu bum*, was to repel ill omens; the third, *yang bum*, was to attract good luck. The jars were all filled with more medicines, specially consecrated and bound in cloth, with a hand-printed description on the lid of each. Once all this was in place and the floor of the chamber almost completely covered, a final round of offerings was sprinkled over everything by hand: dried flower petals, broken-up incense sticks, small fragments of cloth, wheat and dried vegetables.

These and all the other offerings in the First Chamber were there in order to satisfy the earth deities, in this case a naga, a snake-like spirit-creature (called a *lu* in Bhutan) that lives both in water and under the ground.* Lama Sonam told us that today was an auspicious day when the naga was likely to be awake and alert and so would be able to come and accept the offerings. They represented all the things that would satisfy her senses: food, water, medicines, tools, clothes, weapons and so on. After the concentration needed to make sure everything had been put in the right place and in the right order, Lama Sonam and the other monks became more relaxed and took great pleasure in chucking the final offerings of plants and incense wildly into the air, covering each other and many of the bystanders in dust and making them cough.

The filling of the First Chamber had been completed to Lama Sonam's satisfaction. The cavity was then covered with a red cloth, tacked onto the wooden

---

* Many areas in the Himalayas have a whole range of rituals to do with the propitiation of water-dwelling spirits such as nagas because they are believed to be the cause of many illnesses. Modern medicine confirms that waterborne diseases (cholera, dysentery and hepatitis A, for example) are indeed very common in the Himalayas.

chamber lining. Next day the building team would take over and make a two-inch concrete lid to seal the chamber and its contents forever. Then work could begin on the next chamber.

THE SECOND CHAMBER: HAREWOOD, SATURDAY 11 JULY 2004

The Bhutanese had been in England for two months. Today was the day the Second Chamber was to be filled, perhaps the single most important moment in the construction of the stupa.

This was the first of three chambers dedicated to a specific deity, Tara, so the placement of her statue, the building of her mandala and following the correct procedure for making the offerings to her was especially important. It would be a very similar process to the one we had observed Lama Sonam and Cheku carrying out at the stupa in Hongtso. Filling the First Chamber with all the right things and in the right order had been quite intricate, but it had all been done with a certain exuberance and gusto. This next stage would have to be more considered and precise.

This was also the day that the *Sok-shing* was to be erected. Its base would be here in the Second Chamber; the Third and Fourth Chambers would be built around it and its tip would pierce the floor of the Fifth Chamber in the dome. Once the *Sok-shing* was in position, everything properly done and the correct prayers recited, the stupa would no longer be an inert piece of masonry, but something alive, a sacred living thing. This was a turning point.

The statue of Tara had been placed, her mandala created, offerings put carefully in position and all the prayers had been chanted. A small crowd of people waited at the stupa for the *Sok-shing* to arrive. This time they weren't going to be allowed to be mere spectators.

Back at The Hovels, the *Sok-shing* had been carefully loaded onto a trailer, and was trundling slowly towards the stupa location, an incongruous sight on a Yorkshire country lane, but the kind of thing people at Harewood were starting to become quite accustomed to. It was even more heavily swaddled than before, in extra layers for travel protection, and the monks sat with it, cradling it like the body of a loved one. Any slip that might cause it damage would be extremely inauspicious. Bulky and awkwardly balanced, it took four people to carry it the short distance from the trailer to the stupa itself. A sturdy cross-piece made of oak had been fitted securely across the middle of the chamber to take the *Sok-shing*'s weight – not inconsiderable since all the elaborate preparations that had taken place previously – with a small hollow in the middle of it into which the *dorje*-shaped end of the tree would fit. The special mandala made by the young coppersmith in Thimphu was placed centrally on the floor of the chamber, directly beneath it.

Ian and the builders had constructed a scaffolding frame to which the *Sok-shing* could be attached once it had been securely located on the cross-piece and hauled into an upright position. This had been the subject of lengthy discussions between Ian and Lama Sonam, but everyone was happy that this was a system that should – no, that definitely *would* – work. The *Sok-shing* was lifted by hand up onto the temporary platform round the Second Chamber, about eight feet off the ground. This wasn't easy. It seemed to be getting heavier all the time and several of the watchers were pressed into helping. Now it was in position, still horizontal, but poised for the *dorje* to be aligned with the hollow in the centre of the cross-piece.

A delay. Lama Sonam wanted to be absolutely sure the *Sok-shing* was in the right orientation – that the east face of the tree, buried deep under all its layers, was still facing east. He checked the marks: the tree was turned a few degrees. Now everything was correctly aligned. There was quite a crowd of us up on the scaffolding platform by now. I hoped it would bear our weight. How essential we all were was open to debate but everyone was engrossed, wholly committed to helping, determined to make their own contribution, a real group effort. In Buddhist societies, assisting in the building of a stupa is seen as something that brings great merit, but for this group of mainly non-Buddhist Westerners it was an instinctive reaction.

We started to haul the *Sok-shing* upright, hand over

hand, Ian very much in control of the practicalities, Lama Sonam making sure there were no procedural slip-ups. And then it was vertical. Ian had his spirit level out and a large spanner to fit the four lengths of scaffolding that would hold the tree in place.

It was done. People started to drift away. Lama Sonam and the monks performed their pujas. The builders covered the chamber in protective plastic sheeting. The Second Chamber was complete.

THE THIRD AND FOURTH CHAMBERS: HAREWOOD, JULY 2004

The process of filling the Third and Fourth Chambers was essentially the same as for the Second Chamber, but without the erecting of the *Sok-shing*. Where the Second Chamber is dedicated to Tara, these are dedicated to Chenresig and Amitabha, so the mandala in each one is different, as are the offerings, the subsidiary images and the *tsa-tsas* too. Different *tsa-tsas* have different mantras sealed inside them – hence the colour coding – and the mantras have to match the deity.

In the north-west corner of the Fourth Chamber was a little shrine to Tsogda,* a deity of wealth and property specific to the area of eastern Bhutan that Lama Sonam

---

* Tsogda has a similar role to the elephant-headed Ganesh, perhaps the best known of all Hindu deities. He is invoked as a remover of obstacles and worshipped by householders as the protector of wealth.

was from, screened from the rest of the chamber with a purple cloth. There were various offerings quite specific to Tsogda, different from any made so far: special *tormas*, food, money, with a butter lamp placed on top of the image.

'For this chamber we need to make a ninety-nine-fruit offering,' Lama Sonam told me. 'Only dried fruit will do.'

I was taken aback. 'Ninety-nine fruits!' I said. 'I doubt if there are ninety-nine different kinds of edible fruit in the world, let alone dried ones! How many would you find in the markets in Bhutan? About six – if you were lucky!'

Lama Sonam was adamant. That was what it said in the texts. That is what we needed to find.

'You have chosen to make very difficult stupa,' he said, chuckling.

'No – *you* have chosen to make very difficult stupa,' I replied, laughing too.

So the search for ninety-nine different kinds of dried fruit began. There were compromises to make. Nuts counted as fruits in this context apparently, as did cucumber and sesame seeds, though tomatoes, bizarrely, did not. The first shopping expeditions – to Sainsbury's, to a health food store in Harrogate and to an Indian supermarket in Leeds – yielded better results than expected. A sweep of the spice shelf in my kitchen produced a few more. To my surprise, I found we had got up to forty-seven – pretty impressive I thought, but still less than halfway, still fifty-two short.

I gave Lama Sonam the bad news. He shook his head in disappointment. Then he reached into the folds of his *gho* and produced a small plastic sachet containing some undefined grey substance. He held it up to me and gave it a little shake.

'Ninety-nine-fruit powder,' he said. 'I suppose this will have to do.'[4]

On another occasion Lama Sonam suddenly announced that he needed 4,000 little candles, tea-lights, one for each of the *tsa-tsas*, which were due to be consecrated the next day, an auspicious one. The first thousand were tracked down quite quickly (four bags of 250), but it didn't look as if we were going to be able to get hold of the necessary number in time. Once again there was a pragmatic answer.

'We have big butter lamps too. During blessing, if we keep burning, filled with oil, that is OK for other *tsa-tsas*. No need to buy more.'

An industrial-sized can of cheap cooking oil from the Cash and Carry and some extra-long candlewicks solved the problem.

Getting the right substance to mix with flour to make the many *tormas* that we would need was more difficult. Ghee, the clarified butter much used in Indian cooking, was rejected – too soft, it would make the *tormas* difficult to shape, they wouldn't last as long and they would melt in the sun. A relief actually: ghee is much more expensive in England than it is in Bhutan. What had they been using so far, I wondered? Butter, it turned out, far from ideal as it melted even more quickly than ghee. 'A sponsorship deal with Lurpak?' Emily suggested – not the cheapest brand in the super-market, but the monks' favourite it appeared. She even had a slogan: 'Lurpak – the butter that's better than ghee!' Phub Dorji and Kesang, in charge of shopping, thought this was hilarious.

What they said they needed was a substance called *dalda*, some kind of oil but much firmer and waxier and longer lasting than any of the other substances we had discussed. But nobody in England seemed to know what *dalda* was.

'Palm oil?'

'Not palm oil,' said the monks.

We persuaded the nearest Indian supermarket to let us open and prod and sniff all kinds of tins. None were right.

Finally, an Indian friend in Bradford came up with the answer. Dalda (with a capital D) wasn't a substance, it was a brand name, a kind of vegetable oil, quite firm, and, yes, it should be good for *tormas*. You couldn't get Dalda in the UK but they knew where they could get something just like it. 'How much do you need? How much?? Ten kilos??? I'll see what I can do.'

We went shopping for conch shells in London's Billingsgate fish market, for miles and miles of different coloured cotton thread from a wholesale upholstery shop, for buttons and for scraps of cloth as well as for more conventional things like rice and chillies and the monks' other domestic requirements.

'Tomorrow we go Senz-berry for shop,' Phub Dorji would announce and off to the supermarket he would go, accompanied by someone who would drive, help carry the shopping and had a credit card. Gradually each chamber was being filled, the correct offerings to the deities were being made, the pujas properly performed, the proportions of the outer structure built exactly right. Everything was being done in the authentic way, as Lama Sonam had insisted from the very beginning.

THE FIFTH CHAMBER: HAREWOOD, AUGUST 2004

The Fifth and final Chamber is actually inside the *bumpa*, the domed section of the stupa. We had all thought this might be technically the most difficult part of the construction, but once the decision had been made to use Harewood stone and not the cut gritstone from the quarry, the building work went very quickly.

The day the *bumpa* was due to be filled was forecast as a very wet one. Everyone had become so accustomed to Lama Sonam saying what were auspicious and inauspicious days that nobody noticed it was Friday the 13th. Blue plastic had been draped over the stupa to protect it, the contents of the chamber and everybody working on it. In theory this was going to be a relatively simple chamber to fill, with no deity, no mandala, no careful placement of difficult-to-come-by offerings. Basically, it had to house everything that hadn't been put into the other chambers.

There were religious texts, specifically the sutras relating to the Four Noble Truths, one of the root teachings of Buddhism. These were bound into four bundles, each comprising four books and all coated in the same glutinous resin that had been used to seal the *Sok-shing*, before being wrapped in yellow cloth. There were still some small rolls of mantras left from the wrapping of the *Sok-shing*, which would have to be packed, too, and quite a few *tsa-tsas*. Phub Dorji reckoned there were around 2,000 of them left, not much less than half the number that had been shipped from Bhutan.

To these were added a couple of additional items. There was a list of names, written in English and in Dzongkha, of people who had died recently, a list which included Diane's father Jack Howse, Christopher's father Neville and various friends. The Harewood Stupa was to be, in part at least, in their memory.

I tried to persuade my father and Patricia to contribute something, as many people already had. They were keen, but initially found it difficult to come to terms with the idea of putting something precious into the stupa, something that would then never be seen again. It didn't have to be valuable, I assured them. Anything personal would be fine. Their first idea was a family photograph from my father's eightieth birthday party, but this was firmly rejected by Lama Sonam. It was, he said, not a good idea to put an image of a living person into a stupa. (They were originally reliquary tombs, of course, built to house the ashes of the Buddha himself.) Their next idea was to put in a brass box, a tobacco tin – which I thought was quite ironic given my father's extreme aversion to smoking. But this was no ordinary tobacco tin. My grandmother, my father's mother, had commissioned several thousand of them in 1914 and had sent them as a personal gift at Christmas to the British troops serving in the trenches at the start of the First World War. The lid has her profile on it, her initial ('M' for Mary) and the date. So this was something that had a meaningful personal and family connection, but was not especially valuable. Lama Sonam approved. 'Like tin for paan,' he said, which is of course exactly what it is. He opened the lid, saw that the tin was empty and gestured to me to fill it with a pinch of each of the various offerings that were going to go into the chamber.

My father came down to watch, in good spirits despite my having to bully him into dressing appropriately in boots and a warm coat. He was disappointed there was no music and could not be persuaded – very sensibly – to climb the slippery ladder to the scaffolding platform that we were working from. He sat quite happily to one side, chatting to whoever was nearby, sipping coffee laced with whisky from a thermos.

Phub Dorji and Cheku were already inside the

chamber, arranging the first layer of *tsa-tsas*. The chamber was quite small, the same shape as the *bumpa*, with the tip of the *Sok-shing* poking up into it. There didn't seem to me to be any way we would be able to fit 2,000 *tsa-tsas* and all the other stuff into it. But we did. First, a layer of *tsa-tsas*, with the texts and rolls of mantras packed round the indentation made by the niche in which the Buddha statue would finally sit. Then we sprinkled offerings all over them – scraps of cloth, rice, incense powder, dried flowers and great fistfuls of the dry rhododendron twigs and leaves that had been used as packing – until the *tsa-tsas* were completely covered. Lama Sonam flung the dusty twigs and incense around vigorously, chuckling mischievously as it made us – and him – cough and splutter. We kept on repeating this process, layer upon layer, until we reached the top of the chamber and realised that, miraculously, every single *tsa-tsa* had gone.

'Is very good, very lucky, that we fill with nothing left,' said Phub Dorji, beaming and sweating as we finished and covered the chamber with cloth and then plastic against the elements. Indeed it was. And it hadn't even rained that heavily.

A TRIP TO THE SEASIDE: YORKSHIRE, AUGUST 2004

It wasn't all work for the monks. One thing we were all determined they should do was go to the seaside: a typical English summer holiday outing that would be a novelty for the Bhutanese. Their landlocked country is several hundred miles from the sea and only Kesang, a little more travelled than the rest, had ever seen the ocean.

There were heavy showers the morning we had arranged our outing to Whitby and Robin Hood's Bay on the East Yorkshire coast. We looked at the sky and decided to postpone our departure by a couple of hours to see if it got any better. It didn't. 'Let's go anyway,' I said. 'The weather's often better on the coast.'

We set off. The further east we got the worse the weather became. The road on the other side of York was clogged with traffic and there was flooding near Pickering with a long tailback from the roundabout in the centre of town. Lama Sonam was praying loudly in the back of the car. I didn't take it personally any more. He did it on every journey, whoever was at the wheel.

'This next bit of the road is very beautiful,' I said as we drove slowly up onto the North Yorkshire Moors, stuck in a line of cars behind two caravans. 'Great views.'

The higher we climbed, the lower the clouds seemed to get. There was the occasional glimpse across the Moors, fresh heather glowing purple in the murk, but none of the magnificent long vistas I'd been describing so enthusiastically. There is a magical moment as you come down from the Moors towards Whitby when you get the first glimpse of the sea, sparkling in the distance beyond the rolling hills. Today there was just a view of a large blue big top dripping forlornly in a muddy field. The circus was coming to town.

'Do you get typhoons in England?' asked Kesang, whose only previous experience of the sea was in Hong Kong. Under the circumstances it wasn't an unreasonable question.

We parked in the car park at the top of the hill at Robin Hood's Bay and huddled under the tailgate as we assembled wet weather gear for the walk down to the seafront. The road down the hill – the only road in town – is steep and winding. Today it felt more like a water-chute feature in an amusement park than a thoroughfare for traffic. Families in shorts and plastic ponchos huddled in the doorways of the souvenir shops and watched curiously as our unlikely group hurried by.

Fish and chips in a nice café by the sea was the plan. Haddock and chips all round and some crisps to nibble while we were waiting. Lama Sonam fiddled with his crisp packet, unable to get a purchase on the slippery plastic. Suddenly, he pulled a large machete from under his *gho* and sliced the packet open, knife back under cover quick as a flash and before anybody noticed or tried to have us arrested.

We stared out of the window as the rain lashed down on the beach and told tales of sodden childhood summer holidays. We tried to explain that this was, in its way, a very typical English seaside experience.

We finished our fish and chips (another first and a big success with the Bhutanese) and, typical English summer, the rain started to ease. By the time we'd walked past the lifeboats and down the slipway onto the beach it had stopped enough for us to take down our umbrellas. The tide was going out, revealing ribs of stone and salty rockpools, classic beachcombing territory and the Bhutanese proved to be absolute naturals at it. Phub Dorji was keen that each of us English – Diane, Brenda and me – should find a special stone to give him, which we duly did, though he rejected Brenda's first offering, big as a football, as being impractical. Cheku decided to specialise in shells: winkles, whelks and tiny cowries. 'Like little conch,' Phub Dorji said. With some help from Kesang, Lama Sonam ended up with a carrier bag full of carefully selected pebbles and seemed particularly pleased with a couple I found for him, both dark grey with white circular markings: 'Sun and Moon,' he said. They each had brought a bottle to collect 'ocean water'. After an hour of this, it started to drizzle again and we made our way back up to the car, the Bhutanese lingering to lean on a railing high above the beach and look down at the grey breakers rolling endlessly in.

There were a couple of trips to York, one with Harewood House Trust's Director, Terry Suthers. A long-time York resident, Terry is an archaeologist by training and an enthusiastic fount of knowledge about the city's history. He took the Bhutanese on a tour of the city walls and entertained them with stories of Vikings and Romans and ghostly hauntings. They made another visit to York Minster and were amazed once again by the artistry and detail of the stonework. Lama Sonam rubbed his calloused country builder's hand over the smooth curves and delicate carvings and shook his head disbelievingly. But I'm not sure they knew what to make of the choral music by candlelight in the Chancery Chapel, music that is a million miles from the bass rumble and clashing cymbals of Himalayan Buddhist sacred music. A large meal in York's best Indian restaurant afterwards, however, was definitely appreciated.

In Bhutan monks aren't supposed to go to sporting events. When I went to a football match in Thimphu, police came onto the sparsely populated terraces at half-time and brusquely shooed Phub Dorji and some of his monk friends out of the ground. I'd already taken Phub Dorji to a pre-season friendly at Elland Road, much to the astonishment of some of my Leeds United-supporting friends. Now I was driving to Tadcaster with him to watch polo. I'd never been to a polo match before and Phub Dorji certainly hadn't, but we had friends who were enthusiastic players and they invited us along. At the end of the afternoon Phub Dorji was asked to present the trophy. His enthusiasm for new experiences was insatiable and his sociability inexhaustible, though this did create a small problem before the end.

FINISHING OFF: YORKSHIRE, AUGUST 2004

Completing the last sections of the stupa seemed to happen very quickly. Up until the filling of the *bumpa* the speed of progress had been determined by a host of factors, quite outside the actual building work: the gathering together of the right materials for offerings; making sure the necessary pujas were performed; choosing an auspicious day to perform them on, and so on.

Lama Sonam's health was sometimes an issue, too. He was not a young man, in a culture and environment with which he was not familiar. He and the other monks loved the Yorkshire countryside – 'The garden of the gods!' they would exclaim when there was a particularly lush and beautiful English summer's day – and every effort was made to look after them as well as possible. But Lama Sonam was a bit of a hypochondriac. Gastric problems, blood pressure, eyesight – he was always complaining about something. Brenda offered to take him to the doctor, but he wouldn't go with a woman, so Ian showed great patience in making sure his various ailments were addressed when necessary, but not over-indulged. He would return to Bhutan with a bag full of medicines and a pair of new reading glasses, ×2 magnification from Boots.

Now the *bumpa* was filled, the rest of the work was basically structural. The *harmika* – the square section above the *bumpa* – and the thirteen-ringed spire were both made by the stonemasons Ian had recommended, Jim Galt and his company Stonecraft. Lama Sonam found it difficult to understand how the stone was going to be cut so precisely, so Ian took him and the other monks to see Stonecraft's quarry and workshop up in the Pennines above Todmorden. Cranes and fork-lifts clanked and groaned into position like mating primeval beasts and hauled great lumps of Pennine gritstone from the cliff face to the cutting benches where huge band saws sliced through the rock like a knife through soft butter. There, Jim and his team of masons prepared and dressed the cut rock ready to take its place in the stupa. It was an impressive sight and the Bhutanese were fascinated. Maybe my wild claim about the heirs of the masons who had built York Minster wasn't so far off the mark after all. Lama Sonam muttered about wishing he had something like this back home. The image of him at the controls of a JCB on a mountainside in Bhutan or wielding a band saw was an alarming one. We struggled to tear him away.

There was a brief delay when a final misunderstanding about the design spec meant the *harmika* was cut round not square, but that was quickly rectified and everything else slotted smoothly and precisely into place. The protective parasol, crescent moon and sun and its flame-shaped jewel tip – all the copper items that had come from Bhutan – were blessed once more and attached to the very top. And then suddenly the building was finished. There was some whooping from the builders, which the Bhutanese quickly joined, but it all felt strangely anti-climactic. Lama Sonam and his team had one final and very important duty to perform: the consecration of the finished stupa, though we were already making plans for a bigger and more public ceremony the following year.

Diane and I organised a barbecue to give the Bhutanese a proper send-off, expecting a few people to turn up. Around fifty accepted our invitation – nearly everyone they had had any dealings with during their stay. People were genuinely sorry to see them go. 'So, David,' somebody asked, 'are you a Buddhist now?' I gave my usual, rather evasive answer: that I'd been interested in Buddhism for a long time, had read quite a bit about it, always enjoyed being in a Buddhist environment on my various trips to the subcontinent, that I was moved and persuaded by what I understood of Buddhist philosophy. Et cetera, et cetera. I tried to laugh it off. 'But I'm a very bad student!' I said. 'More of a Buddhist by osmosis. Buddh-ish someone once called it.' Afterwards, Phub Dorji took me to task. 'Why do you say that?' he asked. 'Of course you are Buddhist! You make stupa! So you are Buddhist!' I had no answer to that.

We presented each of them – Lama Sonam, Cheku, Kesang and Phub Dorji – with a large album, containing photographs and personal notes of thanks from many of the people who had been involved with the project. Just as they were about to leave, there was an unfortunate wrangle about money – brought about partly by some freelance fund-raising by Phub Dorji on his social rounds (for genuine projects back in Bhutan, but resented by the others more than I had realised) and partly by some unrealistic expectations based on what they had grown used to in England – but mainly my fault for not having agreed everything with them in advance. Then a couple of days as tourists in London before the flight home: a ride in an open-topped bus, Buckingham Palace, a tour of the Houses of Parliament with our local MP (who also happened to chair the Select Committee on Tibetan Affairs), and a turn on the London Eye.

Diane, Judi and Andy and I drove them to Heathrow and made sure they got on the right plane. They were all behaving like seasoned travellers now, old hands at the airport game, and they waved casually back at us as they trundled off to join the queues through security.

We went back to the car and drove up to Yorkshire. It was time for everyone to go home.

The Fifth Journey:
The Consecration

Nearly a year later and I was standing in the Arrivals Hall of Manchester Airport. We were waiting for the plane to land carrying another group of monks from Bhutan, a very different group from Lama Sonam's building team. Lama Baso Karpo, one of Bhutan's most eminent lamas, was bringing six monks over to perform a full consecration ceremony at the Harewood Stupa. With them was Chen Chen Dorji, on this occasion tour leader and head of liaison, but also relishing the prospect of time spent constantly in the company of a lama he greatly respected. I assumed that he would stay with me, but he preferred to be with the monks in their dormitory at The Hovels. This was to be a short visit, with a week or so of pujas in the build-up to the consecration day, then pretty much straight home again. Senior lamas don't like to hang about.

Lama Baso Karpo is a powerful presence. Born in Haa, the same pastoral valley in western Bhutan as both Chen Chen and Phub Dorji, he is based in Phajoding, the monastery on the hill above Thimphu where I had been shown the dragon's egg. Baso Karpo has held important official posts in Bhutan, including that of spiritual adviser to the King, but now he spends more and more time on retreat. His eyes are different colours and his expression is fierce like a hawk's – fierce but compassionate, not unlike Guru Rinpoche's I thought. The monks clearly held him in great respect; they were here to work and he pushed them hard. Phub Dorji was among them. There would be no time for extra-curricular activities on this trip.

Like the stupa builders, the monks were all staying at The Hovels, where every day would start early with a puja. There were pujas most days at the stupa, too, building in length and intensity up to the consecration itself. When the monks weren't doing pujas there was plenty to keep them occupied. There were prayer flags and banners to be strung round the stupa and an ornamental archway built over the bridge at the head of the waterfall, through which all the guests attending the consecration would process. By the day of the consecration the whole area looked splendid, authentically Himalayan. The monks not involved with all this activity were busy making *tormas* and other ritual offerings. No Lurpak this time – now we knew where to get all the materials.

One young monk, Lhap Tsering, also from Haa, spent much of his time creating the sand mandala that was to be the centrepiece for the consecration day puja. Sand mandalas play an important role in Vajrayana Buddhist ritual. A safe place, a divine garden, is created by drawing with coloured sand (actually often marble dust, which is finer and easier to work with) into which the deity particular to that ritual and the qualities that they represent – compassion, wisdom, loving kindness, long life – is invited. Their symbolic presence enhances the power of the ritual being performed. The world they have been asked to temporarily inhabit is a beautiful place. A handsome building stands at the mandala's centre with a courtyard and pillars and eaves and waterspouts which water the trees, plants and bushes in the gardens that surround it, all immaculately created, colour by colour, grain by grain, from the auspicious symbol or mantra at its core to the outer wall and protective flames that surround it.[1]

A sand mandala is usually made by a group of monks, sitting cross-legged round a wooden board marked with a simple grid. They scoop up small quantities of coloured sand in a serrated metal funnel with a pointed end, a little like an inverted fountain-pen nib (*chakpur* in Tibetan) and scratch the serrations delicately to allow a fine line to flow onto the mandala board. Then they take another scoop of a different colour to emphasise or make a shadow for the first line, gradually filling a board that is several feet square with the elaborate shapes and patterns of the mandala. It is painstaking work requiring total concentration, with no room for error or going back over something.

Lhap Tsering's technique was not like anything I had ever seen before. He would draw the intricate patterns of the mandala, not with the *chakpur*, but with a pinch of sand held between his thumb and forefinger. He was drawing – freehand, with sand – forms that many draughtsmen would struggle to draw with a crayon or pencil. And he worked fast, just three days to make the mandala, completely unfazed by the awed spectators who came in an ever-growing stream to watch his extraordinary patience and craftsmanship.

There was one final challenge: how were we to transport the sand mandala the half-mile or so from The Hovels to the stupa site? A sand mandala is obviously a very fragile thing and the track was too bumpy to allow us to drive it there. Normally it would be swept up and dispersed on the final day of the puja, something many people find very hard to fathom. How could something so beautiful, into which so much time and effort and concentration had been invested, simply be thrown away? There are several reasons for this. Firstly, once the puja is over and the deities have returned to their own heavenly realm, the mandala has no further purpose. It is an empty ornament. Making a sand mandala is more like ritual theatre than the creation of a piece of visual art, Lhap Tsering explained.

Like in theatre, once a performance is over, everything is packed up and put away, ready to be used the next time. Secondly, the dispersal of the sand, tipped into running water or shared out among those who had been involved in the ceremony, means that any benefit generated by its creation can be spread out into the world – for the benefit of all beings, a key tenet, as we have seen before, of Vajrayana Buddhist practice.

Lama Baso Karpo had agreed that on this occasion we would not have to destroy the mandala immediately so that we could display it as part of an exhibition about the building of the stupa we had planned in Harewood House later that year. But we still had to be sure it was intact for the day of the consecration – this was very important – and then keep it in storage for a few weeks before it went on display again. We debated ways of fixing the sand, temporarily at least. Could we stick it to the board with a light adhesive? Or spray it all with lacquer? None were practical. In the end a shallow box was made, a Perspex lid put on and Lhap Tsering and Phub Dorji simply picked it up and walked it along the lane, through the gate and onto a table in front of the stupa, chatting and laughing as they went. Easy as pie.

During the days leading up the consecration Lama Baso Karpo required me to participate in many of the ceremonies. I had to look smart, too, wear a suit. Chen Chen even got me dressed up in a Bhutanese *gho*. I sat with the monks during the pujas, making offerings and performing prostrations when required. I had to circumambulate with Lama Baso Karpo, scattering offerings from a tray he was carrying. He strode briskly round in front of me, chanting mantras as he went. Clearly he thought I wasn't concentrating, not walking or making offerings fast enough, and I was amazed at the strength and intensity of his grip as he pulled me behind him.

On another occasion, Chen Chen whispered to me that I should join the monks in meditating silently on the stupa. I closed my eyes and, quite unbidden and quite unexpectedly, a remarkable image presented itself. This is how I described it in my diary:

There was the stupa, as it really was, sitting quietly in an English country garden. Then, quite suddenly, it was bathed in a bright light, as if being lit by a powerful theatrical spotlight. Except that somehow the light was not coming from an outside source, but from the stupa itself; radiating out, not beaming in. After a moment the light started to pulse, before breaking up into rays, into beams of light that streamed outward into the world. The beams were dancing with hieroglyphics that I could not understand but which I took to be mantras.

The chanting resumed. I opened my eyes and the vision was gone. It was an April afternoon in Yorkshire, overcast but bright.

I have always been wary of people talking about their visions: scepticism on my part perhaps, or maybe just a lack of imagination. Though I wrote down what I saw that day, I have never, till now, talked to anybody about it.

The day of the consecration was approaching. We had invited a wide range of people to the event, not just family and friends, but a cross-section of the local community, including representatives of all the faiths: Sikhs, Muslims, Hindus, Christians and many Buddhists, including Akong Rinpoche, one of the founders of Samye Ling in Scotland, the first Tibetan Buddhist centre in Britain.

It was my father's idea to invite Prince Charles. He had been to Bhutan, was known to have an interest in Buddhism and had not long before been quoted as saying he would like to be seen as a 'defender of all the faiths'. My father had written to him some time before and received an initially favourable response. A little later, when Lama Baso Karpo had chosen an auspicious date for the consecration, my father wrote again. Silence. We had more or less given up on the idea, when another, more public announcement from Clarence House told us what must have been the cause of the delay: the date for Prince Charles's wedding to Camilla Parker-Bowles had been chosen and it was less than a week after the day of the consecration. 'Ah well,' my father said, 'it was a good idea, but clearly it isn't going to work.' Then, to everyone's surprise, a message came through: Prince Charles would be delighted to attend, but in a wholly private capacity. He would arrive by helicopter and would only be able to stay an hour or so.

The day of the consecration arrived. The weather forecast was terrible, torrential rain across Yorkshire. A couple of people told me they had nearly turned back because they were sure we wouldn't be able to carry on. But the weather forecast was wrong. We had a couple of showers, but the day was generally fine. Sunshine and rain – very auspicious, the Bhutanese assured me.

All the guests, nearly 200 of them, were welcomed in the Gallery at Harewood House before being ferried down to the stupa site. There was a short Indian dance performance and I said a few words of introduction.

'I may be foolish, but the Harewood Stupa is not a folly. It is the real thing. What you are going to see is not a performance with a beginning, middle and end, but a religious ceremony. The monks will already be in full flow when you arrive and they will carry on after you have left. There will be chanting and music, but I cannot tell you exactly what will happen – because I don't know! You're welcome to move freely round, but please respect the tented area where the monks will be sitting – and please remember, if you want to walk round the stupa, which you're very welcome to, go round clockwise, always keeping it to your right.'

It was as close as we could get to introducing

everyone to the combination of ritual intensity, uncertain waiting around and more or less controlled chaos that typified every large-scale Himalayan Buddhist event I had ever attended.

Everyone set off and a small group of us waited for Prince Charles's helicopter to arrive, which it very soon did, bang on time. A quick briefing and we made our way down. A line of schoolchildren from Bradford's Indian community threw rose petals and sang a short welcoming song as we came through the archway by the bridge and Chen Chen made the most flamboyant presentation of a prayer scarf that I have ever seen. We sat watching the monks for a while before the chanting and the horns and drums and cymbals stopped and there was a natural pause. The monks all presented more prayer scarves to Prince Charles and had their photographs taken with him in front of the stupa. He was introduced to the building team and other people involved with the project. Then the ritual resumed and he watched intently for a while before slipping quietly away, closely followed by the rest of the guests.

The audience had gone, but the monks hadn't finished. I was required to stay with them and conveyed frantic messages to make sure refreshments were sent down to them, too. After another half-hour or so, the rituals were finally complete and the monks returned to The Hovels for a well-earned rest. Their day was not yet finished, however. That evening, after dark, they performed a fire puja in front of the house, masked dancers with burning torches to drive away obstructions, negativity and ignorance, again with full monastic orchestral accompaniment. I encouraged everyone to do what attendees at such an event in Bhutan would do and make offerings of money to the monks, which many of them did, with grace and generosity.

The moon seemed unusually bright that night. I gazed at it intently. The words of some verses in praise of Tara came into my mind: 'Homage to Tara! Holding in her hand the hare-marked moon.' I remembered filming the Tara puja in Boudhanath – twenty-eight years ago I realised, with a shock – and how bright the moon had been the night before the ritual started. We were on the roof of the monastery with the monks playing their long horns and trumpets and Mike nearly fell off when setting one of the lights. Tonight, as the cymbals clashed and the horns brayed and the masked dancers brandished their flaming torches under another bright moon, the memory of the sights and sounds from all that time ago were very vivid, resonating across the years. If we hadn't made the film, if we hadn't filmed in that particular monastery in the shadow of the Great Stupa . . .

Everything you do happens because of everything you have already done.

I continued to stare at the moon. Had Tara hare-marked it tonight?

'What are you doing, David?' Diane interrupted my reverie.

'Oh – nothing,' I replied.

'The lama is asking for you,' she said.

'I'll be right over.'

It had been an extraordinary day, a unique marriage of Himalayan ritual, royal protocol and Yorkshire hospitality. Harewood had never seen anything like it. And now everything had been done that should have been done. Done and done properly. Lama Sonam would have been pleased. The project was completed.

Or I should say that the first part of the project was completed. To understand what building the stupa at Harewood actually meant, not just for me but for everyone involved, was another project entirely. One story ends, another begins. The end of one journey becomes the start of another.

Part Two

Sixth Journeys: Pieces of Eight

NAMOBUDDHA

In a time long ago, Shingta Chenpo, known as the Great Charioteer, was king of a small kingdom to the east of the Kathmandu Valley. The kingdom was prosperous, its people happy and well fed. The king had three sons: Dra Chenpo, Lha Chenpo and Semchen Chenpo, the youngest. The two older brothers were warriors and hunters, hard workers who helped their father rule his kingdom. But secretly Semchen Chenpo was both of his parents' favourite, a gentle and compassionate boy, never happier than when helping others.

One day the three brothers were out hunting, enjoying each other's company as they rode through the forest, when they heard a strange sound coming from a cave. They crept up and found a tiger lying on the ground next to her five newly born cubs, who were whimpering with hunger. Dra Chenpo and Lha Chenpo drew their bows, but Semchen Chenpo stopped them from shooting.

'Can't you see?' he said. 'The tiger is too weak to feed her cubs. What food can we give her that might save them all?'

'Tigers only eat freshly killed meat,' his brothers replied. 'If you want to save her, that is what you must find.'

'But that would mean killing one living being to save another. I cannot do that,' said Semchen Chenpo.

The older brothers were losing patience. 'Come, we are wasting our time here,' they said. 'We are here in the forest to enjoy ourselves. Let's leave this place.'

And all three of them rode away.

After a short while, Semchen Chenpo turned to his brothers. 'You two ride on. I must turn back. I've left something behind in the woods. Don't worry, I'll catch you up.'

But Semchen Chenpo had been thinking to himself: 'I am trapped in the cycle of birth, death and re-birth. I know in my heart that all my life I have only been playing with the idea of giving. Here is a chance to do something truly generous.'

He rode back to the cave where the tiger was. He reached out his hand to touch her face, but she was too weak even to bare her teeth at him. So he cut his arm and allowed her to lick the blood and before long she had regained enough strength to leap on him and devour him.

Dra Chenpo and Lha Chenpo waited for their brother at the edge of the forest. When he did not appear, they began to think about what he had said, and feared he might have returned to the tiger. They spurred their horses on, riding as fast as they could, but when they got to the cave there was nothing there except a pool of blood, a few bones and some scraps of clothing. Utterly distraught, they gathered up their brother's blood-stained clothes and returned to their father's camp.

The queen woke from a bad dream. She dreamed there were three doves flying high in the sky. Suddenly, a hawk swooped down and took one of them. So when her two older sons appeared without Semchen Chenpo, she immediately feared the worst. Hearing what had happened and overwhelmed with unbearable grief, the queen, the king and their two sons returned once again to the cave. There could be no doubt that the tiger had eaten Semchen Chenpo and was now somewhere in the forest with her cubs. They all sat by the mouth of the cave, sobbing uncontrollably.

Meanwhile Semchen Chenpo had been re-born in the celestial realm of Tushita. 'What did I do to merit being re-born here?' he wondered. Looking down from heaven, he saw his mother and father and his two brothers, all so overcome with grief that they were barely able to continue their lives, and he remembered what had happened. 'I must talk to them,' he thought.

'Please do not be unhappy,' he said to them, 'I have

made my choice. By my action I was re-born in the celestial realm. The end of birth is disintegration; the end of gathering is separation. Pursue virtue and we will meet again in Tushita.'

This helped calm the king and queen's grief. Resolving to lead virtuous lives from then on, they put their beloved son's bones into a small casket, which they buried and built a stupa over it.

In the years that followed, people were afraid to travel through the forest where these events had taken place. They thought that they too would be devoured by a tiger. As they walked they recited the mantra 'Namo Buddha – ya!' ('I take refuge in the Buddha!') to help calm their fears.*

It was only quite recently that electricity and a road that cars could drive along came to the little Nepalese village of Namobuddha where the stupa still stands. Before that, at the time of the full moon, a female tiger would often be seen in the vicinity. She would walk three times round the stupa before slipping away again into the forest.

Today, the site of the tiger's cave, just big enough for her and her five cubs, can be found in the middle of the

---

* This story is also told in the Jatakamala, a very popular text among Tibetans, which contains tales from the Buddha's earlier lives. Jataka-mala translates into English as 'The Garland of Birth Stories' or, more wittily, 'Once the Buddha was a Monkey'. This version is taken from a booklet by Khenpo Losel issued by Thrangu Tashi Yangtse Monastery, in which they have added a little local colour (see Bibliography).

large modern monastery complex of Thrangu Tashi Yangtse about two hours' drive east of Kathmandu, presided over by the elderly and very eminent lama Khenchen Thrangu Rinpoche. There are 160 monks based here, both young and old, as it is now an important teaching monastery, where the young monks learn the basics of Buddhist philosophy, metaphysics, logic and psychology and, in the case of Lhakpa Dorji, the very self-assured and knowledgeable young Ladakhi monk who showed me around, pretty good English too.

Building the monastery was a considerable physical feat. Even now the road that leads up the hill to it is absolutely terrible: unsurfaced, dusty and rocky, really only suitable for four-wheel drives, though that doesn't deter the customary medley of motorbikes, overloaded buses and ageing Kathmandu taxis bouncing their way up the mountain track. In the 1990s Thrangu Rinpoche, already quite elderly, would often have to walk the last couple of miles. But the setting is magnificent: beautiful views over classic Nepali terraced valleys; wooded hills above and snow peaks beyond; majestic gold-roofed monastery buildings booming with the deep bass drum beat of Tibetan Buddhist ritual and alive with the flapping red-robed energy of the young monks. Sites associated with the story of Semchen Chenpo are scattered all over: two alternative tigress caves and the site of Semchen Chenpo's father's palace just the other side of a misty hill across the valley.

The stupa which is said to contain the casket with

Semchen Chenpo's bones is a little down the hill to the east of the monastery complex. Though the potency of the legend surrounding it means that the Namobuddha Stupa is regarded by Buddhists with the same reverence as Boudha or Swayambunath, it is on a much more modest scale than either of those, no bigger than the one at Harewood. It stands in a small village square at the end of a single village street, the sort of place you could imagine in a different cultural setting being the perfect location for a shoot-out in a spaghetti western. When I first visited on a cloudy midweek day in November, the square was virtually deserted. A woman was making wooden beads for a *mala* on a small hand-turned lathe. The bell on the large prayer wheel pinged plaintively. We had to knock on the closed door of the café and plead for a cup of tea.

On a sunny Saturday in late February the atmosphere was very different. Cars, buses and motorbikes were double-parked all along the village street and the square was humming with activity. Offerings burned smokily on every corner of the stupa and hundreds of butter lamps were being lit. Women from the village were winnowing wheat along one side of the square. A couple of old men, bow-legged and bent double under their loads, carried twisted bundles of firewood slowly through the crowds. Kids from Kathmandu climbed down from their motorbikes, brushed the dust off their slim-fit jeans and high-heeled ankle boots and posed for selfies. The cafés could barely keep up with the business.

'Ruined by tourists,' I heard somebody mutter, but I couldn't agree. This was all fine, I thought. Stupas are meant to be seen, to be somewhere people can congregate, and Namobuddha village and its famous stupa have become a favourite destination for a day trip from Kathmandu. There were high spirits and loud laughter, but most people were there to bring offerings or circumambulate and everyone was respectful enough in their own way. It has to be better than spending your day off in one of Kathmandu's tacky new shopping malls.

On the corner, where the street meets the square, is a shabby building with a porch and a steep set of steps to a door leading to a very dark interior, with even darker windows on either side. It looks very old. This is Namobuddha Monastery, tiny compared to the magnificent buildings I had just walked down from. Inside, a single monk was chanting and rattling a hand-drum. A steady queue of people brought offerings, lit butter lamps, sat in the dark, greasy interior and rotated their hand prayer wheels. It is this small monastery and its caretaker monk that are responsible for the physical and spiritual upkeep of the Namobuddha Stupa, not the new Thrangu Tashi Yangtse Monastery just up the hill.

I asked if I could meet the caretaker monk.

Lama Sonam Gyalpo said he was eighty-three years old. He had the same wiry mountain vigour as the two Bhutanese lamas who had been at the heart of the Harewood Stupa project: Lama Sonam Choephel and Lama Baso Karpo, both about the same age. We could hear him performing his daily puja in an upstairs room. After about twenty minutes the sounds of the puja, the chanting and the rattling hand-drum, stopped and he shambled out into the bright sunshine, wearing an incredibly scruffy sweater, tracksuit and pink plastic sandals. He circumambulated the stupa three times, spinning every prayer wheel and ringing every bell at each turn, made offerings by the shrine on the eastern side and prostrated three times. Then he came and joined us at our table.

The position of caretaker of the Namobuddha Stupa was a hereditary one, he explained. He was from the Nyingma school of Tibetan Buddhism, where hereditary posts and lineages are not uncommon. He was the thirteenth generation of his family to be the caretaker and he rattled off the names of all the others so fast that even my young monk translator Lakhpa Dorji couldn't keep up. 'The first one was Tsewang Dargay,' he said and shrugged his shoulders. No use asking a date, I realised, but using what is reckoned to be a reasonable measure of a generation on the male side, thirty-five years, that takes us back about 450 years to the mid-sixteenth century. Sonam Gyalpo had been caretaker for fifty-two years, he said, replacing his father when only twenty-two. (Which doesn't add up to eighty-three, I realised later, but the basics hold true: what he was saying was that he had been caretaker for a long time, ever since he was a young man.) His family's tenure had not been untroubled. On more than one occasion the incumbent caretaker had been killed

The Harewood Stupa.

Harewood House: 'A St Petersburg palace on a Yorkshire hill' (p. 13).

The Great Stupa at Boudhanath (p. 32).

The film crew in Ladakh, India, 1977 (p. 35). *Standing, from the left:* Mike Warr and David Lascelles. *Seated, from the left:* Graham Coleman and Robin Broadbank.

Homeward bound (p. 97). *Back row, from the left:* Emily Lascelles, Kesang, Cheku. *Front row, from the left:* Phub Dorji, Lama Sonam, David Lascelles.

Ninzegang, Punakha, Bhutan (p. 58).

Roadside stupas,
Bumthang, Bhutan
(p. 57).

The 108 Stupas, Dochu La, Bhutan (p. 59).

Drukpa Kunley's iron rod: 'A head like an egg, a trunk like a fish and a root like a pig's snout!' (p. 60).

Cheku and Lama Sonam make offerings. 'The smoke billowed thick and white from the burnt offerings, blowing, as smoke always does in the open air, wherever you are sitting, straight into the faces of the spectators' (p. 111).

From the left: Lama Sonam, Kesang and Cheku performing a puja (p. 111).

Phub Dorji in the First Chamber (p. 139).

The First Chamber filled with musical instruments, tools, clothes and offerings (p. 139).

Raising the *Sok-shing* (p. 145).

Lama Sonam makes sure everything is done properly (p. 150).

'Reservoir Monks', Whitby beach (p. 156). *From the left:*
Lama Sonam, Kesang, Phub Dorji, Cheku.

Masked dancers (p. 170).

Lama Baso Karpo and the monks prepare for the consecration (p. 163).

Lhap Tsering's amazing sand mandala technique (p. 165).

Lama Sonam Gyalpo, caretaker of the stupa at Namobuddha (p. 181).

Great Lotus Stupa, Lumbini, Nepal (p. 196).

Mahabodhi Temple, Bodhgaya, India (p. 211).

Vaishali, India: site of the remains of the Buddha's Relic Stupa (p. 240).

Piprahwa, India: one of the sites claimed to be Kapilavastu, where the Buddha lived as a young man (p. 206).

Great Bodhi Stupa, Tsekarmo, Ladakh (p. 264).

'It is rare nowadays to see Ladakhis in traditional costume' (p. 269).

Ladakh: 'The setting sun, its beam tightly shuttered by dark clouds, shines its golden spotlight' (p. 284).

Mount Kailash, Tibet: 'A place of pilgrimage, revered by the followers of four religious traditions' (p. 275).

Old stupas near Tholing, Tibet: 'Strange, ghostly, ruined structures' (p. 282).

Left: Lama Sonam outside his house in Hongtso: 'We have been on a great adventure together' (p. 298).

Below: The re-consecration of the Great Stupa at Boudhanath, November 2016: 'Clouds of magnolia seed pods . . . started to drift down from the sky' (p. 311).

by order of the king or his prime minister, most recently in the early part of the twentieth century. Each time the son had simply taken over from the father. Sonam Gyalpo's own son was here in Namobuddha; he had at least one grandchild, a granddaughter, living abroad, in Belgium. He didn't seem to have any doubt that the inherited position would continue after him.

The physical stupa now standing in the square is only about ninety years old, built over a much older one, something which is true of almost all old stupas in Nepal, including the two most famous ones, Boudhanath and Swayambunath. In most cases nobody knows how many layers deep they go and therefore nobody knows the exact age of the original. It is generally accepted that Swayambunath is the oldest in the Kathmandu Valley. The Namobuddha Stupa needs quite urgent repair, Sonam Gyalpo said. One of the copper Buddhas at the base of the spire was especially unstable. He got up from the table and went back inside, returning, to my surprise, with a smart briefcase, which he unzipped and pulled out a surveyor's report, in English, detailing the costs, both for the construction work and all the accompanying pujas: just short of a million Nepali rupees or about £6,000. I think he hoped I might be a sponsor. He took his responsibilities for the physical as well as the spiritual upkeep of the stupa equally seriously.

What were the spiritual responsibilities, I asked? Every morning he performed the pujas we had heard earlier: to the great tantric master Guru Rinpoche; to

Avalokiteshvara, Chenresig in Tibetan, the embodiment of perfect compassion; and to Amitabha, who embodies, among other things, long life. He would say their mantras 15,000 times every day. Then he would make his circumambulations, offerings and prostrations, as we had seen. On special days, especially in the Nepali month of Chaitra (which approximates to March) and around the time of Saga Dawa (the date of the Buddha's birth, enlightenment and death, in late May or early June) he would perform pujas for the protector of the stupa.

And what if he were not able to fulfil these responsibilities, I asked? What if he fell sick and could not perform the pujas for several weeks? What would happen to the stupa then?

Lama Sonam Gyalpo laughed. 'Nothing would happen to the stupa,' he said. 'And if get sick, I go to the doctor.' He grasped me firmly by the arm and walked me briskly round the stupa. Then he went off to change into his full regalia to have his photograph taken.

WALKING IN THE FOOTSTEPS

The stupa at Harewood was built, but what had we done? Stupas are said to harmonise their environment. In the Himalayas they have often been built in regions that are prone to earthquakes, with the intention that they will calm the restless spirits of the earth, pin down and placate turbulent underground forces. In Tibetan these are called *dudul chorten*, literally 'stupas that subjugate chaotic forces'. Would the Harewood Stupa have a similar effect on its surroundings, subjugating the chaotic forces of Harewood's history and harmonising the contradictions of its present?

This seemed particularly relevant in the build-up to 2007, the Bicentenary of the Abolition of the Slave Trade in the British Empire. Harewood was, as I have already mentioned, built with money made through the sugar trade and therefore the slave trade that supported it. We had to take a position and not be part of what historian James Walvin has called 'a national amnesia' on the subject. Diane and I debated it, night after night. We agreed: let's be damned for what we did, not for what we didn't. There was nothing we could do to change the past – this wasn't *Back to the Future* – but we could be honest about what had happened, we could address the present and inform the future. As Maya Angelou wrote: 'History, despite its wrenching pain/Cannot be unlived, but if faced/With courage, need not be lived again.'[1] I found that what I had learned about Buddhism while building the stupa was a guide and a support: endeavour to see things the way they really are; use whatever knowledge and tools you have to remove obstacles and pacify negativity. Confront those chaotic forces. Pacify those restless spirits.

We decided we should go with our strengths: education, innovative exhibitions, good personal connections with the local Caribbean community, my own experience and connections in the performing arts. We worked with a remarkable woman, Geraldine Connor, and staged her spectacular piece of music theatre, *Carnival Messiah*, in a massive big top in front of Harewood House. Geraldine's musical start point was Handel's great oratorio *Messiah*, performed in her inspired transformation in a Caribbean Carnival style. Its musical influences ranged from calypso to oratorio, from soul to gospel, from reggae to rap. The most famous piece from Handel's original score, the 'Hallelujah Chorus', was performed in the show by a twenty-five-piece Steel Band. The cast was huge, the costumes enormous, the performances unforgettable. *Carnival Messiah* was everything we wanted Harewood's commemoration of the Bicentenary to be: celebratory, inclusive, engaged with the local community, with a very highly visible local presence. It was an exhilarating and transformative experience for everyone involved and the basis of a strong and lasting friendship with Geraldine. 'But would you have had the courage or the clarity to take it on if you hadn't built the stupa?' somebody asked me, sometime after the event. There's no simple answer to that, but the way the timelines overlapped means that, for me at least, they will always be connected.*

After the consecration in spring 2005 much of my time was spent dealing with Bicentenary projects. But I was also very aware that, though I had spent the past

---

* The stupa project: 2002–05 (and still going strong); Bicentenary planning and commemoration: 2003–07 (also still going strong).

few months heavily involved with the building of a stupa, regarded as a highly meritorious activity by Buddhists, there was still much I didn't know or understand. I was doing it all the wrong way round, I realised: doing my research after building the stupa rather than before. (But then I'm someone who had his honeymoon before his wedding: in Bali on the way to Australia, where Diane and I were married in 1990.)

There were still some fundamental questions to which I didn't know the answer: where did stupas come from and what do they mean? Visiting some of the most famous sites in India and the Himalayas seemed to be a good way of getting an insight.

Jean-Luc Godard was once asked what he thought made a good film. 'You must always have a good beginning, a good middle and a good end,' he said, 'though not necessarily in that order.' I seem, without having deliberately set out to do so, to have been following Godard's advice in constructing this book. But in trying to understand what stupas are, where they came from and the different stories behind their making it seemed like a good idea to start at the beginning. So I decided I must visit the Eight Places of Pilgrimage, the places where the first Buddhist stupas were built to house his remains and also where some of the most important events in early Buddhist history took place. There I would be able to see what was left from that time and to feel first hand what being a twenty-first-century pilgrim was like. Walking, as the guidebooks like to put it, in the footsteps of the Buddha. These sites, the Four Principal Places of Pilgrimage and the Four Places of Miracles, are all in the quite small geographical area where the Buddha lived, now contained within the boundaries of northern India's most populous states, Bihar and Uttar Pradesh, with Lumbini, the site of the Buddha's birth, just over the border in Nepal. I was travelling with two companions: Charles Garrad, an old friend who had been with me on a walk round Mount Kailash in western Tibet a couple of years earlier (which I'll describe later), and Namgyal Dorjee, Administrator for the Orient Foundation.

1. Lumbini	Birth	1st Principal Place of Pilgrimage	Heaped Lotus Stupa
2. Bodhgaya	Enlightenment	2nd Principal Place of Pilgrimage	Enlightenment Stupa
3. Sarnath	First teachings	3rd Principal Place of Pilgrimage	Stupa of Many Doors
4. Shravasti	Miracles	1st Place of Miracles	Miracle Stupa
5. Sankashya	Descent from heaven	2nd Place of Miracles	Descent from Heaven Stupa
6. Rajgir	Teachings	3rd Place of Miracles	Reconciliation Stupa
7. Vaishali	Last teaching	4th Place of Miracles	Victory over Death Stupa
8. Kushinagar	Death	4th Principal Place of Pilgrimage	Parinirvana Stupa

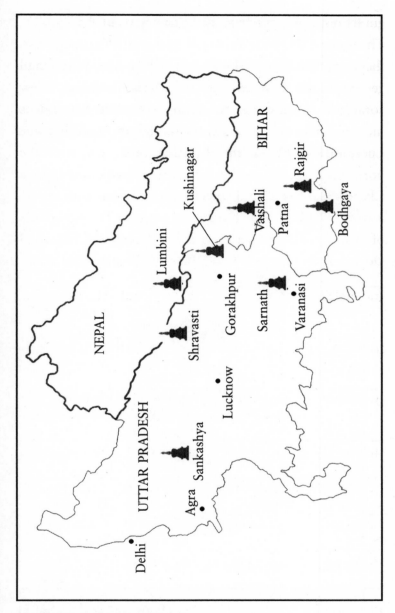

North India Buddhist pilgrim sites

LUMBINI – WHERE THE BUDDHA WAS BORN

Lumbini, the first of the Principal Places of Pilgrimage, is where the Buddha was born. The Lumbini stupa design is called the Lotus Stupa – *Pepung Chorten* in Tibetan. The steps below the dome are rounded and decorated with a design of lotus petals.

Lotus Stupa

We'd had a long drive the day before, but Charles, Namgyal and I left our rooms, about half a mile from the Lumbini Park, at first light. There was still a chill in the air and mist blurred the fields around the monastery guesthouse. We paid the entry fee – 200 rupees for foreigners (about £1.50), free to Nepali and Indian residents – and entered the area round the place of the Buddha's birth, now called the Sacred Garden. In front of us was a simple structure, the Mayadevi Temple, named for the Buddha's mother, Queen Mayadevi, wife of King Suddhodana, leader of the Shakya clan.

When Mayadevi knew her time was close, she left the royal court of her husband and set out for her family home to give birth, as was the custom. At a small village called Lumbini, about halfway between the palace and her home, she gave birth to a son. Emerging from his mother's side as she rested against a tree, the newborn baby took seven steps in each of the four directions – north, south, east and west – and at each step a lotus blossomed.

The child who was to become the Buddha was born Prince Siddhartha, Crown Prince of the Kingdom of Shakya. His mother died soon after giving birth and the boy was brought up by his aunt Mahapajapati Gotami. The family was tight-knit and the palace environment highly protective. Siddhartha's early life was one of luxury and privilege: delicious food, fine clothes, and indulgence in the princely pursuits of archery, falconry and charioteering. He married young, as was traditional in his society, and became a father soon after.

So far, so conventional: the life of a young prince in a minor kingdom on the fringes of the fertile and afflu-ent Ganges Valley in northern India. It was only after leaving his royal home at the age of thirty to follow the life of a wandering holy man that Prince Siddartha began his transformation into Buddha Sakyamuni, the Buddha of the Sakyas. That long journey began here and the building we were about to enter contained the site of his actual birthplace.

The Mayadevi Temple didn't really look like a temple at all, just a simple whitewashed building with a corrugated tin roof topped by a small dome painted with the all-seeing eyes typical of a Nepali-style stupa. We walked up a small ramp, through a modest un-marked door and entered a space that was completely unexpected. Our first impression was right; this wasn't a temple: it was an archaeological dig and the building was simply there to protect the site from the elements. Inside, a false ceiling made out of some kind of insulat-ing material was suspended from a lattice of iron girders over our heads. The lighting was low, the air thick even in the cool of early morning, and there was a distinct smell of incense. A walkway took us round the edge of the building, and on the far side it doubled back on itself towards the centre, over the earth and low brick walls of the dig, the outlines of what once were probably monastic buildings. Although it was still very early in the morning a small group of people was already gathered there, gazing silently over the metal railing. A few feet below, visible through a sheet of scratched and grubby Perspex dotted with flowers and offerings of money, is what is believed to be the exact spot of the Buddha's birth, just a stone slab, but a place of huge significance to Buddhists.

There have always been doubts about whether this actually is exactly where the Buddha was born. A recent excavation has revealed a further, much older wooden structure, below the stone slab. Whether this alters either the date or the authenticity of the exact location of the Buddha's birth is still being debated. There is even one theory that Lumbini is an elaborate fraud, originally perpetrated over a hundred years ago and sustained ever since, for reasons both economic and political, and that the real place of the Buddha's birth is somewhere else entirely.

Buddhist teaching encourages you to test what you are told against your own experience and draw your own conclusions. So what conclusions did the three of us – Namgyal, Charles and me – draw? We each approached our visit to the site with very different sets of expectations, but our impressions were very similar: each of us had a palpable sense that this was somewhere special, a place of power. None of us knew what to expect as we walked through the modest door into the building. We had no preconceptions. There was no heightened sense of anticipation, the building and the entrance to it were very low key. But we all came out feeling the same. Not a scientifically measurable gauge of course, and it is right to look for one, but, given the lack of any absolutely conclusive scientific or archaeological evidence, what else can you do but trust your own instinctive response? I know what I felt and so did the others. There was a palpable aura, a stillness, almost melancholy and suffused with an aroma of incense and floral tributes that were just starting to turn. This was not just an interesting archaeological site; it was something much more than that. 'I wish there was somewhere I could sit for one or two hours,' Namgyal said.

Behind the temple is a brick-lined water tank, the Pushkarini, where Mayadevi bathed herself and her newborn baby. Beyond that, standing in the middle of a large paved area and festooned with prayer flags, is a large *bodhi* tree. Every morning and intermittently during the day, a group of monks sit on a stone platform below it, reciting sutras. As the day progresses, groups of pilgrims arrive: Indian, Thai, Japanese, some Europeans. Many join the chanting monks; others set up their own spot and listen to teachings or say prayers with their own teachers, sometimes harshly amplified through small, portable loudspeakers. A few pose foolishly with the monks, grinning and making peace signs to the camera. Despite all this, it is a very tranquil place, dotted with shady trees with benches beneath them and criss-crossed with brick paths edged with neatly trimmed box hedges. Somewhere you can sit quietly, for as long as you like, just as Namgyal had wished. The Sacred Garden still feels sacred.

Just a couple of hundred yards from the Sacred Garden, you enter another world, Lumbini Park. I'd heard it called the world's first Buddhist theme park and that isn't far off the mark. There have been two monasteries near the Sacred Garden for some time, both quite small and modest. Now a broad footpath is being laid, crossing a moat-like waterway where ducks dabble, cormorants dive, herons and egrets stand and stare, and white and purple lotuses open in the heat of the sun. Across the moat a canal stretches away into the distance, nearly two miles long, dead straight and running due north. An Eternal Peace Flame burns in a stone bowl carved in the shape of a lotus at one end. Elegant Chinese-style bridges cross the canal every few hundred yards. Off to either side, set well back and spread well apart, monastery buildings sprout, brand new, gigantic structures representing every Buddhist tradition on earth: Burmese, Chinese, Japanese, Korean, Laotian, Nepali, Sri Lankan, Thai, Tibetan, Vietnamese, and more. They are impressive structures and clearly every country has gone to considerable trouble to produce fine examples of their indigenous architecture, craftsmanship and design.

We visited the Chinese Temple, which contained a huge, brightly painted Laughing Buddha statue, a pair of enormous drums, and sets of bells and gongs. It still smelled of fresh paint. Opposite it, the Korean Temple awaited completion, a massive grey concrete edifice, still undecorated. A lone cement mixer stood, silent and exhausted, on a driveway the size of an airstrip that led from the locked wrought-iron gates to the temple building beyond. We passed the Nepali Temple, gleaming white and gold like a themed hotel or casino somewhere in the Gulf, and made our way towards the Tibetan Temple, known as the Great Lotus Stupa, with a circular section below the dome decorated with carvings in the shape of lotus petals, the stupa design associated with Lumbini.

The Great Lotus Stupa was built in 2003–04, sponsored by a German charity, the Tara Foundation, and it is finely decorated, both inside and out. There are Life of Buddha frescoes on the walls of the light and airy domed interior and images of the great Nepali stupas of Boudhanath and Swayambunath and a large Wheel of Life on the outside. It is surrounded by a garden, well watered and cared for, with little groups of painted concrete figures depicting scenes from the life of the Buddha. The day we visited was a Sunday and there were plenty of Nepali families there, kids climbing on the giant prayer wheels as if they were merry-go-rounds and being chased off the grass by ferocious guards, blowing their whistles and brandishing large sticks. Something about it didn't feel quite real, though, like a film set, an immaculate re-creation of something rather than the thing itself. No monks were to be seen while we were there, though I was told that pujas are performed there regularly. Maybe it would feel different on one of those days. I came away with a powerful reminder of what I had always been told: that there was more to a stupa than just the form. However perfectly realised it might be on the outside, what was going on – or not going on – inside was what really mattered.

THE KAPILAVASTU CONTROVERSY

Until I started researching the eight stupa sites I wasn't aware of the important role played in their rediscovery by British archaeologists in the nineteenth century. These men were servants of the Raj: soldiers, surveyors, amateur painters, very few of them qualified archaeologists, at a time when that science was still in its infancy and the techniques used often very crude. From the late eighteenth century onwards a series of scholars, linguists, explorers and archaeologists, men like William 'Oriental' Jones, James Prinsep and Alexander Cunningham, dedicated themselves to the investigation and understanding of India's ancient history and in so doing uncovered the roots of Buddhism.

After the Buddha's death, Buddhism continued to have a strong presence in northern India for several centuries, though inevitably its fortunes rose and fell. A high point was the reign of Ashoka. Born in 304 BCE, around 200 years after the death of the Buddha, he was the third emperor of the Mauryan dynasty, ruler of a vast empire that on a modern map would stretch from Karnataka in southern India to Afghanistan, and one of the most extraordinary figures in India's early history.

This was both a dynamic and a violent period and Ashoka's early life was not untypically bloody. He was a usurper, not his father King Bindusara's chosen heir: 'after his father's death, he caused his eldest brother to be slain and took on himself the sovereignty', is how one posthumous account put it.[2] Other accounts say a hundred brothers were killed, a numerical exaggeration not unusual in the chronicles of the time. But the four-year gap between the death of Bindusara and Ashoka's coronation certainly suggests a protracted and probably violent struggle for power.

In 269 BCE, at the age of thirty-five, Ashoka was finally anointed as ruler. He was known as Chandashoka, Ashoka the Fierce, constantly testing the loyalty of everyone around him, his ministers and the women of his harem alike, and executing those he felt he could not trust. About eight years after his coronation he invaded the neighbouring Kingdom of Kalinga, a campaign that climaxed with one of the biggest and bloodiest battles of early Indian history. 'One hundred thousand were deported. One hundred thousand were killed and many more died from other causes,'[3] Ashoka wrote later. He was sickened by the carnage. Full of remorse, he vowed that from that moment on his empire would no longer be ruled by force of arms or state brutality, but by principles based on the Dharma, the teachings of the Buddha.

As described in the histories, this change seems very sudden, very abrupt. But it would seem that Ashoka had had an interest in spiritual matters from before his early, bloodthirsty years as emperor. He is known to have consulted teachers from a range of religious traditions: the Hindu Brahmins who were the most powerful figures in his court, but also followers of the newer traditions of Jainism and Buddhism. His first wife Devi, whom he married some years before he became emperor, was a devout Buddhist, likely to have been a calming and stabilising influence at what must have been a turbulent and uncertain time.

Whatever had gone before, the massacres in Kalinga were the turning point. Ashoka was no longer just someone who was interested in Buddhism, a casual lay follower. He was now a devout practitioner, someone who had taken refuge in the Buddha, the Dharma and the Sangha.* More than that, he was a powerful ruler who was determined to apply those same principles to the way his country was governed. He set out on a series of tours of his huge empire, not to conquer by military force, but to visit the holy places of Buddhism, to see for himself the sites of the eight Relic Stupas, to support Buddhism in any way he could and to make public his newfound faith to his subjects.

Ashoka, describing himself with the immodest honorific 'King Piyadasi, Beloved-of-the-Gods' (he was a Buddhist, but he didn't want you to forget that he was an emperor either), dictated a series of pronouncements, which he had carved into rocks or onto pillars in locations right across his kingdom. Known as the Rock Edicts, they are historical records unlike any

---

* Practising Buddhists take refuge every day in the Buddha (the Teacher), the Dharma (the Teachings) and the Sangha (the Followers of the Teachings).

other: personal expressions of remorse and of strongly held religious and moral beliefs, written by an all-powerful ruler talking directly to his people – something absolutely unheard of at that time – words carved into rock, accessible to everyone. It was as close to mass media communication as you could get in the third century BCE. The edicts cover a wide range of topics: vegetarianism, respect for one's elders, state support for the sick and the elderly, tolerance for all religions. They are first-hand accounts of a ruler's personal philosophy, based on the peaceful and tolerant teachings of the Dharma, and their implementation was amazingly successful: after the war with Kalinga, the Mauryan empire was at peace for nearly thirty years.

Ashoka's other great public expression of his faith was in the building of stupas. It is claimed he built 84,000 of them, almost certainly another exaggeration. (In Buddhist renderings of history, very large numbers – a hundred brothers killed, 84,000 stupas built – tend to mean 'very many' rather than signifying an exact quantity, like we might say 'millions of times' when describing something you had done very often.) It is no coincidence that this is a number that crops up quite often in Buddhism: 84,000 bundles of the Buddha's teachings, 84,000 avenues to enlightenment and so on. On his tour of the Eight Places of Pilgrimage, Ashoka removed some of the relics and divided them many times over to empower the new stupas he was planning to build. At first, the locations he chose were in places with a connection to the life or teachings of the Buddha, but later they were built at the furthest reaches of the Mauryan empire, many hundreds of miles from anywhere the Buddha would have visited. This was his way of spreading awareness of Buddhist teachings and the moral code that they propose. The stupa as a physical embodiment of the Dharma.

Did Ashoka destroy the original stupas after opening them up? It seems highly unlikely. His aim was to spread the benefits of the Buddha's teachings, not to wipe them from the face of the earth. The records stress how careful and respectful he was, with the strong implication that he left some small part of the relics intact in their original location. Ashoka's new stupas in new locations commemorated a whole range of events from the Buddha's life and the lives of those who followed him. It is probable that he built on the sites of the original Relic Stupas, too. Later builders would often build over the ruins of older structures, sometimes many times over, so what looks like the ruins of an ancient stupa may actually have an even older one, maybe several even older ones, beneath it. It is quite possible that Ashoka did that too and the original Relic Stupas are buried deep under those he built 200 years later.

Buddhism in India had mixed fortunes following Ashoka's death. Some subsequent dynasties, such as the Gandharans (first to fifth centuries), the Guptas (fourth to sixth centuries) and the Palas (eighth to twelfth centuries) were supporters. The finest early Buddhist art is from those times. Other rulers, often Brahmins, high-caste orthodox Hindus who saw Buddhism's denial of the caste system as a threat to their own power base, were fiercely opposed. By the end of the twelfth century Buddhism in India was in terminal decline. Muslim armies swept across northern India, and what Hinduism had not replaced or absorbed, they destroyed. Though Buddhism had by this time spread south to Ceylon (Sri Lanka), north to Nepal and Tibet, and east to Burma (Myanmar), Siam (Thailand), China and Japan, it quite quickly disappeared from the country of its birth. Many of its statues, temples and stupas were built over or pulled down. The rest disappeared into the jungle, swamped by strangler figs and tangled up in vines.

The story of the rediscovery of early Buddhist sites is, I think, one of the more unexpected things to grow out of British rule in India in the nineteenth century, the days of the Raj. That said, some of the early conclusions that these men came to were comically wrong-headed. There was early speculation that the Buddha might have come from Africa – because of his curly hair and full lips. Others thought Buddhism might be some kind of tree-worshipping cult – because of the *bodhi* tree under which he achieved enlightenment. Or they believed it somehow involved the worship of snakes – the image of snake-like nagas bowing in obeisance to an unseen figure is quite a common one in early Buddhist carving.

There are mitigating circumstances surrounding these wild misinterpretations. Early Buddhist carvings never showed the actual figure of the Buddha. He was depicted by a tree or a wheel (the wheel of the Dharma) or a footprint, sometimes by a stupa. It was not till the classical Greek-inspired carvings of the first and second centuries from Gandhara, the ancient kingdom that covered the border region between Pakistan and Afghanistan, that the image of the Buddha emerged with which we are familiar today: an elegant figure whether standing or sitting in meditation, wearing an expression of great serenity with half-closed eyes, long ear lobes and hair tied into a tight knot at the top of his head. And trees do figure prominently in the life of the Buddha: his mother Mayadevi gave birth leaning against a tree in Lumbini; he achieved enlightenment sitting under a tree in Bodhgaya; he died lying on a hastily improvised bed between two trees in Kapilavastu. And, as we have seen, the stupa is brought to life when the *Sok-shing*, the Life Tree, is erected within it.

Without the courage and perseverance of these nineteenth-century explorers it is quite possible none of the Buddhist sites in north India would have survived. But their archaeological findings were not without episodes of fierce professional rivalry, controversy and allegations of fraud.

From the time of its rediscovery in the nineteenth century, the exact location both of the Buddha's birthplace and of the city of Kapilavastu has been the subject of particular dispute. Kapilavastu was the capital of the Buddha's father's kingdom, where he lived in his early days, and which is the most likely site of the stupa raised by his family's clan, the Sakyas, to house their share of his ashes. Locating the Buddha's birthplace at Lumbini in Nepal seemed to have been confirmed once and for all by the discovery of a pillar in 1896 with an inscription in ancient script.[4] The pillar was placed there by Ashoka and it still stands in the same place, broken in half by an ancient lightning strike and protected by a high metal fence, just to one side of the Mahabodhi Temple. The discovery soon after of a very early carving on the same site showing Queen Mayadevi giving birth seemed to give further confirmation.

But to this day the location of Kapilavastu is still not agreed. The descriptions by early Buddhist pilgrims on which the searches of British archaeologists were based are ambiguous and sometimes contradictory. They led to fruitless expeditions as far afield as Assam, several hundred miles to the east. The discovery of the pillar at Lumbini seemed to have settled one question, but the hunt for Kapilavastu became the battleground for one of the great archaeological controversies of the time, fought out originally between two figures equally controversial in their own different ways.

The first was Major Laurence Waddell, an army surgeon and one of the first Europeans to study Tibetan Buddhism in any depth. His book *Buddhism in Tibet or Lamaism* draws a lurid and misleading picture of

Vajrayana Buddhism as decadent and devil-worshipping. He described it as 'the most depraved yet interesting form of Buddhism'[5] – which sounds more like an expression of the prejudices of his own strict Scottish Presbyterian background than anything else – but unfortunately this quickly became the generally accepted view, largely because there was no other, and it coloured the attitude of the Raj towards Tibet for some time to come. Waddell was clearly a difficult man: opinionated, quick to take umbrage, a bearer of grudges.

The other was Dr Alois Führer, a German-born archaeologist who was curator of Lucknow Museum and Archeological Surveyor for the United Provinces (now Uttar Pradesh). It was Führer who confirmed the authenticity of the pillar at Lumbini, though failing to credit Waddell's previous work that had led to its discovery – not the first time Führer had been guilty of appropriating other people's work as exclusively his own, as Waddell was not slow to point out. So when Führer then discovered an extensive network of ruins close to Lumbini, in a location that fitted earlier pilgrims' descriptions of Kapilavastu, there was plenty at stake. His professional reputation, dented by the row with Waddell about the Lumbini pillar and other allegations about his high-handed working methods, needed a major coup. The pressure was on. Führer launched into a high-speed excavation, so fast that they virtually levelled the site, though not before he was able to make a series of assertions about the discoveries they had made that established beyond doubt, he said, that this was indeed Kapilavastu. So far so good. Then disaster struck. Führer received an unexpected visit from another distinguished archaeologist, Vincent Smith, an associate of Waddell's who was serving as a District Officer nearby and had heard of the spectacular discovery. Smith caught Führer red-handed putting fake artefacts into the small stupas at the site, 'impudent forgeries' Smith called them, artefacts that would have authenticated the alleged dates of Führer's great discovery. The matter was hushed up, but Dr Führer's reputation, with considerable encouragement from the ever-vindictive Dr Waddell, was ruined. He resigned, swiftly left India and disappeared from sight.

At exactly the same time, December 1896 and January 1897, spurred on by the exciting discoveries being made over the border, William Peppe, manager of an estate at Birdpur in India that ran right up to the Nepali border, just south of Lumbini and Führer's Kapilavastu site, decided to investigate several large and intriguing mounds on the northern edge of his estate. He was particularly interested in a very prominent one near the village of Piprahwa. He quickly realised that this was the remains of a very old Buddhist stupa and, digging further, found a huge stone coffer containing three small vases, which revealed fragments of bone, jewels and an array of tiny gold ornaments. On the lid of one of the vases was an inscription in a language that nobody at that time recognised. An accurate translation is still not universally agreed. This is a version from the early twentieth century by the French orientalist Auguste Barth: 'This receptacle of relics of the blessed Buddha of the Sakyas is the pious gift of the brothers of Sukirti, jointly with their sisters, with their sons and wives'.[6] Does this suggest that Piprahwa might be the site of one of the original eight stupas? Or was it something built later, by Ashoka or his successors?

More than a hundred years later, the controversy rumbles on. In 1973, the Archaeological Survey of India discovered terracotta seals with the inscription 'Community of Buddhist monks of Kapilavastu' at Piprahwa. In 2001, a UNESCO-sponsored archaeological expedition to Lumbini uncovered ceramics known to be contemporary with the time of the Buddha near a Nepali village called Tilaurokot, not far from Führer's site. So is Kapilavastu in India or Nepal? Both countries would love to claim Kapilavastu as their own. National pride is at stake here, not to mention substantial tourist income.

I visited both Tilaurokot and Piprahwa in 2012. The Tilaurokot site in Nepal has extensive ruins, blurred outlines of buildings half-smothered by forest. We were shown round by an enthusiastic young man who said he had worked on the dig as a boy with his father under a Japanese archaeologist. The Piprahwa site in India is very different. The brick dome of the stupa is surrounded by an immaculately kept garden, completely deserted when we were there, with densely planted flowerbeds and sprinklers playing on the lawns. Did it really matter which was the authentic location, I wondered? But then I'm not an archaeologist. Everyone agreed that both sites were within the borders of the Sakya kingdom and that they were very close together. There clearly had been grand buildings at both. Perhaps the royal family moved between residences – because the weather or the hunting was better, or simply to be seen by their subjects. It seems to me entirely possible that the young Buddha and his family spent time at both places and that Tilaurokot and Piprahwa are both Kapilavastu.

The controversy doesn't stop there. There is a dissenting view – no surprise in archaeology – that the discovery of the stone coffer and the inscription on the lid of the vase at Piprahwa was also a Führer-inspired fake. There are photographs of him at the site with William Peppe, though there is no evidence that he interfered with it. The dissenters go on to claim that there has been a century-long conspiracy of silence involving several generations of archaeologists and the governments of both India and Nepal to maintain the status quo, and that the real site of Kapilavastu is somewhere else entirely.

Real or fake, some of the Piprahwa relics went to Siam (Thailand) soon after their discovery at the request of the King of Siam, a devout Buddhist, before being returned to the National Museum in Delhi. I stood in the special room where they are now kept, wondering whether I should ignore the guard and the signs saying 'No Photography'. Two young Tibetans strode in, prostrated three times, scrutinised the ornate teak and gilt pagoda, made in Thailand, in which the relics are housed, before circumambulating and leaving. Neither of them said a word. Clearly they believed the relics were real.

Charles Allen has written extensively on the Kapilavastu controversy and on the role of officers of the British Raj in rediscovering India's ancient Buddhist sites.[7] I've taken much of the above, in heavily truncated form, from his books on the subject, to which I'm much indebted. In 2006 Charles organised a day-long conference at Harewood on the Piprahwa controversy at which several distinguished academics, a Singhalese monk and William Peppe's grandson were present. They all visited the Harewood Stupa at the start of the day and I was able to say, not too smugly I hope, that I was in the fortunate position of knowing exactly what was inside, when it had been put there and by whom.

BODHGAYA – WHERE THE BUDDHA ACHIEVED ENLIGHTENMENT

The second Principal Place of Pilgrimage is Bodhgaya, the holiest of all places to Buddhists. This is where the Buddha achieved enlightenment. The associated stupa design is known (unsurprisingly) as the Enlightenment Stupa – *Jangchup Chorten* in Tibetan – with plain square steps and a niche for a statue set in the dome. It is the most widely seen of all the Tibetan stupa designs and the one we used at Harewood.

Enlightenment Stupa

In the grey light before dawn Namgyal and I sat on a low bench under a tree and drank cups of well-boiled, very sweet tea before setting off down the wide pedestrianised avenue that leads to the temple complex gate. An early start to avoid the crowds we thought. Not many of the shops were open, but soon they would be displaying a variety of wares: offerings to take to the temple and an array of other religious objects, but also plastic guitars, Buddha-in-a-snowglobe and bootleg DVDs. Bodhgaya is a major pilgrimage site, with all the commercial trappings that go along with that.

At the entrance there was already a steady flow of people, even at this very early hour. We left our shoes and went through the security gates, recently erected after a threat from a Hindu fundamentalist group. The Mahabodhi Temple does not conform to any of the classic stupa shapes. It looks more like one of the great, towered, brightly painted Hindu temples of South India, but with little stupas and Buddha statues in the many niches, and topped by the distinctive thirteen rings, sun, crescent moon and jewel tip. Its architectural origins are not entirely clear, but it was never intended as a receptacle for the Buddha's ashes. Ashoka is generally accepted as the temple's founder, but this building is 700 or 800 years later, fifth or sixth century, heavily and not always sympathetically restored by British archaeologists in the nineteenth century.

By the time the Buddha arrived at Bodhgaya, he had long since renounced his life of courtly luxury and set out into the world looking for spiritual truth, spending many years wandering, receiving teachings from sadhus and nearly starving himself to death living as an ascetic in the forest. Eventually he arrived at the shores of the River Neranjana. There, emaciated and exhausted, he broke his long fast by accepting a bowl of curd from a milkmaid from the village of Senani, just outside modern Bodhgaya. Refreshed, he spread a grass mat under a *bodhi* tree and vowed to sit in meditation until he achieved enlightenment.

The forces of Mara, the great tempter, did everything they could to break his meditative concentration. They bombarded him with every kind of hostile weather: rain, flood, thunder and lightning. They sent demons to threaten him and beautiful women to seduce him. But his meditation grew deeper and deeper until finally, at dawn on the full moon, on the same day of the year on which he was born, he attained enlightenment. Now he was no longer a seeker after truth, a bodhisattva, but an enlightened being, the Buddha, the Awakened One. His insights during that intense period of meditation form the basis of all his subsequent teaching.

The Mahabodhi Temple is a fine, tall building, but the shrine room inside is quite small. It was already full of people, some trying to make prostrations in the confined space, others meditating or making offerings to the large Buddha statue, serene and glowing gold under his bright yellow robe at the far end of the room, placed exactly where the Buddha himself would have sat. I crammed myself into a corner and sat quietly for a while.

After a little time, I started to walk round the temple, joining a growing number of other circumambulators, even though it was still barely light. The marble floor was cool underfoot and remained so even later in the day when the sun grew hot. At the back of the temple, clinging to its west wall, was the *bodhi* tree itself, ancient, tall, with thick overhanging branches and leaves slowly turning autumn-brown. High stone railings surrounded the tree and strong wooden props held up its ageing limbs. Ashoka's daughter took a shoot from the original to Sri Lanka – where it still flourishes – and this one is a cutting from that tree, as are several other holy *bodhi* trees, the one in Lumbini, for example. Layers of history, as at all the eight sites.

There is a constant murmur of activity round the Mahabodi Temple and the gardens surrounding it – sometimes more than a murmur when a full-scale puja begins. All day and every day there are several hundred monks and lay people scattered round the garden, sitting in meditation under the trees or clustered round the many smaller stupas that fill the garden. Devout practitioners performed full-length prostrations, their hands and knees padded against the repeated impact. A group of Korean ladies prepared elaborate offerings: flowers and colourful packets of confectioneries. A solitary Western devotee, dressed in full Tibetan garb, his long hair oiled and swept back in a ponytail, was performing a puja, reading from a text, punctuating his chanting with bursts from his ritual bell and hand-drum.

There was a little ripple of excitement. 'The Dalai Lama's sister is here,' someone whispered, and there she was, just her and a companion, circumambulating quietly and leaving offerings, modestly acknowledging the attention of her fellow pilgrims.

I sat for a while on one of the benches near the *bodhi* tree. Occasionally, an autumn leaf would drift down from the branches overhead. It would be nice to take one home, I thought, looking at a fine specimen that had landed a few feet in front of me. The thought was not even complete before a tiny and very determined Sri Lankan lady darted forward and picked it up.

I watched a fashionable young Indian, bearded, long-haired, all in black, looking like someone from the Mumbai art scene. He was walking very slowly along the south wall of the temple, a walking meditation, one foot carefully placed in front of the other, perfectly balanced, totally focused, his concentration absolute. Then, suddenly, the spell was broken. He reached into his pocket and pulled out a mobile phone before turning rapidly, phone to ear, and walking back in the opposite direction, anti-clockwise, seeming quite agitated now, all too quickly back in samsara, the mundane world of stress and constant interruption.

Along the north wall of the temple is Ratnachakarma, the Jewel Walk, where the Buddha walked back and forth for a week after achieving enlightenment, his footsteps marked by carved lotuses, strewn daily with flowers. On a rise to the north-east is the Animeshlochana Stupa, the Stupa of the Unblinking Gaze, where he stood for another week, staring back at the *bodhi* tree. A group of Bhutanese pilgrims had gathered there. To the south is a water tank and in the middle of it is a brightly painted statue of a large hooded cobra with a small Buddha seated below it. The cobra is the King of the Nagas, who sheltered the Buddha from a wild storm during his meditation. The gardens are full of stupas, hundreds of them, big and small, standing alone or in groups, their designs echoing the different architectural traditions of the Buddhist diaspora.

I went to a large rough shed just outside the main garden to make an offering – fifty butter lamps, one for each member of my family – and received a brief teaching on moderation from the presiding monk. 'Too much donation not good. Too little not good also,' he said. 'Same for food, reading, meditation. Everything.' The Buddhist Middle Way. Namgyal filled a large bottle with water and we went on a complete circuit of the garden, putting a small amount in each of the offering bowls, about 850 of them, as we went round.

On our last day there it rained, quite heavily. An auspicious sign, but we had to take extra care on the slippery marble floor as we circumambulated the temple for the last time. Our feet were wet but our spirits were lifted.

SARNATH – WHERE THE BUDDHA GAVE HIS FIRST TEACHINGS

The third Principal Place of Pilgrimage is Sarnath, about fifty miles from Bodhgaya. This is where the Buddha gave his first teachings after achieving enlightenment. The design associated with Sarnath is known as the Stupa of Many Doors, *Gomang Chorten* in Tibetan. The steps below the dome are square and punctuated with many niches, representing doorways through which the Buddha's teachings can be released into the world. They are also doors through which other teachings can be welcomed in. Buddhism has always prided itself, with good reason, as being open to the teachings of other religions. The Buddha walked here from Bodhgaya, where he met five of the fellow seekers after truth that he had known during his time as a wandering ascetic. They were surprised to see him, doubtful at first about his claims, thinking he had abandoned his search as being too demanding. It was to them that he gave his first teaching and the five ascetics became the first members of the Sangha, the Buddha's first followers.

Stupa of Many Doors

It was late afternoon and the Deer Park at Sarnath was crowded. It usually is. Crowded, but calm. A large group of white-clad pilgrims from Sri Lanka gathered at the foot of the great mound of the Dhamekh Stupa, left offerings and chanted in unison. Another group sat in a circle on the grass in silent meditation. As the light started to fade and the sun became a deeper orange in the grey Gangetic haze, a whistle was blown and security guards started to hustle the pilgrims unceremoniously past the beggars and the hawkers and out of the park. Then the sound systems started in the marketplace, great booming bass notes like blows to the chest, harshly amplified Hindi pop songs blaring from the stacks of loudspeakers. It was the start of the great Hindu festival of Dasheera, in honour of Durga, the warrior goddess, the fiercely protective mother, always ready to unleash her anger against those who threaten her children.

That night the streets of Varanasi, just a few miles from Sarnath and Hinduism's most holy city, were heaving with people. The nightly Festival of Arthi on the banks of the Ganges, when Brahmin priests propitiate the many deities in the Hindu pantheon and make offerings to Mother Ganga, the mythical river from which all life flows, was even bigger and louder and more crowded than usual. We jumped into a couple of cycle rickshaws for a hair-raising and hilarious ride through the city, my Tibetan companion Choedar shouting out Durga's mantra 'Hari Hari Made' at the top of his voice and roaring with laughter as we made our way through the crowds. It seemed like the population of the whole city, all one and a quarter million of them, was having an enormous street party.

The thoughtful tranquillity of the Buddha's teachings and the noise and exuberance – sometimes near hysterical exuberance – of modern India. Would it have been so very different in his day? Without the deafening sound systems of course.

For many centuries Sarnath was one of Buddhism's most important centres. Ashoka built stupas here and left a pillar topped with a four-headed lion. When India became independent in 1947 this was the image chosen to symbolise the new nation. The original carving is in Sarnath's Archaeological Museum, in perfect condition, having – miraculously – survived a fall of some thirty-five feet when an invading army toppled the pillar on which it sat.

In the seventh century, 1,200 years after the Buddha's death, Sarnath is said to have still had thirty monasteries and 3,000 resident monks. One hundred years later an army of Huns swept through northern India and left the town and its religious buildings in ruins. Sarnath recovered, only to be sacked again by Muslim invaders in the eleventh century. Once again it recovered, once again it was sacked. By the sixteenth century, though much reduced, it was still important enough to be acknowledged by the great Mughal Emperor Akbar as part of his attempt to reconcile the different religions in his vast empire.

When the British archaeologist Alexander Cunningham* came to Sarnath as a young man in the 1860s he found it almost deserted. He excavated the remains of the Dharmarajika Stupa† and found that it contained relics. Could this have been one of the original eight Relic Stupas? The monsoon came and Cunningham's excavations had to stop. His findings were taken to a warehouse in Varanasi, where they lay waiting for his return. Called away on military service, he was not able to continue his excavations the following year. Nobody in Varanasi knew what the piles of earthenware and old stones were any more, or cared. The stone carvings were used as building materials. The relics were thrown into the Ganges.

It was at Sarnath that the Buddha spoke of the Four Noble Truths to the five ascetics who were to become his first followers. This is one of the most important, one of the most fundamental, of all Buddhist teachings.

The Truth of the Reality of Suffering
The Truth of the Causes of Suffering
The Truth of the Cessation of Suffering
The Truth of the Path to the Cessation of Suffering

---

* Cunningham (1814–93) was an officer in the Bengal Engineers and the first head of the Archaeological Survey of India. He was exceptionally energetic in his field surveys during this time and rediscovered many of the ancient Buddhist sites of India, which had fallen into disrepair or been swallowed up by the jungle.
† This is not the same as the Dhamekh Stupa and is no longer standing.

The Dalai Lama describes the Four Noble Truths as 'all-encompassing'[8] and Khenchen Thrangu Rinpoche calls them typical of the Buddha's way of conveying what he had himself learned: 'The Buddha taught whatever would enable a person to develop, so that he or she could progress gradually towards the very deep and vast teachings.'[9] There are many discourses on the subject from teachers throughout Buddhism's long history. The Four Noble Truths are devastatingly direct, very concise, and contain within them the essence of the Buddha's teachings. Their layers of meaning could take a lifetime to comprehend.

I tried to find a quiet place in the Deer Park to think about the Four Noble Truths. The *bodhi* tree near the entrance was too close to the marketplace, where the sound systems for the Durga celebrations were cranking up the volume. Sitting on the grass near the Dhamekh Stupa was little better. I got up and started to walk round the stupa. It reminded me of something: its looming, pyramidical shape, its imposing mass, the shadows and discolouration of age on the curved lower tier, the niches higher up where statues would once have stood, the remnants of the carved texts that would once have covered it.

As I walked, I realised what it reminded me of. It reminded me of Mount Kailash, the holy mountain in western Tibet where Charles and I had walked a couple of years earlier.

Dharmek Stupa

Mount Kailash

SHRAVASTI — WHERE THE BUDDHA WOULD SPEND THE RAINY SEASON

The fourth Place of Pilgrimage, the first of the Places of Miracles, is at Shravasti. This stupa is known as the

Miracle Stupa, *Chotrul Chorten* in Tibetan. The steps leading up to the dome have projecting central sections on each of the four sides and sometimes four niches for statues in the dome as well.

Miracle Stupa

The Jetavana Grove is large, several acres of parkland dotted with mature trees and with many excavated outlines of buildings scattered among them, cared for nowadays by the Archaeological Survey of India. In the Buddha's time the grove would have been far bigger. It stood just outside the walls of Shravasti, one of the largest cities in India, occupying a strategic location at the junction of important trade routes that ran south-west to the Godavari River, south-east to Rajgir and west through the Rajput Desert to Gandhara. Shravasti was the capital of the Kosalans, one of the richest and most powerful clans in the north of India, ruled by King Prasanjit.

Jetavana Grove was famed for its beauty. Sudatta, a rich merchant from a neighbouring kingdom and a follower of the Buddha, wanted to buy it as a resting place for his teacher. The land belonged to Jeta, one of the king's younger sons. The Kosalans were traders, known for driving a hard bargain, and Jeta said that he would only allow Sudatta to buy as much land as he could cover with gold coins. Such was Sudatta's devotion that he laid his entire fortune on the ground, and such was his wealth that it covered almost the entire grove. Impressed, Jeta let Sudatta have the land and offered to pay himself for the building of the first monastery there.

The Buddha spent more time in Shravasti than anywhere else, twenty-five rainy season retreats it is said, each three months long, surrounded by his closest followers and probably thousands of other devotees, giving teachings and instructions. Even now, in the hot, flat plains of northern India, with its crazy roads and overwhelming numbers of people, it is a peaceful place. But for the Buddha it would have been more demanding, somewhere he would have been bombarded constantly with requests, pressed for advice or swamped with offers of hospitality. I've observed this when travelling with Tibetan lamas in India or Nepal. Wherever they go people want their own little piece of them: a moment of time, to talk, to be given a blessing, to name a child or simply an invitation to eat or take tea. The motivation is good, everyone genuinely wants advice or the opportunity to make a generous gesture or an offering. But for the lama it is exhausting.

Because of the length of time he spent there, it is not surprising that there are more stories about the Buddha in Shravasti than anywhere else. The one that gives the stupa its name, the Miracle Stupa, is perhaps the most striking.

Challenged, not for the first time, to a definitive debate by the representatives of rival schools of religion and philosophy, the Buddha eventually and reluctantly agreed. He made just one condition. The debate must take place under the broad-leaved shade of the largest mango tree in Jetavana Grove. The other debaters agreed. A great hall was built to accommodate the event and to house the many eager spectators. The night before, his challengers tried to put the Buddha at a disadvantage by cutting down all the mango trees in Shravasti. The Buddha was normally reluctant to perform miracles in public, but in this case clearly he felt the need to make an exception. He strode into the hall, nonchalantly sucking on a mango. He threw the mango stone onto the ground where it immediately sprouted into a great tree. Then he transformed himself. His lower body became engulfed in flames and he projected spouts of water from his upper body. Next, he reversed the process, shooting flames from his upper body and gushing water below. Then he appeared as an enormous bull with a quivering hump, snorting and stamping his hooves, first in the west, then in the east, then in the north, then in the south. The Buddha performed twenty-two of these transformations, known as the Miracles of the Pairs, before sitting down calmly on a lotus and multiplying himself so many times that he not only filled the hall but all the space right up into the heavens. There was no need for a debate.

It was also in Shravasti that the Buddha encountered the brutal robber and murderer known as Angulimala, who had the gruesome custom of cutting a finger off each of his victims and wearing them round his neck (Angulimala translates as 'the Garland of Fingers'). He had vowed to kill a thousand people and he wore the fingers to help him keep count. Knowing that Angulimala was lying in wait for his thousandth victim, the Buddha transformed himself into the murderer's own mother and so confused him that when the Buddha assumed his own form he was able to persuade Angulimala to reflect on who he had been and what he had done. Even after being persuaded to repent of his evil ways and follow the Buddhist path, Angulimala was often insulted or assaulted by people who knew him from his earlier days – an example, the Buddha would say, of the inevitable karmic consequences of past negative acts.

I heard a variation of this story from the manager of the hotel where I was staying. In this version,

Angulimala was not a dacoit (a bandit or street robber) but high-born, the son of a king, handsome and intelligent. As a young man he was sent away to an ashram to be educated. He was the most gifted in his class, so much so that his fellow students became jealous and turned their guru against him. On the day they all came to graduate it was the custom for each student to ask the guru what they should give him as an offering of thanks for his teaching. A hundred gold pieces, the guru said to the first. Two water buffalos, he said to the second, and so on. When it came to Angulimala's turn, the guru, his head filled with the poison the other students had been feeding him, said the gift he wanted was the fingers of a thousand people Angulimala had killed.

This was an interesting twist on a Buddhist tale, one influenced by orthodox Brahmin thinking perhaps. For Buddhists, the moral of the story is that it is possible to confront and try to address your own karma, however negative it may be, though it will never be possible to escape from it entirely. The Brahmin version becomes the tale of a high-born person returning to his original state of grace – thanks to the Buddha in this instance, but a return to the proper order of things, a very different interpretation to the revolutionary transformation of evil into good that the Buddhist story tells. The idea of a low-born person, a thief and murderer, attaining a higher state would have been anathema to the Brahmin-dominated Hindu caste system.

Today Shravasti is another important stop on the Buddhist pilgrim trail. Approaching from the west along the busy Lucknow road, dodging the bicycles and the bullock carts, hoping not to be wiped out by the overloaded trucks and buses, the flat and featureless Uttar Pradesh skyline is dominated by the golden spire of a huge Thai stupa. The scale of it feels strangely incongruous, vainglorious even. But perhaps the seven-storey Gandhakuti, the Hall of Fragrance, where the Buddha gave many of his teachings in Shravasti, felt like that in his day: a consciously majestic architectural statement, meant to be seen from afar, like the great cathedrals of the flatlands of East Anglia or northern France. It sits about half a mile from Jetavana Grove, with facilities for large gatherings of the international Buddhist community, but it was closed for restoration when I visited. There is a move to make Shravasti a more active centre for such gatherings, somewhere to rival Bodhgaya or Lumbini in the future.

Jetavana Grove itself is very busy, especially towards the end of the day and early in the morning. Large groups of pilgrims swirl around the site and settle like murmurations of roosting starlings at its holiest places: the *bodhi* tree, grown from a cutting from the original in Bodhgaya; the Gandhakuti, now just a series of low brick walkways and walls covered in gold leaf and offerings of flowers; the Kosambakuti, where the Buddha actually lived. Spending a day there, it was not so hard to imagine the place in the Buddha's time:

devotees constantly on the move, making offerings, saying prayers, the ebb and flow of large numbers of people in a holy place. There are the remains of many stupas here, too, one built on top of another in most cases, with the oldest from around 250 BCE, the Ashokan era, the most recent from the ninth or tenth century.

There are more stupas about a mile away in an area that is still largely unexcavated. One is for Mahapajapati Gotami, the Buddha's stepmother and aunt, who brought him up and later became a devoted follower. There is another to mark the well where he drew water to drink. There is one for the reformed murderer Angulimala and one where Sudatta, the merchant who bought the grove for the Buddha, built his house. None claim to be a Buddha Relic Stupa. At the Sudatta site, several have been built over time, one on top of another, with a Hindu shrine the uppermost of all, not an unusual configuration. There was substantial restoration work going on, piles of new bricks and a workforce that was untypically animated. A boisterous Indian family I'd noticed earlier at Jetavana Grove was there and quite a few other people were climbing to the top of the stupa and taking pictures of each other. A couple of particularly arrogant-looking Brahmin priests strutted about. I wondered whether the restoration work was of the old Hindu shrine, history repeating itself in India's current mood of fundamentalist nationalism, trying to obliterate a piece of Buddhist history from the landscape.

This is a tune that has been played many times over

the last 2,500 years. The Buddha was a reformer, opposed to the orthodoxies of the Brahmin priests who were the most powerful religious force in India during his lifetime and from whose teachings what is now known as Hinduism was born. He taught that enlightenment, release from the wheel of life, death and re-birth, was possible for anyone, and this challenged at its very root the caste system on which the power of the Brahmins was based. An uneasy relationship between Buddhism and the more traditional forms of Hinduism continues to this day.

Dr B. R. Ambedkar (1891–1956) was independent India's first Law Minister and a key figure in the writing of India's constitution. Born into one of Hinduism's 'Untouchable' castes, he battled discrimination all his life and gave particular importance to equality across caste, gender and religion in the constitution – a cornerstone of the Congress Party's founding ideal of a secular India. He resigned from the government when he felt these ideals were being compromised. He had studied Buddhism all his life and in 1956, not long before his death, converted publicly along with some half a million other members of the Untouchables, thereby removing both himself and them from the caste system, something which still, more than sixty years later, angers Hindu extremists. As recently as March 2018, there was a spate of vandalism across India of statues of figures who did not conform to the views of those who supported India's current hardline

version of Hinduism. A statue of Ambedkar in southern India was among them.

SANKASHYA – WHERE THE BUDDHA RETURNED
FROM TUSHITA HEAVEN

The fifth Place of Pilgrimage, the second of the Places of
Miracles, is at Sankashya. It is the least known and least
visited of the eight ancient stupa sites. A thriving town
in the time of the Buddha, it is now just a small village
on a mound, surrounded by further mounds, some made
of brick, and a small pond, Nagasara, the Pool of the
Snakes, which pilgrims sometimes circumambulate.
There is no temple or monastery or resident body of
monks and there has been very little excavation. It is in
a remote spot, not easily accessible, but the story behind
its significance, why it is a Place of Miracles, is a beautiful one.

The Buddha was in the heavenly realm of Tushita. He
was giving teachings to his mother, Mayadevi, who died
shortly after he was born and who now dwelt in Tushita
Heaven. Back in the earthly realm his many followers
were growing concerned. Would he ever return to them,
they wondered? They entreated the Hindu gods Brahma
and Vishnu to approach the Buddha on their behalf and
ask him to return and give further teachings. The Buddha
agreed quite readily. It had always been his intention to
return. The place he returned to was Sankashya, his

journey from Tushita Heaven facilitated by the building of a great triple staircase of gold, silver and turquoise. The Buddha descended the central golden staircase, with Brahma and Vishnu on either side. The three flights disappeared into the ground, leaving only thirty-three steps visible. It is said that when Emperor Ashoka came to Sankashya, he instructed his men to dig to see how far the steps went, only giving up when they reached the water table, deep underground.

The design associated with Sankashya is known as the Descent from Heaven Stupa, *Lhabab Chorten* in Tibetan. Three rows of thirty-three steps descend from the dome. Sometimes the figure of the Buddha is depicted, descending the stairs. Sometimes he is represented simply by a footprint at the bottom of the stairway.

Descent from Heaven Stupa

RAJGIR – WHERE THE BUDDHA TAUGHT

The sixth Place of Pilgrimage, the third Place of Miracles, is at Rajgir. The stupa associated with Rajgir is known as the Reconciliation Stupa – *Yendum Chorten* in Tibetan. The steps leading up to the dome are arranged not in a square, but as an octagon.

Reconciliation Stupa

In the Buddha's time, Rajgir was the capital of one of the most powerful kingdoms in the area, Maghada, renowned for its prosperity and stability – and for the size and efficiency of its army. The ruler of Maghada, King Bimbisara, and King Prasenajit of Kosala married each other's sisters and the two great military powers of the region co-existed in a sometimes uneasy equilibrium for many years.

Rajgir (literally 'royal mountain') is about two hours' drive north-east of Bodhgaya, quite a scruffy place now, with no immediately clear focal point. There are ruins, scattered over a wide area: the outlines of the walls of monasteries and palaces, mighty defensive ramparts, stupas and other buildings, which the road from Bodhgaya weaves through before taking you to a car park at the bottom of one of Rajgir's many hills.

There you have two choices. To the left is a scary-looking cable car, which you can ride up to the Peace Stupa, its dome shining white and bright at the top of the hill.*

Or you can do what I did and follow the favoured routine for most pilgrims here and walk straight ahead, up another hill, on a path originally laid out by King Bimbisara, to the places where the Buddha and his students would gather for teachings. The lower section

---

* The first Peace Pagodas were built in Japan just after the Second World War under the guidance of Nichidatsu Fujii, a Japanese Buddhist monk and founder of the Nipponzan-Myōhōji Buddhist Order. Fujii was a great admirer of Mahatma Gandhi and dedicated his life to promoting non-violence, chiefly through the building of Peace Pagodas (or Peace Stupas) all over the world. Now there are more than seventy of them, in Asia, Europe and North America, including the Peace Pagoda in Battersea Park in London.

of the path was lined with beggars and sellers of trinkets. Pilgrims gave generously as they trudged upwards. An elderly Japanese lady bobbled by in a palanquin. Then the old road gave out – Bimbisara insisted on walking the last stretch. You pass the rocky outcrop whose distinctive shape gives the hill its English name, the Vulture's Peak, and climb past a series of small caves where the Buddha meditated and taught.

One of the Buddha's followers was his cousin Devadatta. He was an adept pupil, but ambitious. 'You are old and your health is failing,' Devadatta told his cousin. 'Now is the time for you to follow a life of solitary contemplation. Let me lead the order.' But the Buddha was wary of Devadatta's motivation and the offer was firmly declined. Angry at the rejection, Devadatta decided to turn to more violent methods. He hired assassins, but they fell to their knees in worship as soon as they saw their intended victim. He released a mad elephant to trample the Buddha to death, only for the creature to prostrate itself at his feet. He hurled a rock as the Buddha passed beneath him – but the rock cracked in half and caused just a small cut to his foot.

Devadatta decided to try something more devious. He stirred up a schism among the Buddha's followers on a range of subtle points of doctrine. This was a more difficult problem to resolve and the Sangha was for a little while in some disarray, but in time the Buddha was able to reconcile all internal differences – hence the name the

Reconciliation Stupa. Devadatta was forced into exile, a disappointed and embittered man.

At the top of the hill, the ground flattens out and forms a kind of rocky platform. At the far end is a low wall with a small shrine, open to the elements, festooned with garlands of flowers and other offerings, the bricks daubed with gold leaf. There is a long view out over the wooded plain below, hazy in the heat. This is where the Heart Sutra was first taught and pilgrims prostrate and sit and meditate on its meaning.[*] With devastating succinctness, the Heart Sutra expresses one of the most complex and profound Buddhist teachings, the concept of Emptiness:

> In Emptiness there is no form.
> In Emptiness there is no feeling.
> In Emptiness there is no thought.
> In Emptiness there is no will.
> In Emptiness there is no consciousness.

There is not very much to see at Rajgir, no impressive buildings, no spectacular archaeological remains, no well-kept gardens with trees under which to rest in the shade. Just a place, an open space on the top of a hill and some caves. But, as a lama said to me when I was

---

[*] Most Tibetans follow the Mahayana Buddhist tradition, which believes that the Vulture's Peak at Rajgir is where the Heart Sutra was first taught. Though the location is disputed by some other traditions, the teaching itself is core to all Buddhists.

on my way to Mount Kailash, 'In the end the mountain is just a lump of rock. It is no more and no less than what you bring to it.'

In all the places of pilgrimage there are now only traces of what had been there in Buddha's time; memories of what had once been great cities and magnificent buildings; a mound of bricks or a trench dug into the clay where there was once a stupa; low brick walls smeared with gold leaf where there was once a monastery; places that may or may not have been where an incident in the Buddha's life occurred.

And what of the resting places of the relics themselves? Once so fiercely contested, then redistributed across a continent, then lost or thrown – carelessly, accidentally – in the river or put on display in a museum?

Form and no form. Form and formlessness. Perhaps what is not there is as important as what is.

VAISHALI – WHERE THE BUDDHA GAVE HIS LAST TEACHING

The fourth and last of the Places of Miracles, the seventh Place of Pilgrimage, is at Vaishali. This stupa has three rounded steps leading up to the dome. It is known as the Stupa of Victory over Life – *Namgyal Chorten* in Tibetan.

Victory Stupa

The Buddha and his followers were resting in Vaishali, the capital of the Licchavi Republic. It was thought to be the finest city in the region, famous for its elegance and prosperity, with handsome buildings and beautiful gardens. The Buddha had visited often. On his first visit after his enlightenment he had helped rid the city of a terrible plague. It was here that he ordained the first women into the Sangha and where the famous courtesan Amrapali became his disciple.

But now the Buddha was feeling his age. His health was failing him and he knew he did not have long to live. He gathered his disciples in a mango grove in Amrapali's garden and told them that the time of his death was close. Such was their distress at this news, however, that he agreed to prolong his life for a short time. But he also told them this was the last teaching from him they would receive.

Shortly afterwards he left the city and started to make his way slowly towards Kushinagar, where he knew he would end his days. A crowd of Licchavis rushed in pursuit of the sombre procession. They implored the Buddha to stay with them, not to leave their city and not to leave this life. He turned calmly to make his last farewell and handed them his begging bowl. Then he crossed the river, heading north. As soon as he reached the far bank, the river swelled and flooded, leaving the Buddha and his followers on one bank and the distraught townsfolk on the other.

Today, Vaishali is in transition. It is an important place on the 'Buddhism's Holy Places' pilgrim trail, but not a major draw like Lumbini or Kushinagar. Not yet. The setting is very rural. Until recently there were few facilities, just some very basic guesthouses and a handful of roadside teashops. But that is starting to change. Charles and I were booked to stay at a hotel called the Vaishali Residency, brand new, very empty, equipped with all mod cons – most of which were not working – with very inexperienced staff. 'What time is breakfast?' I asked when we arrived. Look of total panic from the young man on reception: 'Breakfast, sir? Breakfast???' The next morning the cavernous reception area was unexpectedly filled with a long neat row of very smart, brand new suitcases. Outside was a large air-conditioned bus. A group of Korean pilgrims had arrived late the previous night and were having an early breakfast before whizzing round the sights and then on to their next stop – probably Kushinagar. Next to the hotel was an area called the Buddha Fun & Food Village with restaurants, a children's play area and, bizarrely, a plastic dinosaur looming over the wall. Like the hotel, it too was completely empty.

You could say Vaishali is a lesson in impermanence: a great city in the Buddha's time, a beautiful place, the world's oldest republic; all that history destroyed and buried deep for many hundreds of years; now being reanimated as a twenty-first-century destination for pilgrim tourists. How long will this new version last, I wondered?

But perhaps that history was not so far from the surface after all. We walked a couple of miles to the remains of the Kutagarasala Vihara, the monastery where the Buddha usually stayed when he came to Vaishali. It is an extensive site, with the remains of several brick stupas, a large water tank and a well-preserved Ashokan pillar with nineteenth-century graffiti scratched on by British visitors. 'R. Benton 1825', says one. 'J. Finch 1817', says another, with an elegant curlicue beneath it.

Our walk to the Vihara took us past freshly greened fields growing rice and potatoes and through villages that I don't think it is too romantic to say didn't feel as if they had changed all that much since ancient times.

The timeless quality of rural India. Brahmin priests squatted outside their temples taking offerings from passing travellers; mothers washed and de-loused their children's hair under the village pump; water buffalos munched lugubriously as their flattened cowpats dried on the walls of the huts; cormorants sat by the water tank, their wings spread wide to dry in the sun.

Everything had changed – and nothing had.

Close to the hotel was another large water tank where elected members of the Vaishali assembly were anointed. Next to the tank an iron gate led into a well-tended garden and inside the gate was a large sign, mottled and discoloured by weather and time. 'Buddha's Relic Stupa', it said.[10] A brick path between trimmed box hedges led towards the remains of the stupa, surrounded by iron railings, protected by a green corrugated metal dome. There wasn't much to see under the dome, just the outline of some walls, some made of brick, some of mud. The sign said that the mud walls were the remains of a stupa, dating back to the fifth century BCE, the time of the Buddha. It was later encased and enlarged by as many as four others made of brick from the Ashokan period and later. If these dates are right, this could indeed be the site of one of the original Relic Stupas. The location fitted, too, close to somewhere the Licchavis would gather together. Why, then, was there not more publicity about it?

This stupa was only fully excavated in 1958 and at the lowest level a relic casket was found, which is now housed in the museum at Patna, capital of Bihar, India's most densely populated state. We drove there the following day, through the noise and smell and congestion of a massive urban sprawl. 'What is Patna famous for?' I asked our driver. A short pause. 'Corruption,' he said. I later discovered that it had once been a place of major historical importance: Paliputra, the capital of Ashoka's huge empire, though almost all traces of the ancient city have disappeared long ago, buried beneath the concrete and the tarmac.

The Patna Museum is a typical public building of the latter days of the Raj, a classic piece of Victorian gothic, a more modest version of the Victoria & Albert Museum in London, set in a large garden, the only piece of open space for some distance around. Inside there is a grand entrance hall and a big central staircase but the exhibition spaces are dark, badly ventilated, crowded with exhibits, randomly distributed and smelling strongly of mould and formaldehyde. There are some wonderful exhibits: a fine set of early twentieth-century *thangkas*, very moth-eaten, and some magnificent stone carvings from the eighth century and earlier, but none of it is well displayed or well looked after.

The relics from Vaishali are kept locked in a special room, for which you have to pay extra. We were escorted up the main staircase by a tall, straight-backed and heavily mustachioed security guard, obviously ex-military, with a wooden leg, carrying an enormous bunch of keys. He painstakingly unlocked the multiple padlocks and we were shown into the room where the relics were displayed in a kind of low-key theatrical tableau, quite dimly lit, all behind heavily reinforced glass. No photography allowed. Inside the case was the small stone relic casket with its contents removed and laid out around it. They were just as described on the notice at the Relic Stupa site: 'Ashy earth, a small conch, two glass beads, a fragmentary piece of gold leaf and a copper punch-marked coin.'

We stared, strangely mesmerised, at the ancient relics. Quite plain, but beautiful too. Almost certainly authentic. A link to the time, 2,500 years ago, when the first stupas were built.

The security man stood by stony-faced, fiddling with his keys and occasionally stroking his moustache.

KUSHINAGAR – WHERE THE BUDDHA DIED

Kushinagar is the last of the Four Principal Places of Pilgrimage: birth in Lumbini, enlightenment in Bodhgaya, first teachings at Sarnath and here, Kushinagar, the place that the Buddha's disciple Ananda had called 'this backwoods town', where the Buddha died and attained Parinirvana, release from the endless cycle of birth, death and re-birth. This is the Parinirvana Stupa – *Nyangday Chorten* in Tibetan. It has no steps, just a bell-shaped dome rising directly from the base. There is no longer any need for steps to show the path. Parinirvana, Full Enlightenment, has been attained.

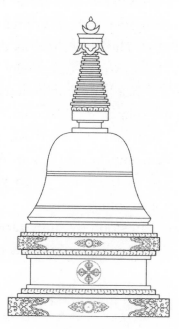

Parinirvana Stupa

The line of pilgrims stretched down the steps that lead to the Parinirvana Temple and spread into the surrounding garden. There were around fifty of them, Burmese, easily identifiable as a group by their matching yellow baseball caps and by the length of gold and orange cloth they were carrying shoulder-high between them. They shuffled slowly, calmly, silently towards the door of the temple.* Inside is one of Buddhism's most famous statues, a twenty-foot-long reclining figure depicting the Buddha at the moment of his death. He is lying on his right side, his head resting gently on his arm; his eyes are closed, his expression serene. All that can be seen of the statue are the head and the feet, burnished with a rich patina of gold, the result of many thousands of tiny smears of gold leaf left as offerings by pilgrims over the years. The rest of the body is draped with a long piece of orange cloth and it was this that the pilgrims waiting patiently outside had come to replace. Two priests placed the new cloth carefully over the old and accepted an offering of money, discreetly wrapped in a prayer scarf. The Parinirvana Temple is a narrow space with just enough room to circumambulate and the Burmese pilgrims walked slowly round in single file, lighting candles as they went, 108 of them, before gathering at the head of the statue and praying quietly for a few minutes.

Behind the temple is the Parinirvana Stupa, a simple white dome, shaped like a giant saltshaker and topped with three small umbrellas, the shape of the classic Ashokan stupa. This is quite a new structure, but, as so

* Remembering my visit to Kushinagar some years later, I couldn't help wondering whether these gentle, devout people might have been among those involved in the brutal, genocidal persecution of the Rohingya minority in their own country. It hardly seemed possible. But then, sad to say, being a Buddhist doesn't necessarily mean you are not capable of the worst excesses of human behaviour.

often, it is built over the site of a much older stupa, maybe several of them. Layers of history; palaces, temples, monasteries and stupas built by glorious and all-powerful rulers, dynasties and structures that in time will all crumble and fall, and be superseded by other builders who also believe that what they are creating will last forever. Nothing is permanent.

About a mile away another, much older structure, a huge and uneven mound of bricks, the Ramabhar Stupa, marks the place where the Buddha was cremated. There was a small improvised altar on its eastern face, with a copper bowl full of rice, a few prayer scarves and some flowers. Incense sticks smoked lazily. I circumambulated in the hot late morning sun. Lichen and little sprigs of green foliage grew out of the brickwork and the façade was smeared with gold leaf. Here and there were pools of soft wax where candles had been left to burn. It was a peaceful place, surrounded by a garden, very neat and tidy with a few benches placed thoughtfully under the trees. I felt a connection here to something very ancient, more so than at the main temple.

Could this be one of the original Relic Stupas, I wondered? There seems to be no archaeological evidence one way or another, no signs like the one at Vaishali, no claims or counter-claims. It's a romantic response I know, but I would like to think that this place, where the Buddha's earthly body was reduced to ashes, the place where he reached Parinirvana and was released forever from the cycle of birth, death and re-birth, might also be the site of the first Buddhist stupa ever built.

Seventh Journeys: Something Old, Something New

I had visited many stupas by now and started to understand their many different functions. I had seen
reliquary shrines, *dungten* in Tibetan, built to contain
the relics of a saint or great teacher. In the Potala in
Lhasa, for example, the main residence of the Dalai
Lama since the seventeenth century, there are eight
dungten. The two largest are for the 5th Dalai Lama
(1617–82), who was responsible for creating the
Potala that we see today, and for the 13th Dalai Lama
(1876–1933), the predecessor of the present one, which
is a monumental fifty feet and three storeys high.

Dungten are not always built on this scale. There is
a *dungten* containing the bone relics of one of the
twentieth century's greatest lamas, Dyilgo Khyentse
Rinpoche, in Kyichu Lakhang, a small monastery in

the Paro Valley in Bhutan. Kyichu is little more than a cluster of buildings huddled round a small courtyard where a miraculous orange tree grows, one that bears fruit all through the year – something I can bear witness to from several visits at different times. The monastery was for many years Dyilgo Khyentse's home and it is where he died. Born in Kham in eastern Tibet in 1910, Dyilgo Khyentse spent his early years studying with many great teachers from all the lineages of Tibetan Buddhism and on long solitary retreats. After the Chinese invasion of Tibet in the 1950s he and his family escaped to Bhutan where he was based for the rest of his life. He was an inspirational figure, a living embodiment of what he taught for his many followers, who ranged from students in the West to the Dalai Lama himself. His *dungten* stands in the newest of the three temples at Kyichu, about three feet high, made of silver, beaten copper and gold, with his image in the niche and the triple stairway that characterises the Descent from Heaven Stupa. For his many students Dyilgo Khyentse was indeed a Buddha who had descended from Tushita Heaven to bring his teachings to this earthly realm.

One of old Tibet's most revered sites was the gold-and-silver-encrusted *dungten* in Ganden Monastery near Lhasa that contained the body of Tsongkhapa, founder of the reformist Gelukpa school in the early fifteenth century and one of the most influential lamas in Tibet's history.* In the dark pre-dawn hours of a spring morning in 1969 a group of monks broke open the *dungten* and removed Tsongkhapa's embalmed body, taking it to a quiet location a little way from the monastery. There they burned it. A terrible act of vandalism, of heresy even, you might think. But just a few days later a large group of Mao's Red Guards arrived at Ganden, as the monks had been secretly informed they would. The Red Guards loaded anything that might be valuable into trucks and smashed everything else. Then they dynamited the monastery buildings. The monks had acted just in time and saved their revered founder from public desecration and abuse. Today much of Ganden has been rebuilt and Tsongkhapa's stupa, known as the Golden Reliquary at Ganden, has been restored, part of China's supposedly more tolerant attitude to Tibet's cultural history. There is of course no longer a body inside.[1]

Not all stupas are primarily concerned with dead lamas or their bodies or relics, however. These other kinds of stupas are known as *chorten* in Tibetan, literally 'receptacles for offerings', a more complex meaning than the simple translation of 'mound'. As we have

---

* Tsongkhapa (1357–1419), literally 'the man from the onion valley', is one of the most important figures in the development of Buddhism in Tibet. The first of the great Gelukpa monasteries, Ganden, was founded by him in 1409. The Dalai Lama is a Gelukpa, but Tsongkhapa's reincarnation, the Ganden Tripa, is still recognised as the spiritual head of the school.

already seen, it is what is inside a stupa, the many offerings and so on, that empowers it.

Often a chorten will simply mark a place where something important has happened – a commemorative stupa. There are thousands of chortens all across the Himalayas, built to mark where a great lama was born or lived or meditated, where holy texts had been translated, where a miraculous event had occurred, or simply somewhere geographically significant like the confluence of two rivers or the top of a mountain pass. In this context the building of a chorten pinpoints an important place or historical moment for all to see and to remember. But they are more than just monuments, as you might find a pillar marking the site of a battle in Europe. They are more like acupuncture points, where pins focus the energy of particular points in the body, calming that energy or releasing it, transforming it or harmonising it. A chorten can be built to create energy points in a landscape as the following story – part history, part legend as so often – illustrates.

Songtsen Gampo was the ruler of Tibet in the seventh century, a Buddhist who dedicated his reign to unifying the country. He introduced a law code based on Dharma principles, instigated the translation of many texts from Sanskrit, developed the Tibetan script and built the country's first Buddhist temples. He was also politically astute, marrying princesses from both

Nepal and China, thereby creating alliances with his two most powerful neighbours. Both princesses brought priceless statues with them to Lhasa as part of their dowries and Songtsen Gampo promised to build temples for each of them. But as diligently as his builders laboured during the day, by the next morning all their work had been reduced to rubble. It seemed that negative forces were conspiring during the night to thwart the king's will and obstruct the establishment of the Dharma in Tibet. The king's Chinese wife, Gyaza Kongjo, was known to be well versed in the ancient art of Chinese divination, so Songtsen Gampo asked for her help in discovering the source of this obstruction and her advice about how to remove it. Gyaza Kongjo's divinations revealed that the geomancy of the region was dominated by an enormous female demon, Sinmo, who sprawled across the Tibetan plateau and into the neighbouring Kingdom of Bhutan. So Songtsen Gampo built 108 monasteries, stupas and temples – in one night, the legend says – across his kingdom and beyond. The twelve most important were placed on the power points of the demoness Sinmo's body: her shoulders, hips, elbows, knees, on the palms of her hands and on each foot. Kyichu Lakhang (where Dyilgo Khyentse's Relic Stupa is) pins her left knee and Jampa Lakhang in Bumthang (where a spring flows cool in the summer and warm in the winter) pins her left foot. The great Jokhang Temple in Lhasa, still the holiest place in Tibet, stands over her heart. The demoness was immobilised, the obstruction was removed, the Dharma could be re-established.

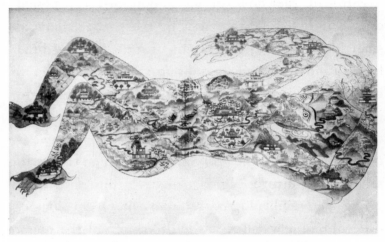

The sprawling ogress – drawing at Kyichu Lakhang

When I visited Lhasa in 2002 the Barkhor, the area surrounding the Jokhang, was one of the few parts of the old city of Lhasa relatively untouched by Chinese modernisations. Approaching the temple I became aware of a strange sound, a kind of rhythmic swishing, like autumn leaves being swept by a giant broom. It was the sound of hundreds of pilgrims making their prostrations: hands raised in a gesture of prayer above the head, in front of the mouth and over the heart. Then a full-length forward prostration, forehead touched to the ground, hands stretched out in front. Stand up again, walk to the point your hands had reached. Repeat till you reach your destination, which could be one circuit of the Barkhor or a pilgrimage halfway across Tibet.

I joined the flow of circumambulators, a real cross-section of Tibetan society, every age and type: smartly dressed city folk, some of the women in high heels; ruddy-cheeked nomads from Amdo or Kham, hair wild and matted, wearing tattered *chubas** and gym shoes; young men with hair oiled and braided, coiled on top of their heads or hanging in twists down their backs; and women with heavy headdresses and coral and turquoise beads woven into their hair. There were embroidered fur hats, snappy trilbies, a little boy in a woollen hat with 'ART' written on it. One old lady who asked me for alms was wearing a smart curly brimmed white straw number that would have looked good on a country and western singer.

I made my way inside. It seemed there had been a big ceremony the day before and the monks' robes were still propped up where they had been sitting, upright and empty, as if their occupants had just dematerialised. An old man was scraping melted butter from the lamps off the floor. Otherwise the place was unexpectedly, eerily empty. Statues of the

---

* A traditional Tibetan robe, usually made of yak wool and lined with sheepskin.

Buddha and Guru Rinpoche stood in the centre of the hall, *thangkas* hung from the pillars, photographs of the late Panchen Lama were propped up on one of the thrones. No image of the Dalai Lama, though – strictly forbidden by the Chinese government. In pride of place behind the main altar is a magnificent golden statue of Jowo Sakyamuni, the Buddha as a twelve-year-old prince, part of Gyaza Kongjo's dowry for her Tibetan husband. He sits serenely, draped in the finest brocade and encrusted with jewels. Huge butter lamps glow gold in front of him. Giant serpentine nagas coil protectively round the pillars that surround him.

Off the main hall is a series of small shrines, each with its own statue, all behind doors with heavy metal grilles, opened only on special days. A group of pilgrims arrived, villagers from just outside Lhasa, come to make offerings at Songtsen Khampo's shrine. The offering they brought was *chang*, home-brewed barley beer. They were in high spirits, quite boisterous – they had clearly been sampling their offering on their way into town. Every one of them paused in front of the Jowo Sakyamuni statue, quiet for a moment, a mantra muttered, a mudra (symbolic hand gesture) offered, a forehead touched to the railing. Then back to business, the metal gate to the shrine was opened for them and they slopped *chang* messily into a large pot-bellied container topped with a silver camel's head that stood next to Songtsen Gampo's statue,* swigging some themselves to help it all along, laughing and merry. A tall elderly man in an elegant fur hat began to sing and the others quickly joined in. Then a row of women, eight of them, began to dance in a line, shuffling their booted feet and swinging their legs, singing in unison. If the Jokhang is the beating heart of Tibet's embattled culture, as many people insist it still is, then, despite decades of oppression, perhaps that heart pulses stronger than the Chinese government might like you to think.

SOMETHING OLD . . .

In Tibet you will find stupas that act as gateways, with an archway through which you pass on the way to somewhere important. If you go on a pilgrimage to Mount Kailash, Asia's holiest mountain, you begin your circuit of the mountain by circumambulating and then walking through the Kangyi Chorten and leaving an offering on its rough stone steps. Kailash is holy to Hindus as well as Buddhists and I photographed a

---

* This silver container is said to have been hidden as a treasure by Songtsen Gampo and discovered by Tsongkhapa. It was Tsongkhapa who returned it to the Jokhang in 1409 when he staged the first Great Prayer Festival, the Monlam, one of the great celebratory festivals of the Tibetan Buddhist calendar, following a major renovation of the Jokhang and its sacred statues.

group of rather disoriented-looking pilgrims from India. They had flown up from the sweltering heat and humidity of Delhi to Kathmandu, then been packed onto buses which drove rapidly up to the fierce mountain landscape of western Tibet before depositing them at the foot of Mount Kailash. Delhi is less than 1,000 feet above sea level, with June temperatures of as much as 40°C; the Kailash circuit starts at about 15,000 feet and climbs to over 18,000 feet for the final pass, Drolma La, with temperatures that even in June can drop to below freezing at night. It snowed when we were there. It is about as extreme a shift in climatic conditions as could be imagined. The pilgrims are often woefully underprepared and ill-equipped and many suffer from altitude sickness. We saw a jeep carrying the body of someone who had died on their way round the mountain. To die on a pilgrimage is supposed to be very good karma: for the pilgrim maybe, but what about for the get-rich-quick tour operators who have not taken proper care of their clients?

A photograph from 1904 shows British soldiers under the command of Francis Younghusband entering Lhasa, the climax of one of the most ill-conceived and tragic British imperial ventures of the early twentieth century. They are about to march through the chorten that was the ancient gateway to the city. It is supposed to be a victorious moment, but to me it has always seemed more pathetic than triumphant, both absurd and incongruous, the little stick-figure soldiers dwarfed by the chorten and by the mass of the Potala looming beyond it, looking somehow as if they know that they really shouldn't be there.[2]

British troops entering Lhasa, 1904

A stupa can be any size. The biggest, one of the largest religious structures of any kind in the world, is at Borobudur in Indonesia, well over one hundred feet high.* At the other end of the scale is the *kadam* chorten, designed to be carried, often worn round the neck so as to be close to one's heart, small enough to carry in the palm of your hand. The Indian Buddhist

---

* The Great Stupa of Universal Compassion now under construction in Bendigo in South Australia will be even bigger – over 164 feet tall.

philosopher Atisha, a very influential figure in the teaching of Buddhism in Tibet, carried a *kadam* containing the ashes of his own teacher with him throughout his life.

Stupas have many different purposes: different shapes, different sizes, different manifestations, different functions. But they are always places of spiritual significance, never built for the glory of a secular ruler or to celebrate a military triumph. Spiritually, making a stupa has always been seen as a highly meritorious undertaking for all concerned, for the actual builders as much as the sponsor – but always built for the benefit of others, not for personal aggrandisement or glory.

. . . SOMETHING NEW

A newly built stupa won't carry the kind of historic spiritual resonance of the ancient chortens of Tibet or Ladakh or Nepal or Bhutan. Located in countries with no history of Buddhism, building one must have a twofold function. It creates merit for the sponsor but it also has to disseminate that merit out into the wider world. In this way everyone who comes into contact with it also comes into contact with the Buddha and with Buddhist teachings, making those teachings very accessible, whether you are actively seeking them or not. What must motivate the building of a stupa today is a wish to create something that is a positive benefit, however small, to the place in which it is located – and beyond. New stupas will often have names, sometimes a little grandiose, to emphasise this: the World Peace Stupa, the Great Stupa of Universal Compassion and so on.

The Harewood Stupa has settled comfortably into its landscape. It looks as if it has always been there. A thick wall of bamboo is its backdrop; rhododendrons and Himalayan blue poppies flower in the open spaces around it. The Himalayan Garden in which it sits has matured now and a stroll through it is the best way to approach. You walk down a little man-made rocky gorge, alpine flowers nestled in its crevasses, then brush past a Bhutanese pine with its delicate cones and feathery needles, before entering a hidden valley carpeted with primulas and more than twenty varieties of flowering rhododendron. Orchids, blue poppies and cobra lilies lurk among the rocks. The path leads to a Chinese-style arched bridge over the Beck – no need to wobble over the stepping-stones any more if you don't want to – and then up the slope on the other side towards the stupa. I take this walk often. Early morning is best when the sun strikes the east face of the stupa and Buddha Sakyamuni in his niche glows gold in its rays. I walk round three times and leave an offering. I've even managed to persuade my dogs to circumambulate in the right direction.

Over a couple of years I collected together images of these offerings and made a small photographic book,

108 Offerings, a visual almanac of a calendar year described by the plants, flowers and other objects I had collected along the way or brought from home: rhododendron flowers in the spring, strawberries in the summer, plums and apples in the autumn, holly and mistletoe in winter and so on. I left a heart-shaped biscuit on Valentine's Day and three chocolate hares wrapped in foil on Easter Sunday. There are often offerings left by other visitors, too – flowers, a photograph, a candle, sometimes prayer flags or prayer scarves tied to the bamboo clumps. We have had visits from Mongolian musicians, from Gurkha soldiers stationed at nearby Catterick, from Western Buddhists and from many eminent lamas who have circumambulated, led prayers or supervised the putting up of new prayer flags. Some have made suggestions about improvements: a small solar-powered light for the Buddha statue, bells or wind chimes in the trees around. One told me, kindly but quite sternly, that leaving offerings was good, but the Buddha's niche should be cleaned more often. I promised him it would be.

Harewood has more than 200,000 visitors a year and the more energetic will walk round the lake and through the Himalayan Garden on their way to look at the vegetable plots and fruit trees of the eighteenth-century Walled Garden. Very few will be Buddhists. I sometimes hang around near the stupa to see how people respond. Almost without exception it seems to calm them, slow them down a little. Some will stop and read the short notice explaining what it is and how it came about. A few will circumambulate three times, as the notice suggests they do, before continuing on their way. The Harewood Stupa has become an integral part of people's experience of visiting the gardens here.

TSEKARMO

Khenpo Rangdol beamed across the desk in his small office in the Drikung Kagyu Monastery in Dehra Dun. 'You must come to Ladakh!' he said. 'We are building a big stupa there!' Khenpo Rangdol is a tall and charming Ladakhi with a rich baritone voice and excellent English, and he has a position of some responsibility at the monastery – he is an able administrator and a highly effective fund-raiser. I had been showing him pictures of the Harewood Stupa and he responded by telling me about the project he was involved in near his home village. 'Work is nearly finished now,' he said. 'Come to the consecration, August time next year. Weather in Ladakh very good at that time.'

Ladakh is an area of what is technically known as high-altitude cold desert sandwiched between Kashmir and Tibet, part of the state of Jammu and Kashmir, a hotly and often violently disputed focus of tensions between India and Pakistan since partition. Kashmir is mainly Muslim in the west and predominantly Buddhist in the east and Ladakh's strategic location means that for a long time there has been a highly visible Indian military presence there. When I first visited in June 1977, when we were making the *Trilogy*, we drove over the high passes from Kashmir, following an army convoy in our battered VW minibus, snow still piled roof-high on either side of the road. At Kargil, about halfway between Srinigar in Kashmir and Leh, the main town in Ladakh, people pointed out the ridge just a few miles away that had been the front line of the ongoing border dispute between India and Pakistan not long before. The military were still very much in evidence when I visited again in 2011, local heroes now because of their rescue work a year earlier when a highly unusual and devastating flash flood had swept down from the mountains one August night, washing fields and bridges and houses and livestock away. More than 250 people died and many more lost their homes.

Normally the average annual rainfall in Ladakh is only four inches, so Ladakhis rely on the rivers for washing and drinking water and to irrigate their crops. The main river of Ladakh is the Indus, one of the great waterways of Asia, which rises just north of Mount Kailash in western Tibet, weaving through Ladakh and Baltistan before curving south, swelling and slowing into the huge, sluggish brown ribbon of water that irrigates the green core of Pakistan. Typically, a Ladakhi village will be clustered close to the river – the Indus or one of its many tributaries – with a patchwork of irrigated fields surrounding it and the monastery perched on a rocky outcrop above it. The village of Tingmosgang, where Khenpo Rangdol was from, and the monastery of Tsekarmo, where he had his early training as a monk, are laid out in exactly this way.

An old monk called Konchok Rinchen from Tsekarmo had a dream of building a stupa on a high hill, opposite the monastery and above Tingmosgang, where he intended it would act as a protector for the village. But building a stupa is expensive (as I had learned) and there were no sponsors. The project stalled till a committee of laymen and monks, including Khenpo Rangdol, decided to put their weight behind it and go about finding the funds. With the help of local sponsors they organised a group of Lama Dancers from Ladakh to go on an extensive tour of Europe, from which the bulk of the money needed was raised.

By this time it had been decided to move the site from the hilltop to a more accessible location up the valley from the monastery – a stupa should be somewhere that many people can visit. A small stupa would be built on the original site in honour of Konchok Rinchen, who had passed away by now. The project's ambitions had grown, too. As well as the stupa, there would be a retreat centre and a kind of retirement home for old monks, where they could be well looked after by younger monks and receive proper medical care, something that is not always possible within the monastery. In the future Khenpo Rangdol told me there were plans to build educational facilities there, too, including a library and museum: somewhere that Ladakhis, particularly the young, many of whom leave to study elsewhere, can learn about Buddhism and their own language and culture.

With the funds from the Lama Dance tour, building could be completed. The finest painters from Nepal were employed, painting onto cloth that was then attached to the walls – quite unusual in the Himalayas where painting is almost always done onsite. The Great Bodhi Stupa at Tsekarmo is an Enlightenment Stupa, like the one at Harewood but far bigger, with a large main chamber that you can walk into. With larger stupas, the *Sok-shing*, the Life Tree that Khenpo Rangdol described as 'the central channel', begins above this chamber, linking it to the dome and thirteen-ringed spire. An impressive array of offerings, texts and relics had been collected: juniper from Drokpa, very old handwritten books from Tibet, relics from high lamas including scraps of Milarepa's* clothes and Guru Rinpoche's hair.

The old monk Konchok Rinchen had wanted to build the stupa as a protector for the village and it seems to have worked. In the flash floods of 2010, Tingmosgang was relatively untouched, with no loss of

---

* Milarepa (1050–1135 approx.) is perhaps Tibet's best-loved mystic, a teacher and poet, the embodiment of the Vajrayana path, a flawed human being who achieved enlightenment within one lifetime, for the benefit of all. He is said to have written 100,000 songs, composed spontaneously while in deep meditation.

life, and the village's school, hospital and other major buildings were largely undamaged.

A couple of weeks before I was due to leave for Ladakh, my father died. It wasn't entirely unexpected. He'd been in poor health for some years and had never really recovered from having a pacemaker fitted, normally a fairly standard operation but one where in his case there had been several complications. But when the end came it was very sudden. He was working through his morning routine, not a particularly complex one: get up, have breakfast on a tray in his room, take his pills, get dressed and so on. But it seemed to get more and more drawn out as time went on. That morning, at about nine o'clock, he was sitting on his bed watching Patricia get ready, when he told her he felt a little faint and, almost before he'd finished the sentence, had a major heart attack. An ambulance was called and nearby family – both my half-brother Mark and I live within five minutes' drive, Patricia's son Michael was visiting from Australia – hurried to the scene. The paramedics arrived and did what they apparently have to do by law: the full emergency procedure of CPR, artificial respiration, electric shocks, the works. As I drove up to Harewood House my father was being wheeled out to the ambulance at high speed, surrounded by paramedics, wired up, oxygen mask on, hair wild, only partially dressed. About as undignified as could be. I wish to this day that had not been my last sight of him. I followed the ambulance to the hospital where they told us he was dead on arrival. Privately, we were told that he'd already died by the time they got him into the ambulance. Why all the equipment and melodrama then, I could not help but wonder? In the small hospital room where his body now lay Patricia solemnly handed me his signet ring, a surreal moment that I didn't know what to make of. He'd just had the ring reduced to stop it falling off his bony, ageing finger and it was much too small for me.

My father died on Monday, 11 July 2011. My brother Mark and his fiancée Judy were to be married the following Saturday, 16 July. What to do? The family conferred and quite quickly we decided that we should go ahead as planned. We also realised that the funeral had to take place before the wedding – both Patricia and Mark were especially positive about this idea. The show must go on, we all agreed. My father had worked in theatres much of his life and it really is what he would have wanted. The family was gathering anyway for the wedding, there was a marquee next to the church – many of the components were already in place. So my father's funeral was rapidly arranged for the Friday, just four days after he died and the day before Mark and Judy's wedding. Villagers and people who worked on the estate lined the drive and a policeman stopped the traffic and saluted as we drove out onto the main road on the way to the crematorium. The maelstrom of arrangements meant there had been little time for expression of emotion. Everyone had reacted in their own way and in their own time. Much to my surprise, it was the saluting policeman that did for me.

I had another personal dilemma: should I go ahead with my trip to Ladakh? I weighed up the pros and cons. Patricia had both her sons there and plans for a memorial service were still a few months away. There wasn't actually anything for me to do and, more unconsciously than consciously perhaps, my connection with the Himalayas, and especially the growing significance of Buddhism in my life, was becoming an increasingly important counterbalance for me to the pressures and assumptions and expectations of what Diane and I in our more irreverent moments called 'Bizarrewood'. Like it or not, I had now inherited my father's title. A little time away to reflect on that would be no bad thing. Diane encouraged me to go. So I went.

In Leh I met up with an American friend, Robert Chilton, whom I knew through his work with the Orient Foundation. We visited Stakna, a small monastery in the Indus Valley, about an hour's drive from Leh and quite close to Thiksey, where we had filmed all those years before in 1977. At Stakna there was a gathering of monks performing a puja, in honour of the previous abbot we were told, a Bhutanese, who had died exactly a year previously. Robert and I kept a suitably discreet distance, anxious not to disturb them, and sent in offerings as a mark of respect. As the monks filed out a little later one of them came up to us, speaking excellent English, said he had noticed our respectful behaviour and wondered if we were Buddhists. We got talking and he was delighted to learn we had both spent time in Bhutan. I started to show him pictures of the Harewood Stupa, built by Bhutanese I told him. As I scrolled through the photographs on my camera, up came an image of my father's funeral, just a few weeks earlier. I froze, transfixed – and then, quite unexpectedly, burst into tears, sobbing more violently than at any time since my father's death, much to the astonishment of both Robert and the young Bhutanese monk.

We said an affectionate farewell a little later and Robert and I walked down to the car, pausing to circumambulate a stupa at the bottom of the hill. I was still feeling emotionally raw as we walked slowly round, so it was a moment or two before I noticed that Robert too was crying. He told me he was thinking of his grandmother who had died a couple of years earlier. 'She was one of the people who first interested me in Buddhism,' he said. We looked at each other, tears streaming down our faces. And then we started to laugh.

Stupa consecrations are long affairs. I knew that from Harewood. This one lasted two weeks. First, there was a week of pujas and offering ceremonies before the arrival of His Holiness the Drikung Kyabgon Chetsang, the head of the Drikung Kagyu school, who had been invited to preside over the consecration and inauguration and to give teachings to his many followers in Ladakh. His arrival was a grand affair. A long procession of cars made its way slowly up the narrow road, newly surfaced and lined with prayer flags, through the village, past the old monastery and up the valley to the new stupa and the little cluster of half-finished buildings around it. Crowds of Ladakhis waited, prayer scarves at the ready.

It is rare nowadays to see Ladakhis in traditional costume, but for this very special occasion everyone wore their finest. The women's costumes in particular were spectacular. They had silky-haired goatskin cloaks draped over their brocade dresses, with stunning headdresses, *peraks*, encrusted with row upon row of lumps of turquoise, some the size of a pigeon's egg, that reached halfway down their backs. A turquoise-encrusted peak, hooded like a cobra's head, curved over their faces and giant ear-pieces fanned out like woolly bat's wings on either side. They wore heavy necklaces of coral, bone, gold and yet more turquoise, heirlooms that indicated a family's wealth and status. Other women had simpler headgear, with a high, round crown and an elegantly curled brim, like small, stylish witch's hats. Many people had travelled from beyond the Indus Valley to be there. There were men in bright yellow brocade tunics and black, pointed hats. There was a small group of young women, olive-skinned and giggly, making eye contact then lowering their eyes flirtatiously, very different from the dark, self-contained, mountain-weathered Ladakhis. They wore loose trousers and their bright blouses had epaulettes of beaten silver and beads and pearl buttons, with elaborate headdresses decorated with more silver, skeins of bright wool and large bunches of flowers, some silk, some freshly picked. These were Drokpas from the Dha-Hanu region near the Pakistani border, the descendants of Greek soldiers from Alexander the Great's invading army.

And there were us foreigners, a motley bunch: a majority of Germans and Swiss (many of them sponsors of the project), a fair sprinkling of Eastern Europeans (Poles, Latvians, Ukrainians and Estonians), a couple of Japanese and Vietnamese, a few Americans. I was one of only two Brits.

The arrival of the Drikung Rinpoche marked the end of the preparations. The purification puja that had been going on for a week was over and it was now time for the large sand mandala that had been made in the main chamber to be revealed. Drikung Rinpoche presided over a fire puja in front of a table laden with offerings – be careful not to let your shadow fall on them, I was warned. Then the sand mandala was swept up and disposed of in a spring that rose in the hillside behind the stupa, its benefits flowing into the world as the water from the spring flowed into the river. The sun came out and Ladakhis and foreigners sat in the garden round the spring drinking butter tea.

The next day, 3 August, was trebly auspicious. It was the day the stupa was to be formally inaugurated, it was the day the Buddha first turned the Wheel of the

Dharma when he gave his first teachings at Sarnath – and it was Drikung Rinpoche's birthday. There was a lengthy round of speeches, all translated from Tibetan first into Ladakhi, then German and then English. There was even a very ragged rendition of 'Happy Birthday' from some of the Westerners.

Drikung Rinpoche's teaching began. He talked about stupas, how important it was that as many people as possible saw them, and that they should never be seen simply as a decoration or a monument, but as the Buddha himself. As he spoke a lone white butterfly flew slowly over the assembly and, though there was no sign of rain, a rainbow appeared in the bright blue sky above the hill behind the stupa. The next morning, just before Drikung Rinpoche was due to continue his teaching, a halation appeared round the sun, followed after about half an hour by another, fainter outer ring which slowly faded, leaving the inner circle even more intense. This unusual meteorological phenomenon, correctly called a 22° halo but more poetically known as an icebow or oriole, is caused by light interacting with ice crystals in the atmosphere. We were high up, over 10,000 feet, it was a fine day in the middle of the Ladakhi summer and the sky was a bright Himalayan blue. Not normal conditions for an icebow.

Since then, every 3 August, the anniversary of the inauguration, whatever the weather I was told, a rainbow or, more rarely, an icebow appears in the sky over the hill above the Great Stupa of Tsekarmo.

Eighth Journeys: Natural Born Stupas

KAILASH

In the early summer of 2010, my sixtieth year, I went on a pilgrimage to Mount Kailash in western Tibet, the holiest mountain in Asia. Getting there meant a long walk. I have a metal hip and dodgy knees. Camping was the only option. I hadn't spent a night under canvas for twenty years or more. What was I doing setting off on a three-week trek at altitude in one of the wildest landscapes on earth? Once we reached Tibet we would never be below 14,000 feet. It was going to be a challenge. Kailash seems to have that effect on people.

There were six of us – two old friends of mine, Paul Dolan and Charles Garrad, and my three sons, Ben, Orly and Eddy. Three old fellas and three young fellas. Only Ben had experience of trekking in the Himalayas, but this was something I had wanted to do since I first started reading about Tibet in my teens and the others were all crazy and curious and open-minded enough to agree to come with me.

We walked into Tibet from Simikot, a smoky, dusty, scruffy Himalayan village, a magical place built of mud and stone on a steep hillside. Straw and wood piled round a crisp new solar panel. Shiva's trident on the roof next to a satellite dish. Snot-moustached kids smiling quizzically from the doorways of their homes. Simikot is the district capital of the province of Humla in north-west Nepal, one of the poorest and least populated parts of the country, with no roads or industry. Subsistence farming is the rule, but the winters are long and the growing season short, so life is tough. Slicing through the province north-west to south is the Karnali River and this was our way into Tibet, six days' walking, the path sometimes steep, precarious and high on the valley wall; sometimes flat, broad and close enough to the rushing river to splash our faces with its icy water; sometimes crossing on precarious footbridges, hoping not to meet a herd of goats coming the other way. A majestic valley, a beautiful landscape, this year's crops ripening in the sun before the monsoon comes.

We climbed steadily, through the fine mist of the mountain clouds, a campsite surrounded by fields of wild marijuana, fewer trees but more wild flowers, a slow trudge up to the highest pass, Nara Langna, at 15,000 feet. Then a spectacular first vision of the Tibetan plateau fringed by snow peaks, a knee-jarring descent to the border, a final crossing of the Karnali, and we were in Tibet. Kailash was now just a day's drive away.

Of all the books about Tibet I read when I was younger, Lama Anagarika Govinda's *The Way of the White Clouds* left the strongest impression. Govinda calls himself 'an Indian national of European descent and Buddhist faith, belonging to a Tibetan order and believing in the Brotherhood of Man'.[1] The book describes his travels across the Himalayas during the late 1940s, one of the last Westerners to spend time in Tibet before the Chinese invasion in 1950. He says this about Kailash:

> There are mountains which are just mountains and there are mountains with personalities. The personality of a mountain is more than merely a strange shape that makes it different from others – just as a strangely shaped face or strange actions do not make an individual into a personality. Personality consists in the power to influence others and this power is due to consistency, harmony and one-pointedness of character . . . If these qualities are present in a mountain we recognize it as a vessel of cosmic power and we call it a sacred mountain.[2]

Kailash is physically very striking. Set back from the main Himalayan range, it stands alone on the Tibetan plateau, over 22,000 feet tall, shaped like a pyramid, with clearly defined slopes facing in the four directions. It is around 50 million years old, formed when the great tectonic masses of Gondwanaland and the northern Eurasian plate collided to form the Himalayas. Before this the Tibetan plateau, today one of the highest places on earth, was an ocean, the Tethys Sea, and Kailash would have been an island. Four of the great rivers of Asia have their sources in its foothills. Rising to the north is the Indus, which irrigates much of Pakistan; to the south is the Karnali, our route in and a major tributary of the Ganges; to the west is the Sutlej, which flows through the ancient Kingdom of Guge before joining the Indus; and to the east is the Tsangpo, which traverses Tibet before changing its name to the Brahmaputra on its journey south into the Bay of Bengal. These rivers are crucial waterways, the very lifeblood of Tibet, Nepal, Pakistan and India.

That's the geography and the geology. But they're just the start of it because, as Govinda's description suggests, Mount Kailash is also a holy place, a place of pilgrimage, somewhere that is revered by the followers of four religious traditions.

For Hindus it is the abode of Shiva, its conical shape evoking the lingam, his universal symbol. He sits on the top of the mountain in perpetual union with his consort Parvati.

Buddhists know the mountain as Kang Rinpoche, the abode of the fierce tantric deity Chakrasamvara*

---

* A wrathful protective deity, often called upon as a focus for meditation and purification practices.

and his consort, Dorje Phamo. It also has a strong association with the Tibetan poet and mystic Milarepa, who meditated in its caves, living on a diet of nettles.

To followers of the Jain religion it is known as Astapada, the place where Rishabha, one of their founders, achieved enlightenment.

And to Bon-pos, followers of the animistic belief system that pre-dated Buddhism in Tibet, it is Tise, where their great teacher Shenrab Miwo descended to earth.

Pilgrims from all four religions circumambulate the mountain as they would a stupa. Because of its spiritual significance, nobody has ever climbed it.

Mount Kailash is often equated with Mount Meru, the mythical mountain that stands at the centre of the universe, the axis of the world. Meru's pinnacle, immeasurably high, reaches up to the heavens; its slopes are the abode of the gods; the foothills of the Himalayas are where it makes contact with our world and it descends as deep into the underworld as it reaches high up into the heavens. And Mount Kailash is the source of the River Ganga, the mythical river that rises in heaven and from which all life flows (not to be confused with the geographical River Ganges, which emerges mysteriously from the Gangotri Glacier on the other side of the Himalayas).

There is a story about a contest for control of the mountain between Milarepa and a Bon-po magician, Naro Bonchung. They agree that the winner will be whoever reaches the summit before dawn on the following day. Early that morning, Naro Bonchung can be seen moving rapidly towards the peak, wearing a green cloak and playing his shaman's drum. Milarepa, in deep meditation in a cave at the foot of the mountain, seems unconcerned. Then, at the very last moment, he wakes, snaps his fingers, puts on his own cloak and appears in an instant on the summit, just as the first rays of the morning sun strike it. Naro Bonchung is so astonished that he drops his drum, which bounces down the mountainside. The clearly defined scarred striations that can be seen on its eastern slopes are said to be the marks left by his drum.

Ancient myths and scientific facts. With Mount Kailash it is difficult to tell where one ends and the other begins.

We made it round the mountain in three and a half days, breathless but exhilarated. Some Tibetans do it in a single day, setting out well before dawn. Others prostrate all the way round. A cave in one monastery on the circuit has the imprint of a yak horn on its wall. This is where Gotsangpo, a much-revered Tibetan meditator of the thirteenth century who was described to me as the first person to circumambulate Kailash, was led by a white yak to shelter from a storm. Another has the cave where Milarepa meditated before racing the Bon-po magician to the peak. Here there are footprints and a hoof-print embedded in the rock. At the highest point of the pass, Drolma La, over 18,000 feet above sea level, is a large boulder, buried under prayer flags and offerings left by pilgrims. Gotsangpo was led to the pass by a pack of twenty-one wolves. As they reached the top, the wolves vanished into the rock. Twenty-one wolves. Twenty-one Taras in the pantheon of Buddhist deities. Drolma La. Tara's Pass.

You could say that Kailash is the biggest stupa in the world. Naturally formed, not man-made of course, but with all the attributes – and more – that a stupa builder strives to emulate. Going on a pilgrimage there, Buddhists believe, can harmonise discord, reconcile differences and ultimately show the way to liberation. For me there was also another, quite unexpected outcome.

After we got back, I gave a couple of talks about our journey. This was a year or so before my father died and he and my stepmother Patricia attended one of them. She came up to me afterwards. 'You do realise what the date was when you reached Drolma La, don't you,' she said. I looked puzzled. 'June the eighteenth, you said. Quite a coincidence!'

On 18 June 1815, my great-great-great-grandfather Henry fought in and was wounded at the Battle of Waterloo. His battle medal hangs below his huge portrait in the dining room of Harewood House. He is sitting on his favourite horse, surrounded by fox-hounds, an image not without irony because not long after he had a bad fall while out hunting and died of his injuries. Exactly one hundred years later, 18 June 1915, my grandfather was wounded at the Second Battle of Artois, one of well over 100,000 Allied casualties that day. German casualties were 73,000. The Allied advance was less than two miles. On 18 June 1944, as the Allied armies pushed up through central Italy, my father was on a night patrol that ran into the enemy frontline. He was wounded and captured and spent the next nine months as a prisoner of war.

I was aware of the significance of the date, but I suppose I'd buried the knowledge, on the basis that if I didn't dwell on it I would never be affected by it. So was it just a coincidence? Maybe, if you believe in such things. I prefer a different interpretation. It was the healing power of the mountain. A family curse exorcised, I believed, for me and for future generations.

BEYOND KAILASH

A day's drive west of Kailash is the town of Tholing, a place of great importance in the spread of Buddhism into Tibet 1,500 years ago, now wholly Chinese in character apart from what is left of the old monastery. We'd all been looking forward to staying in a hotel, however basic, after more than a week under canvas, but found that our room reservations had been cancelled for use by visiting Chinese officials, far more important than us. After a desultory trudge around town looking at some pretty grim accommodation, we were directed to an enormous, brand new hotel. Very modern, we were told. We would be the first guests.

The rooms were fine, though far from fully functional. The wet-room floor sloped towards the door so every time you turned the shower on the bedroom flooded. There was no hot water. Binod Rai, our Nepali tour leader, by some distance the lightest member of our group, sat on the only chair in my room, which immediately collapsed beneath him. But all the rooms had plasma TVs, fully functional once you'd peeled off the protective plastic coating. I forced myself awake one night to watch England grind out a feeble goalless draw with Algeria in the World Cup. The kitchens and dining room weren't operational yet, so we catered for ourselves and ate in our mess tent in the car park. From this bizarre base we were able to visit probably the most extraordinary landscape I have ever been to.

Buddhism had gone into a steep decline in Tibet from the reign of King Langdarma (863–906) onwards. Its revival was hampered by the lack of good teachers and experienced practitioners. Yeshe O, ruler of the Kingdom of Guge in western Tibet, vowed to put this right. On the recommendation of Rinchen Zangpo, known as the Translator,* a monk and spiritual adviser

---

* Rinchen Zangpo (958–1055) translated many texts from Sanskrit into Tibetan from his base in Tholing. He was also responsible for the magnificent frescos in the monastery there, which, along with his work in the temples of Sanchi in Ladakh, are perhaps the finest Buddhist wall paintings to be found anywhere in the Himalayas and some of the few that have a known and named creator.

to the king who was already resident in the monastery in Tholing, Yeshe O sent an emissary to the great Buddhist university at Nalanda in India.

This was where he would find someone who could help reintroduce Buddhist teachings to Tibet, Rinchen Zangpo said. The emissary soon realised who was the right man for the job: the great Indian master Atisha, already revered as one of the foremost scholars and most inspiring teachers of his generation. But Atisha was happy where he was and did not want to go to Tibet, a wild and uncultured place by all accounts, so the emissary returned empty-handed. Undeterred, the king sent another emissary, with the same result. Yeshe O was a determined man and he decided to lead a third mission to Nalanda himself. The journey was a difficult one, through wild and often hostile country, and he was taken prisoner and held to ransom by a neighbouring ruler who demanded the king's body weight in gold for his release. Yeshe O's nephew Jangchub O gathered together the wealth of the kingdom and set off to pay for his uncle's freedom. But when he reached his destination he discovered that the ransom was short, by the weight of Yeshe O's head it is said, and his captor refused to release him. Yeshe O took his nephew to one side. 'I am an old man now,' he said, 'not worth the ransom money. Leave me here and use the gold instead to persuade Atisha to come to Tibet.' He would not be dissuaded and with a heavy heart Jangchub O set off for Nalanda. Atisha did not care about the gold, but he was deeply moved by Yeshe O's dedication. Here was a man who was prepared to sacrifice everything, even his own life, for the greater good. Atisha travelled back to Guge with Jangchub O and remained there for the rest of his life, one of the key figures in what is often known as 'the second diffusion' of Buddhism in Tibet.

Atisha, Rinchen Zangpo and many of the other Indian masters who followed them passed this way, travelling along what was then a major trade route from India – climbing from the Ganges plains into Kashmir, then through Ladakh and on into Guge (whose long-abandoned capital Tsaparang is just to the west of Tholing) and Tholing itself, before crossing the 17,000-foot Bogo La pass onto the Tibetan plateau and following the Tsangpo River east towards Lhasa.

This is a landscape unlike any other in the world, great sandstone gorges with panoramic views of the north face of the high Himalayas, the soft stone sculpted by ice and wind into dramatic architectural forms: arches, pyramids, delicately balanced pinnacles and rock formations shaped like stupas, almost indistinguishable from the ruins of the many man-made versions that are scattered across the valley floor.

One morning, Charles, Paul, Eddy and I walked along the Sutlej Valley floor just outside Tholing, up close to these strange, ghostly, ruined structures. The damage seemed to have been entirely from natural causes, eroded by wind and weather, though you couldn't rule out Red Guards or thieves looking for treasure. Many of the stupas were hollowed out. Hundreds of *tsa tsas* and other little lumps of baked earth just about recognisable as figures were tumbling out, like the stuffing of a broken sofa or the innards of a disembowelled creature. I remembered the description I had used when trying to explain the process of filling a stupa to people at Harewood a few years before: how an empty stupa was 'like a bowl without water or a body without guts'. We picked up a couple of the *tsa tsas* and debated whether we should take them home as souvenirs. In the end, we decided they were better left where they were.

There is a large and important stupa just by Tholing Gompa, a Descent from Heaven Stupa, unusual in having steps in all four directions, containing the relics of Rinchen Zangpo. It was vandalised by Red Guards during the Cultural Revolution, as was the monastery next door, but it has been restored with some sensitivity and now looks to be in better condition than when it had been photographed by Lama Anagarika Govinda sixty years earlier. It has a rough-hewn quality to it, as if it had erupted out of the rocky ground, not been built upon it. Directly opposite the neat municipal park that its present-day Chinese guardians have chosen to surround it with is the police station, a brutal block of concrete, heavily guarded by stone-faced men with automatic weapons.

The ochre red and off-white bands that make the Tholing Stupa so distinctive are also a feature of another of western Tibet's special places, Thirthapuri, near Mount Kailash. There are hot springs here, bubbling sulphorous but soothing from the rock, somewhere pilgrims go to soak their weary limbs after walking round the holy mountain. Many will make another circumambulation, a short walk circling the small monastery that has been built round a place where Guru Rinpoche once meditated, weaving in and out of the crowds of stupas old and new, passing mani walls* and piles of carved yak skulls. Here it is difficult to tell the difference between what is man-made and what is natural. What Tibetans call 'self-born' stupas seem to be growing out of the red and white striped rock formations – and at the same time are being absorbed back into it.

I remembered the Indus Valley in Ladakh. It too is scattered with stupas: at the approaches to monasteries, by the river, in the middle of fields. The older ones, their whitewash fading, are the same dusty grey as the rocky desert landscape in which they sit. In the evening the setting sun, its beam tightly shuttered by dark clouds, shines its golden spotlight on them, and they glow as if they are on fire.

These are environments where a rock can turn out to be a stupa, or a stupa a rock. Where a whole landscape

---

* A wall made up entirely of stones with mantras carved onto them.

is a giant mandala, and where a text telling how to draw a mandala in coloured sand is also a description of a landscape.

The special power of the Himalayan stupa grows, in part certainly, from this close relationship with the natural world. The square base connects with the earth, emerges from it, a solid shape that blends into the smoothly rounded form of the dome above it, before tapering to a point that reaches upwards towards the sky – and towards enlightenment. Natural forms shaped by natural forces adapted to a profound symbolic and spiritual purpose. Sacred geometry.

THIRTY-SEVEN STEPS

I had visited many stupas by now. I'd become wholly familiar with their sculptural form and the many variations thereof, across nations and cultures, both man-made and natural. I had come to understand how it represented the enlightened mind of the Buddha and experienced first-hand how that manifested, whether that was at Boudha or at Mount Kailash; at a rough brick mound that was all that remained of one of the eight Relic Stupas or at a small, untidy roadside stupa in Bhutan or Ladakh. But what of its other meaning – as a guide to how to achieve enlightenment yourself?

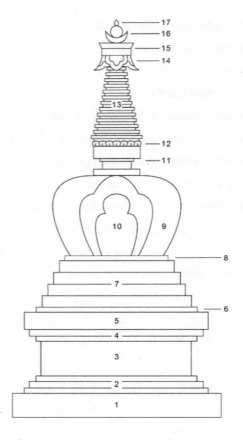

1. The foundation
2. The three small steps
3. The lotus seat
4. The base of the building
5. The balcony
6. The ten virtues
7. The four immeasureables
8. The vase seat
9. The vase (*bumpa*)
10. The vase gate
11. The throat (*harmika*)
12. The lotus base
13. The thirteen wheels of the Dharma
14. The parasol
15. The rain cover
16. The moon and sun
17. The jewel tip (*norbu tok*)

This drawing of the Enlightenment Stupa shows the names of all its component parts. When these were first explained to me and I was given books to refer to, I was puzzled. Why were the names not always the same, and why in some cases was the same name used for different parts? The explanation was quite simple: they were different translations of Tibetan or Sanskrit words with some variations according to the teachings of different traditions. The names on this diagram are simply those that seemed the clearest and most descriptive.

It was explained to me that the different parts of the stupa represented the Thirty-Seven Steps Towards Enlightenment: in other words that it not only represented the enlightened mind of the Buddha but was also a guide to how to achieve that enlightenment for yourself, finding the essential Buddha-nature that Buddhists believe is within each and every one of us.

Once again, the various Buddhist traditions describe these thirty-seven steps in different ways, and here I've settled on the translation that seemed clearest.[3] The Thirty-Seven Steps Towards Enlightenment break down as follows: the Four Foundations of Mindfulness, the Four Right Endeavours, the Four Bases of Success, the Five Faculties, the Five Powers, the Seven Factors of Awakening and the Eight-fold Noble Path.

Each part of the stupa represents one of these steps. The Vase Seat, for example, the small rounded ledge below the dome that is sometimes painted or carved to resemble the petals of a lotus, represents the Five Powers – Faith, Effort, Mindfulness, Single-Pointed

Concentration and Wisdom. The *harmika*, the square section below the spire onto which the all-seeing eyes of the Buddha are sometimes painted, represents the Eight-fold Noble Path, a fundamental teaching.

These are complex subjects about which many, far more learned than me, have written and taught. To try to explain the path to enlightenment as described by the thirty-seven steps is beyond the scope of this book and beyond my knowledge or learning.

What I had gained, however, both on my travels and through being involved with building a stupa, was an understanding of the relationship between aesthetic elegance, the purity of geometry and a deeper spiritual meaning – between outer form and inner meaning and how that inner meaning can become absorbed deep inside you. The shape of the stupa, its rising steps, its upward-thrusting architectural energy are no accident. The point of the thirty-seven steps is that they lead somewhere. They lead to enlightenment. Sitting on the very top of the structure is *norbu tok*, the jewel tip. The element associated with the jewel tip is called *akasa* in Sanskrit, a word for which there is no real English equivalent, though it is usually translated as Space. *Akasa* describes something that is all-encompassing, that surrounds everything, that is above everything, below everything – but that is also within everything.

Once you have reached the jewel tip there is nowhere else to go. Above it, there is nothing. You have both literally and symbolically reached the very tip, the end point. Conceptually not unlike the place where my attempt to understand sacred geometry started: the single point that has no inside, that has no outside and that has no dimension. Where it all begins. And ends. The academic Adrian Snodgrass in his book *The Symbolism of the Stupa* describes it like this:

> Having ascended the levels of the stupa in meditation, the yogin has reached the ultimate pinnacle of its structure. From here, he steps into the void. He has reached total Enlightenment and realized the Buddhahood concealed within him. He steps beyond the symbol into silence.[4]

The stupa grid is far more than a diagram for a construction project. Someone described it to me as 'a road map of the path to enlightenment', where the dynamic upward thrust of its component parts invites the practitioner to embark on a journey, to rise by his or her own efforts from the mundane world of samsara to the wisdom gone beyond.

THE THIRTY-SEVEN FACTORS OF THE ENLIGHTENED MIND

Four Foundations of Mindfulness	4
Four Right Endeavours	4
Four Bases of Success	4
Five Faculties	5
Five Powers	5
Seven Factors of Awakening	7
Eight-fold Noble Path	8
	37

The Four Foundations of Mindfulness
  (i)   Mindfulness of Body
  (ii) Mindfulness of Feeling
  (iii) Mindfulness of Mind
  (iv) Mindfulness of all other Phenomena

The Four Right Endeavours
  (i)   Aspire that non-virtuous actions, which have not yet occurred, do not develop.
  (ii) Aspire that non-virtuous actions, which have already occurred, cease to develop.
  (iii) Aspire that virtuous actions, which have not yet occurred, do develop.
  (iv) Aspire that virtuous actions, which have already occurred, may continue to develop.

The Four Bases of Success

  (i)   Single-pointed cultivation of Will

  (ii) Single-pointed cultivation of Mind

 (iii) Single-pointed cultivation of Effort

 (iv) Single-pointed cultivation of Analysis

The Five Faculties

  (i)   Faith

  (ii) Effort

 (iii) Mindfulness

 (iv) Single-Pointed Concentration

  (v) Wisdom

The Five Powers

  (i)   The Power of Faith

  (ii) The Power of Effort

 (iii) The Power of Mindfulness

 (iv) The Power of Single-Pointed Concentration

  (v) The Power of Wisdom

The Seven Factors of Awakening

  (i)   Mindfulness

  (ii) The Investigation of Truth

 (iii) Effort

 (iv) Joy

  (v) Flexibility

 (vi) Single-Pointed Concentration

(vii) Equanimity

The Eight-fold Noble Path
   (i)   Right Understanding
  (ii)   Right Motivation
 (iii)   Right Speech
 (iv)   Right Action
  (v)   Right Livelihood
 (vi)   Right Effort
 (vii)   Right Mindfulness
(viii)   Right Meditative Concentration

Ninth Journeys: What Goes Round

Lama Sonam was sitting in the sun on a low bench by his house. He was wearing a characteristically shabby maroon gho and a bizarre red hat, a cross between a sparkly party wig and a bathing cap. He got to his feet, quite sprightly, smiled broadly and gestured for me to follow him up the stair-ladder into his house. I remembered it had caused me problems before. Let's see if I could negotiate it with a little more dignity this time.

I hadn't seen Lama Sonam for nearly twelve years, not since my last visit to Bhutan in 2005. When I had left England for Nepal a month or so earlier I didn't even know for certain whether he was still alive. If the date in his passport was correct – something I'd always had my doubts about – he was seventy-seven when he came to Harewood, which meant he would be eighty-nine now. I had e-mailed his daughter Sangay telling her that I was hoping to visit Bhutan and asking if she could tell me how he was. Correspondence with Bhutan is a stop-start affair at the best of times but shortly after I arrived in Nepal I finally heard back from her: her father was indeed still with us, still living in the same place, but in poor health so not travelling around much any more. I started to make arrangements for a short visit.

Bhutan had changed quite a bit in twelve years. The road from the airport is two-lane blacktop now, no more skittering along precariously close to the road's edge to allow a truck to trundle by on the inside. Thimphu sprawls along the valley, twice the size, with a lot of new buildings. Even the most modern-looking concrete and glass ones still had traditional Bhutanese painted ornamentation round the doors and windows. There was considerably more traffic, a proper rush hour, but Thimphu was still small-town enough for me to be hailed through open car windows, not just once, but twice by people who recognised me – and I really don't know that many people in Thimphu. A huge new statue of Buddha Sakyamuni dominates the valley, more than 150 feet tall and visible from everywhere in the town, built in the grounds of an ancient ruined palace and designed to both fulfil an ancient prophecy and commemorate a hundred years of the monarchy. Long delays in the building schedule meant the centenary deadline was missed by several years, so with characteristic Himalayan pragmatism the anniversary was quickly changed to become a celebration of the sixtieth birthday of the previous King instead.

The road to Lama Sonam's home village Hongtso winds up towards Dochu La, the first pass on the long west–east Bhutanese highway, where the 108 stupas are. We turned off just before the checkpoint and parked a little way up the track that leads into the village. It was, if anything, even rougher and rockier than I had remembered it. We passed the group of eight stupas I had seen on my very first visit, a sort of Lama Sonam showroom as I'd then thought. They now stood in the courtyard of a nunnery, empty except for a caretaker over the winter months, the nuns due to return in a few weeks. The stupas had been brightly painted with colourful garlands and clouds and bunches of flowers, a very traditional design.

'Not everyone like,' Sangay said.

'Lama Sonam not like?' I asked.

'Oh yes, *he* like,' came her reply. 'But younger generation . . .'

The single stupa next to his house that had been under construction twelve years ago was still there too, with rows of white prayer flags on either side, flapping briskly in the breeze.

The stairway safely negotiated, Lama Sonam wedged himself into his low chair in the corner of the main room of the house. All was much the same as before, except there was now a large photograph in pride of place on the wall, just above one of the windows: my father and stepmother standing in the gardens at Harewood with Lama Sonam, all smiling at the camera. I told him that my father had died five years ago and that my mother, whom we had visited in London just before the stupa builders flew home, had died recently as well, but that my stepmother was still alive and well.* He nodded, said that his second wife had also passed away, which was the reason for all the white prayer flags by the stupa outside. He added something else half under his breath and chuckled his characteristic wheezy chuckle. 'What did he say?' I asked. 'He said: That means now you are lord.' Lama Sonam pointed at my father's beard in the photo and my beard as if somehow that proved it.

He seemed quite lively, though definitely more frail; the same as before but shrunken somehow, smaller, more stooped, his face more wrinkled, his beard more wispy and his eyes narrowed into even tighter slits. I told him that many people from England had asked me to pass on their good wishes. He nodded again as what I said was translated by Sangay and her half-brother Kesang, who had also of course been part of the stupa building team. He seemed pleased. Kesang was very attentive, both to his father and to me, playing the role of head of the household, though he wasn't around all that much according to Sangay, often in Hong Kong. Since Lama Sonam's second wife had died it was his

---

* Patricia passed away two years later, in May 2018.

other daughter, Sangay's half-sister, Kesang's full sister, who really looked after him. She is much younger than either of her siblings, bright and confident and competent, but she was about to leave home to go to college in India, leaving Lama Sonam with fairly minimal family support.

'Are you still a monk?' I asked Kesang. He grinned rather sheepishly. 'Lay monk. Like my father,' he said. ('He's married with two children,' Sangay told me later, 'and he still drinks too much.')

I asked about Cheku, Lama Sonam's long-time assistant, the fourth member of the stupa building team. Still living in Hongtso, quite well, but away visiting his family in eastern Bhutan. I was sorry not to see him.

Though he shinned up the ladder nimbly enough and was alert and engaged when the conversation involved him, Lama Sonam's health was generally not good. Occasionally, he would bow his head, squeeze his eyes shut and hold the bridge of his nose tight between his fingers. 'He get headache,' Kesang said. 'Daytime mostly OK, but night-time very bad, so he not sleep.' ('It's his breathing, not headache,' Sangay said on the drive back. She and her half-brother didn't see eye to eye about much, though they did agree that it was night-times that were worst.) All this meant that he didn't leave home very much any more, except to go to Thimphu occasionally to see the doctor. Most days, Kesang said, he just sits at home praying. He had made seven more stupas since coming back from England,

Kesang told me. There was a big one in Phuntsoling in southern Bhutan, the main border crossing point between Bhutan and India – I remember him mentioning this during our very first visit – and the previous year he had made one in Gaya, up in the mountains north of Punakha. 'I think this his last one,' Kesang said, a little sadly.

I gave Lama Sonam a copy of my little photographic book, *108 Offerings*, and explained how it had come about. He seemed to find this quite amusing and went through it page by page, asking what everything was. Sangay crouched at his feet translating my explanations. *Etho-metho* is Dzongkha for rhododendron, I remembered. There are quite a few rhododendron flowers in the book. He seemed genuinely pleased that the stupa at Harewood was being properly cared for, that offerings were being made there and so on. I told him that it was visited regularly by other Buddhists and occasionally by lamas from Nepal or India, in England to give teachings.

We went outside to take photographs by the stupa. 'We have been on a great adventure together,' I said to him. I think he understood what I was saying even before it was translated for him and he laughed his characteristically wheezy laugh. I felt quite emotional saying goodbye. I wondered if I would ever see him again.

About eighteen months later, October 2017, I had a message from Sangay to tell me that her father had died peacefully in his sleep. I made a small offering to help pay for the funeral costs and Sangay sent me photographs of the cremation by the stupa just outside his house. Cantankerous old country builder though he could be, I wish him a good re-birth with all my heart.

LAMA BASO KARPO

I phoned Phub Dorji from my hotel. 'I'll come and get you in my car,' he said. That was a surprise. I didn't know he had a car. But it wasn't a surprise to hear that he had been very active since I had last seen him. He had used the money from England to build a retreat place in Phajoding (I remember him pointing out the site); he had been in Japan with a lama for a brief visit and was now involved in a scheme to make affordable prints of *thangkas*. I worried that his entrepreneurial energy, admirable in many ways, would lead him into trouble. With him was his friend Lhap Tsering, the sand mandala maker, who had not long finished a three-year retreat. His warm smile and his calm presence seemed even more serene than before.

We were on our way to see Lama Baso Karpo, the lama from Haa who had presided over the consecration at Harewood. Lama Baso Karpo is probably even older than Lama Sonam, though I doubt if anyone would dare ask him directly and I never saw his passport. He appeared unchanged, though maybe his gaze was a little less fierce, his energy less focused. Perhaps this was because he was now in a relaxed social situation, not in full Vajrayana ritual mode. He did seem a little tired, unsurprising perhaps, as he had been at the royal palace for several days, saying prayers and overseeing pujas for Bhutan's new Crown Prince, born just a few days earlier to great national rejoicing.

With him was his attendant, his nephew Tshewang Namgay. 'How's your English coming on, Namgay?' I asked him. He laughed. When they were in England for the consecration I remember it dawning on me that Tshewang understood much more English than he was letting on.

Phub Dorji, Lhap Tsering and I presented prayer scarves to the lama. Phub Dorji showed him one of his prints, of a *phurba* mandala. The old lama scrutinised it carefully, checking every detail for accuracy before nodding his satisfaction. Phub Dorji seemed pleased – and a little relieved. I gave him a copy of *108 Offerings*, which he went through page by page, as Lama Sonam had. He picked out a couple of images with feathers in them: found on the ground along the way like everything else, not taken from a living bird, I assured him. Like Lama Sonam, he seemed happy that the stupa was being properly cared for. I was told that he had asked about it on several occasions over the years. I mentioned to him my idea of eventually building eight more small stupas in the Himalayan Garden, which he was very enthusiastic about.

Food came: chicken, beef, rice, dal and plenty of chillies, and we ate quietly. I asked about the other monks who had accompanied Lama Baso Karpo for the consecration. The two younger ones, Tsewang Dorji and Norbu Gyeltshen, were in the monastery and were well, I was told. But Rinchen, the oldest of the consecration party after Lama Baso Karpo, had died a couple of years earlier of lung cancer. Lhap Tsering sat quietly to one side, not saying much. After a while, he took the prayer scarf from round his neck and started to fold it very carefully, very gracefully, very meticulously, before tucking it into the sleeve of his robe, absolutely precise and effortlessly elegant in everything he did, as always.

'Why is it so important to build stupas?' I asked. The old lama looked quizzically at me.

'Do you not know by now?' his expression seemed to say.

THE RE-CONSECRATION OF THE GREAT STUPA: BOUDHANATH, NOVEMBER 2016

My plane was late and it took forever to get through the friendly chaos of Kathmandu Airport so it was nearly midnight by the time I got to the Hotel Tibet International in Boudhanath. I made my way wearily up to my room on the sixth floor, where there is a balcony with a view of the stupa. The last time I'd been here, ten months earlier, January 2016, it had been a depressing sight. The stupa had been structurally damaged by the earthquake the previous year and everything above the dome had to be dismantled, a majestic structure reduced to a grubby stump. By the time I had left Nepal a couple of months later, work had begun on the restoration, but no one was optimistic about how long it would take: at least a year was the guess, probably longer, depending on the amount of bureaucratic interference. Now, several months ahead of schedule, the transformation was spectacular. The great dome, brightly lit in vertical bands of blue, white, green, red and yellow, gleamed above the nighttime roofscape of jumbled wires, satellite dishes and water tanks. The spire radiated a dazzling shade of white-gold. Everything was ready for the ceremonies of purification and re-consecration that were due to take place over the next couple of days.

I set off for the stupa early the next morning. It was only when I got there that I realised the scale and ambition of what was going on. The outer ring was already busy with circumambulators, but this was not the focus of attention. The whole of the first tier of the stupa was full of monks from all four schools of Tibetan Buddhism – Nyingma, Sakya, Kagyu and Gelukpa – and each was performing its own version of the long and elaborate purification pujas that were preparing the way for the consecration the next day. In brief, these pujas are for the purification of self, of others and of one's environment – in this case especially the Great Stupa itself – for the sake of all beings, mediated through chanted prayers, meditation and the symbolic use of ritual objects and offerings. Although the aim of the pujas was essentially the same, each school has its own tradition, each with its own imagery and practices. The Kagyus were performing a puja dedicated to the deity Chakrasamvara, his body blue, with four heads and twelve arms, locked in eternal embrace with his wisdom dakini consort.* The Gelukpas were focused on Yamantaka, the wrathful version of the bodhisattva Manjushri, who embodies the knowledge and wisdom of all the Buddhas. For the Sakyas it was Hevajra, another fierce protective deity particular to their lineage. The text for the Nyingmas' puja was Longchen Nyingthig, a *terma*, a teaching hidden by Guru Rinpoche and discovered by the *terton* Jigme Lingpa (1730–98). He found himself flying through the sky riding a white lion till he reached what he realised was the Great Stupa at Boudha. There he was given a casket containing five scrolls and seven beads of crystal. One of the scrolls was the Longchen Nyingthig and, by eating the crystals, he came to a true understanding of its meaning.

Each school occupied one segment of the stupa: the Kagyus to the south, the Sakyas to the west, the

---

* Most male deities will have a female consort, often called a wisdom dakini.

Nyingmas to the north and the Gelukpas to the east, each with their own altar, statues, *thangkas, tormas* and a wide range of offerings appropriate to their own particular practice.

Khenpo Dorjee hailed me from the upper tier (how on earth did he pick me out from the swirling crowds?) and, brandishing my VIP badge, I stooped past the security guards and through the low and narrow doorway up onto the stupa. I had met Khenpo Dorjee on my previous visit, but I had never seen him like this, greeting me like an old friend, bouncing with energy and beaming with joy. He introduced me to Norbu Sherpa, a Nyingma monk, General Secretary of the Boudha Area Development Committee and official spokesman for the event. He will answer all your questions, the Khenpo confidently assured me.

I followed Norbu Sherpa to somewhere quieter, away from the amplified chant and boom of the pujas, to a little yard behind the ring of buildings round the stupa, where we sat drinking tea. 'Do you know of the Buddhist Federation?' he asked. I shook my head. 'All arrangements for these days made by the Buddhist Federation,' he said. 'Many of the people sat here,' he gestured around him. The Federation was set up in 2004 as a forum for all the four schools of Tibetan Buddhism active in Nepal and they take it in turns to take the chair. Their aim was to find areas of common interest, where and how they could work together, and this was their biggest and most important project. 'This has never happened before,' Norbu Sherpa said. 'Four pujas simultaneous transmission. And tomorrow, as well as Nyingma, Gelukpa, Sakya and Kagyu, Theravadan monks from Nepali Vihara and Newari Vajrayana also.* Never before. Each school one hundred five monks, but they send more, so tomorrow total more than seven hundred I think.'

Each school had recognised the importance of the occasion and sent very senior lamas to preside over the pujas, quite possibly the biggest gathering of eminent practitioners from all the traditions ever gathered outside Tibet.

'But how has all this happened so quickly?' I asked. 'This must be the first major heritage building project in the whole world to finish ahead of schedule!' Norbu Sherpa laughed. 'Volunteers,' he said. 'Volunteers made it happen.' Almost all the work had been voluntary, from the manual labour of sifting and washing and carrying of bricks to the sponsorship of statues and donations for the sixty-eight pounds of gold needed to re-gild the tiles that encase the thirteen steps of the spire. 'Better on the stupa than in the bank for good Buddhist!' said Norbu Sherpa. Forty-six of the sixty-eight pounds of gold were from one donor, I discovered later – a rich

---

* Theravadan Buddhist practitioners are mostly found in South Asia (Sri Lanka, Thailand, Cambodia, Laos and Burma) but there are Viharas (monasteries) in Nepal as well. Newari Vajrayana Buddhism is native to Nepal and is sometimes claimed to be the closest to the Buddhism practised in India after the Buddha's death.

Tibetan businessman. There is no doubt this has been the secret: private finance, voluntary labour, minimal government interference.

'Proof that we can rebuild our heritage,' the Nepali Prime Minister boasted to the press. But the fact is that they haven't. At most of Kathmandu Valley's damaged heritage sites, work had barely begun, eighteen months after the earthquakes. A UNESCO representative blamed 'No clear decision-making line'. Mix this with a bucket or two of corruption and a wheelbarrow full of inefficiency and it was hardly surprising not much had been done.

Back at the stupa, the day had settled into its rhythm. The sounds of the different pujas echoed and merged and then separated again: the hypnotic drumbeats of the Nyingmas, the rattle of 105 Kagyu *damaru* (hand-drums), the basso profondo rumble of the Gelukpa chants, the gentle treble melody of young Chinese Mahayana monks.

Queues of devotees, getting longer and longer as the day went on, formed to offer prayer scarves to the senior lamas and money to the monks, small denomination notes to each one, always seeming to have exactly the right number to go round. A distinguished-looking Tibetan lady arrived with an entourage and accumulated so many *kadas* that she looked like she had fallen into a snowdrift. An attendant smoothly removed them from round her neck and she moved on. Another tiny woman scuttled forward, bent almost double with humility as she approached the lama, almost tripping over herself and her bundle of *kadas* in her eagerness.

And so many cameras: grizzled Westerners draped with telephotos, a slender Nepali girl in traditional costume with a video camera almost as big as her, monks extracting cameras with unfeasibly large lenses from inside their robes.

The prayer flags attached to the stupa blew gently in the wind, their shadows rippling like running water on the white of the dome and the gold of the spire. The eyes on the *harmika* were shielded with a curtain of yellow cloth, to be taken down on the day of the consecration. The wind caught the curtain and for a moment an eye was revealed, as if it were winking at the crowds below. And the sun shone, perfect Himalayan weather, with even a hazy glimpse of a snowy peak beyond the hills to the north.

A refreshment break. Women appeared with plastic cups that they filled with tea (salty and buttery in the morning, sweet and milky in the afternoon), then bananas, biscuits and rice dotted with sultanas. The logistics (all volunteers, remember) were challenging to put it mildly, but the organisation was quite invisible. Everyone was used to this, they'd done it before, and they all seemed relaxed and happy despite the pressure of heat and smoke and crowds. I don't think I saw an angry face or heard a raised voice in two days.

There was a surreal moment when Khenpo Dorjee introduced me to a tall, broad-faced Nepali in a black suit. 'Chief of Police,' he said. It seemed that the Chief of Police, come to offer *kadas* to the lamas like so many others, wanted to chat. 'Press? TV?' he asked. I told him that I was here writing a book, but that I used to produce TV shows and some movies. 'I am a big lover of movies,' said the Police Chief. 'What have you made?' I gave my standard answer: 'Lots of different things but probably the best known, a long time ago now, was an English TV show called *Inspector Morse*.' He gestured to an aide and got him to write it down, my name too, heavily mis-spelled. 'Try to get the DVD,' I said, and he nodded and shook my hand and moved on. I'd like to be a fly on the wall for that screening. I suspect policing methods in Morse's fictional Oxford and modern Kathmandu don't have much in common.

The next day, consecration day, was the same only more so. At the start of the day a series of groups processed in through the main gate and made their way slowly round the stupa. First, the monks themselves, with their long horns and cymbals and red-plumed hats. Then, dancers dressed as snow lions or wearing traditional costume, including a wondrous range of headgear. There were schools and sports clubs and groups representing many of the districts of Nepal. There were pipe and drum marching bands and trumpets and battered old horns and tubas that looked like they hadn't been played for a very long time indeed. And the smoke drifted over them all from the smouldering offerings of juniper as their music mingled with the chanting of the monks.

Khenchen Thrangu Rinpoche arrived, his car swathed in prayer scarves, people reaching through the widows to be blessed by him. He was eighty-three, one of the few surviving lamas to have been brought up in pre-Chinese-invasion Tibet and is recognised as one of Tibetan Buddhism's greatest living scholars. His presence, frail and stooped but radiating loving kindness, gave added gravitas to the day's proceedings. Sitting on the throne next to him was a much younger lama, Yongey Mingyur Rinpoche, fluent in English, the writer of best-selling books on the overlap between neuroscience and advanced meditation techniques. The ancient wisdom of Tibet and its modern application.

The energy levels felt more intense than the previous day. Over in the Gelukpa quadrant, a fire puja was going on. A senior lama from Ganden Monastery, shielded from the bright sun with a colourful umbrella, threw offerings of food and plant material into the flames. The queues to make offerings and receive blessings grew longer, the senior lamas smiling and blessing, and blessing and smiling again, never missing a ritual beat, not a single verse of the text, not a single elegant mudra. The pressure of devotees grew fiercer, the accumulation of blessings more intense. I started to feel out of place and uneasy. It all seemed strangely competitive, everyone's motivation more materialistic than spiritual, I thought. Or maybe they were just having a good time and I was being a prig.

I mentioned this to an American friend, a long-time resident in Nepal, and he laughed. 'The old Tibetan ladies are the worst!' he said 'Sharp elbows!' He went on to describe what had happened to him that afternoon. 'I was queuing to offer a scarf to one of the lamas and there was a monk in front of me, quite plump, very sleek and complacent looking with some acolytes in tow. Chinese I thought, my inbuilt anti-Chinese feelings rising quickly to the surface. Then I thought – no, this is wrong, this is not how I should be thinking on a day like this. So I very humbly offered him my scarf and asked for his blessing. At that moment the door to the upper level opened and the monk and his attendants went past the security guards and up the steps. I followed him, unchallenged by the security guys – they thought I was part of his retinue. As I walked round I looked down at the section where my teacher was. I hadn't been able to get anywhere near him to get his blessing, the queues were so long. At that moment he looked up, straight at me and gave me a little wave and a smile. I had my blessing after all.'

At 11 a.m. Thrangu Rinpoche was helped up from his throne and, supported on all sides, started to make his way slowly and painfully up the short but steep flight of steps that led to the next tier. The greater the effort, the broader his smile became. He reached the top and the horns started to play and the monks started to process round the dome, a key moment of the consecration. A yellow helicopter appeared and started to circle (in a clockwise direction of course), flying quite low. TV, I assumed, getting some good aerial shots. Then clouds of magnolia seed pods (*champaka* in Tibetan), much used in rituals and to decorate *tormas*, started to drift down from the helicopter. They fluttered in the gentle breeze, turning slowly and flashing in the sun to be gathered like blessings from the heavens by the crowds down below. It was as if Thrangu Rinpoche himself had orchestrated it. Perhaps he had.

A few hours later it was all over. The Great Stupa at Boudhanath, where I had first felt the power of such places some forty years earlier, where in a sense the road to the building of the stupa at Harewood began, was re-empowered in the most spectacular way. The wheel had turned a full circle. I had come back to where I started, which is pretty inevitable if you walk round a stupa, I suppose.

What inspired the idea of the Harewood project was how these were places that were accessible in the widest sense, had a human touch, a feeling for place, that they were a vehicle for an understanding of Buddhism that reached out to ordinary people, not just the learned or the initiated. People who visit the Harewood Stupa seem to respond to that, consciously or unconsciously. And what I had just been fortunate enough to witness at Boudha was how many thousands of people, from a whole range of backgrounds and walks of life, from beggars to the Chief of Police, from some of the greatest living lamas to spiritual tourists from the West, can engage with and celebrate something extraordinary together under the all-seeing eyes on the golden spire.

In the Legend of the Great Stupa, Guru Rinpoche tells his listeners:

> The benefits and favours received by any creature who with a pure heart prostrates before the Great Stupa, circumambulates it, and adores it, are inconceivable and incalculable.[1]

In the sutras, the Buddha explains the many benefits of circumambulating, how you will be healthy, happy, blessed with good fortune and guaranteed a good re-birth:

> One hundred maidens of Kamboja wearing jewelled earrings, with circlets of gold upon their arms and adorned with rings and necklaces of the finest gold; one hundred elephants, snowy white, robust and broad-backed, adorned with gold and jewels, carrying their great trunks curved over their heads like ploughshares, could not even begin to equal one sixteenth part of the value of one step of one circumambulation.[2]

Engaging with a stupa is not difficult. It doesn't matter who you are. All you have to do is put one foot in front of another and walk on round.

Try it. Walk round a stupa. The exercise will do you good. The benefits may well be immeasurable.

The Tenth Journey: Ashes to Ashes

My father and Patricia's wishes were expressed very clearly in their wills. They both wanted to be cremated and their ashes mingled, before being divided into three parts. One part was to be scattered on the pitch at Elland Road, home of Leeds United. They had both been Honorary President of the football club, my father for nearly fifty years, Patricia – to her great delight – for a few months before her death. A second part was to be scattered on the lake at Harewood and the third was to be put into the family vault. So when Patricia died in May 2018, we – that is me, my stepbrother Michael (Patricia's son from her first marriage) and my half-brother Mark – set about fulfilling their wishes.

We decided to tackle the third part of the request first: the family vault. This was trickier than it might sound. It had last been used when my grandmother died in 1965, fifty-three years earlier, and there were not many people still around who had been at the funeral. So nobody was sure exactly where the vault was. We knew it was under Harewood Church and we knew the opening had been turfed over, but those were the only things we were at all confident about. I was one of the people who had been there, an awkward and gangly fourteen-year-old in a dark coat that I remember being slightly too small for me (which made me feel even more awkward and gangly, of course), and I was pretty certain it was somewhere along the south wall, but Eric White, a young estate carpenter at the time, now long retired, remembered it being at the eastern end of the church, under the altar. There were no obvious visual clues. A set of worn steps, slippery with moss, on the north side of the church turned out to lead to a room that housed the old boiler, long defunct. We had visions of having to dig all along the south wall of the church, a long job.

Then someone Googled 'Princess Mary's funeral – 1965' and we were quickly led to a short Pathé News piece on YouTube. There were black and white images of members of my grandmother's family, both Lascelles and royals, including the Queen and a young Prince Charles, also tall and gangly in a dark, rather better-fitting coat, arriving at Harewood Church, inter-cut with various politicians and other dignitaries making their way into Westminster Abbey, complete with plummy and reverential voiceover. Then – gold dust! Images –

shot from a discreet distance across the graveyard – of the coffin being carried along the south side of the church to where a group of priests and family members were standing round a large hole in the ground. Eric and I were both right: the vault was under the south-east corner of the church, behind the final buttress before the church narrows to the chancel, the area around the altar.

Back to the present and the mechanical digger, driven by Ian 'Diesel' Harrison, one of the team who had been involved in building the stupa, got to work and, lining up opposite a small air vent at the bottom of the wall of the church, quickly uncovered four hefty stone slabs. Ian Copeland, 'Lama Ian Action', chiselled out the lime holding the slabs in place and levered two of the slabs up and out of the way.

'There'll be a door down there,' Ian had said before work had started, 'and there'll be a key to that door and I know where the key is – in the safe in the Estate Office.'

'How do you know that?' I asked.

'Because it has a label on it saying "Key to Vault",' he replied.

My son Ben and I clambered down a ladder into the stone chamber and ducked under the two stone slabs. Sure enough, at the far end was a rough oak door. I couldn't see the keyhole at first and imagined having to lever the door open, but Ben spotted it, quite low down on the right-hand side, full of cobwebs, which were quickly blown away. The heavy metal key slid easily into the lock with a satisfyingly dramatic echo, as if there was a very large space behind it, and turned as smoothly as if the lock had only just been used, not buried underground for more than fifty years. A gentle nudge from my foot and the door opened.

I had no idea what to expect inside. I had no memory of going down there when my grandmother was buried; very probably I didn't. So, though what Ben and I saw by the light of our torches was not exactly a surprise, neither of us had expected it to be so clean and tidy and orderly, no hint of damp or dirt, no cobwebs or mould. In front of us was a stone chamber with a vaulted ceiling, around twenty feet long and easily high and wide enough for two six-foot men to stand side by side in. Along either side of the central corridor were three stone shelves divided into openings wide enough and deep enough to take a coffin slid in lengthways. There were thirty-eight niches in total, twenty-five of them sealed with a stone slab on which was carved the name and dates of the person inside. The oldest was of Edwin Lascelles himself, the builder of Harewood House, the founder of the dynasty some might say, who died in January 1795. He was tucked discreetly away at floor level in the far right-hand corner. The most recent, unsurprisingly, was of my grandmother, Victoria Alexandra Alice Mary, the Princess Royal, on the top shelf above Edwin. All those Christian names were slightly too long for the stone-mason to fit comfortably onto the slab so he had been forced to cut into the wall and extend it by just enough to fit the 'Vi' of 'Victoria' on the left-hand end.

The next day Michael and I mingled the ashes. Michael is self-confessedly and comically dyscalculic (can't make sense of numbers), so he had a little difficulty at first trying to work out how we were to divide the ashes from two separate urns into three parts, but we got there in the end, rolled up our sleeves and mixed them like flour for bread in a huge bowl. We had managed to find an urn from the undertaker's catalogue that didn't look like something out of *Ali Baba and the Forty Thieves* before we realised that the urn would be sealed in, never to be seen again, so it didn't really matter what it looked like. Nevertheless, theirs were probably the first cremated remains down there and certainly the first where an Earl and Countess would be sharing a niche, so it seemed only right that their mingled remains should be contained in something that was as dignified an object as we could find at short notice.

The weather had turned the day we put the urn into the vault. We had had more than a week of glorious sunshine, but that Friday, exactly a week after Patricia's funeral, it was raining and gloomy. Somehow, it seemed appropriate. A small group of us huddled under brand new blue umbrellas – bought for the funeral but not needed that day – as the rain spattered the gravestones and made a puddle at the bottom of the ladder down to the vault. We had all agreed that the three sons should be the only ones there when we put the urn into its final resting place. We stood there for a few minutes, Michael, Mark and I, quiet and sombre, and I read four lines from *The Tibetan Book of the Dead*:

> The end of collecting is dispersal.
> The end of building is disintegration.
> The end of meeting is parting.
> The end of life is death.

It was done. The door to the vault was locked and the stone covering replaced. The rain continued, not heavy, but persistent. In a week or two the slab with my father and Patricia's names and dates engraved on it would be put into position and the vault sealed until it is time for the next one to go in. Which will probably be me.

We'd decided to do the scattering of the ashes on the lake the following day, the last before Michael was due to fly back to Australia. Scattering of ashes in the open air is notoriously prone to black comedy, like the scene near the end of *The Big Lebowski*, where the Dude and Walter are disposing of the cremated remains of their bowling buddy Donny into the Pacific Ocean and the wind changes. Something similar had happened when my uncle's ashes were scattered from a boat on Harewood Lake some years earlier.

I suggested an alternative. 'Why don't we scatter the ashes from the bridge at the head of the lake?' I proposed. 'From there they'll wash down over the waterfall and into the stream. Just as good as the middle of the lake. This is what the monks did with the sand mandala they made for the consecration.' Everyone thought this was a great idea and we agreed to meet on the bridge early, before the gardens opened to the public.

The weather was back in benign mode and it was a perfect May morning, cool but sunny, as Michael and I carried the second urn, wrapped in a prayer scarf, through the Himalayan Garden to the stupa, collecting some flower offerings along the way. When we arrived we found that Binu Rai, a Nepali Buddhist who had been one of Patricia's carers during the last years of her life, was there already and the stupa had been well prepared: candles, incense and flowers covered the four steps. We placed the urn carefully among the offerings and waited for the others to arrive. Then Michael, Mark and I walked the urn three times round, one circumambulation each, the others following behind before we processed the short distance up to the bridge. I unscrewed the lid and we all took it in turns, oldest (Michael and me) to youngest (Michael's grandson Wolfgang, aged three), to pour the ashes down into the water. Some drifted like smoke over the lip of the waterfall, some caught the flow of the water and hurried over the edge, some lingered in the shallows under the bridge, waiting to be washed slowly away over the next few hours.

Over the days that followed my thoughts kept on returning to the disposal of the ashes, those two consecutive days, how different they were. In some ways they seemed to sum up many of the things I felt, that I feel, about Harewood.

The vault was heavy with the weight of history. Solid, immovable, buried deep, literally carved in stone. And very hidden away. Those makers of Harewood and their wives and offspring (mostly sons, not many daughters) are very well sealed into that vault indeed: their bones are in wooden coffins; the coffins are cemented in behind a stone slab; the whole vault is locked behind a thick wooden door; the door is covered by more very substantial stone slabs; the stone slabs are covered in turf. Unless you know where to look it isn't easy to find. Access to the final resting place of my ancestors is for the chosen few only, while their memory lingers on in the building – Harewood House – that they built and furnished and lived in. But the vault is an immaculately crafted place, elegant in its way, understated, built to last. Harewood in microcosm perhaps: a house and a landscape with a fascinating and often surprising history, but somewhere that often feels to me to have too much of the wrong kind of reverence for the past, with something dead in there too perhaps – unless you can find a way of breathing new life into it, which many of its owners have tried to do of course, though it must be said that some have tried harder than others.

And that's what pouring the ashes into the Beck from the bridge at the head of the lake, right next to the stupa, felt like – a breath of new life. There was a younger and fresher energy at work here, an energy that treated the past with respect but looked at it with a degree of what I've heard described as positive scepticism, too, an energy that is fuelled primarily by the need to engage with today and tomorrow. The original stupas were built to house the ashes and other remains of someone who had just died. So was the family vault, but their function could not be more different. For Buddhists death is seen as a beginning as well as an end, as a liberation, as a moment when the possibility of enlightenment is as strong as it is ever likely to be in your lifetime, stronger, when the concept of beginnings and endings is no longer relevant, just another turning of the wheel, when you can achieve a better re-birth or, just possibly, escape from the cycle of birth, death and re-birth altogether. The dark, silent vault was very much a final resting place, somewhere to contemplate the reality, the inevitability, of death. The sunlit, flower-strewn stupa was somewhere you could celebrate its infinite potential.

Notes

Epigraph

1. Based on Martin Willson's chantable translation of the 'Praises to the Twenty-One Taras'. Translation made for the Foundation for the Preservation of the Mahayana Tradition Education Services, Taos, New Mexico, USA, 2001.

Prologue

1. Bhikku Nanamoli, *The Life of the Buddha*, Buddhist Publication Society, Kandy, Sri Lanka, 2006, pp. 309–22.
2. Ibid.

Second Journeys: A Seed Is Sown

1. Keith Dowman, *The Legend of the Great Stupa: Two Termas from the Nyingma Tradition*, Dharma Publishing, Berkeley, CA, 1973, p. 29.
2. Ibid., p. 5.
3. Ibid., p. 59.
4. Ibid., pp. 50–1.
5. Ibid., p. 54.

6. Ibid., p. 15.
7. www.orient.org.

Third Journeys: Bhutan and Back Again

1. https://treasuryoflives.org/biographies/view/Pema-Lingpa/3000.
2. Keith Dowman, *The Divine Madman: The Sublime Life and Songs of Drukpa Kunley*, Pilgrims Publishing, Varanasi, 2000, pp. 120–1.

The Fourth Journey: The Harewood Stupa

1. Miranda Lundy, *Sacred Geometry*, Wooden Books, Glastonbury, 2006, pp. 2–5.
2. Robert Beer, *The Encyclopedia of Tibetan Symbols and Motifs*, Serindia Publications, Chicago, IL, 2004, pp. 3–32.
3. Ibid., p. 132.
4. The ninety-nine dried fruits: 1) date; 2) pineapple; 3) papaya; 4) mango; 5) golden raisin; 6) black raisin; 7) green raisin; 8) sultana; 9) cranberry; 10) apricot; 11) plum; 12) apple; 13) pear; 14) peach; 15) banana; 16) prune; 17) fig; 18) nectarine; 19) tamarind; 20) pomegranate; 21) lime; 22) mulberry; 23) senjed; 24) harhuri; 25) juniper; 26) star anise; 27) clove; 28) white cardamom; 29) nutmeg; 30) orange; 31) lemon; 32) sugar cane; 33) black sesame; 34) white sesame; 35) coconut; 36) pecan nut; 37) brazil nut; 38) almond; 39) walnut; 40) hazelnut; 41) pine nut; 42) peanut; 43) chestnut; 44) betel nut; 45) cashew nut; 46) pistachio nut; 47) macadamia nut; 48–99) Lama Sonam's ninety-nine-fruit powder.

The Fifth Journey: The Consecration

1. Based on a description on the Tashi Lhunpo Monastery UK Trust website, www.tashi-lhunpo.org.uk.

Sixth Journeys: Pieces of Eight

1. From Maya Angelou's poem 'On the Pulse of Morning', first read as part of her address at the inauguration of Bill Clinton as President of the United States, 20 January 1993.
2. Nayanjot Lahiri, *Ashoka in Ancient India*, Harvard University Press, Boston, MA, 2015, p. 101.
3. Ibid., p. 115.
4. Ven. S. Dhammika, *Edicts of King Ashoka*, https://www. accesstoinsight.org/lib/authors/dhammika/wheel386. html. The full text reads: 'Twenty years after his coronation, Beloved-of-the-Gods, King Piyadasi, visited this place and worshipped because here the Buddha, the sage of the Sakyans, was born. He had a stone figure and a pillar set up and because the Lord was born here, the village of Lumbini was exempted from tax and required to pay only one eighth of the produce.'
5. Charles Allen, *The Buddha and Dr Führer: An Archaeological Scandal*, Haus Publishing, London, 2008, p. 121.
6. Ibid, p. 240.
7. Both *The Buddha and Dr Führer* and *The Buddha and the Sahibs* (see Bibliography).
8. The Dalai Lama, *The Four Noble Truths*, The Lama Yeshe Wisdom Archive, https://www.lamayeshe.com/ article/four-noble-truths.
9. Khenchen Thrangu Rinpoche, *The Four Noble Truths,* Namo Buddha Publications, Boulder, CO, 1994, p. 3.

10. The full text of the sign by the Vaishali Relic Stupa: 'This is one amongst the eight original relic stupas built over the corporeal remains of Buddha. According to Buddhist traditions, after attaining parinirvana his body was cremated by the Mallas of Kushinagar with a royal ceremony befitting a universal king and the mortal remains were distributed among eight claimants including the Lichhavis of Vaishali. Seven others were Ajatshatru the king of Magadha, Sakyas of Kapliavastu, Bulis of Alakappa, Koliyas of Ramagram, a Brahmin of Vethoweep and Mallas of Pava and Kushinagar. This was originally a small mud stupa measuring 8.07 metres in diameter raised in 5th century B.C. Later during Maurya, Sunga and Kushan periods it was encased with bricks and enlarged in four phases which increased the diameter to 12.00 metres. The Ayaka projection noticed towards south and east is probably the earliest example of Ayakapattas. Excavation of the stupa was conducted by Kashi Prasad Jayaswal Research Institute, Patna in the year 1958. The most remarkable discovery is the relic casket of stone partly filled with ashy earth besides a small conch, two glass beads, a fragmentary piece of gold leaf and a copper punch marked coin.'

Seventh Journeys: Something Old, Something New

1. Thupten Jinpa, *Tsongkhapa: A Buddha in the Land of Snows*, Shambala, Boulder, CO, 2019, pp. xiii–xiv.

2. Sir Francis Younghusband (1863–1942), sometimes described as the last great imperial adventurer, led what started off as a Trade Mission to Tibet in 1904. The British were convinced that agents for Tsarist Russia,

their great political rivals in Central Asia, were gaining excessive influence there. The Trade Mission quite quickly became an invading army and several thousand people, most of them primitively armed Tibetans trying to prevent the foreigners reaching their holy city, were killed before Younghusband reached Lhasa. The trade agreement he reached with Tibetan officials was quickly overturned by the British government in London.

Eighth Journeys: Natural Born Stupas

1. Lama Anagarika Govinda, *The Way of the White Clouds*, Ebury, London, 1966, author's biography on book jacket.
2. Ibid., p. 199.
3. R. M. L. Gethin, *The Buddhist Path to Awakening*, Oneworld Publications, Oxford, 2001. This was the translation recommended by Thupten Jinpa.
4. Adrian Snodgrass, *The Symbolism of the Stupa*, Motilal Banarsidass Publishers, New Delhi India, 1992, p. 352.

Ninth Journeys: What Goes Round

1. Dowman, *The Legend of the Great Stupa*, p. 40.
2. Elizabeth Cook, *The Stupa: Sacred Symbol of Enlightenment*, Dharma Publishing, Berkeley, CA, 1997, p. 240.

Bibliography

Allen, Charles, *A Mountain in Tibet: The Search for Mount Kailas and the Sources of the Great Rivers of Asia*, Abacus, London, 1982

—— *The Buddha and the Sahibs: The Men Who Discovered India's Lost Religion*, John Murray, London, 2003

—— *Duel in the Snows: The True Story of the Younghusband Mission to Lhasa*, John Murray, London, 2004

—— *The Buddha and Dr Führer: An Archaeological Scandal*, Haus Publishing, London, 2008

—— *Ashoka: The Search for India's Lost Emperor*, Hachette, London, 2012

Baas, Jacquelynn, *Smile of the Buddha: Eastern Philosophy and Western Art from Monet to Today*, University of California Press, Berkeley, CA, 2005

Beer, Robert, *The Encyclopedia of Tibetan Symbols and Motifs*, Serindia Publications, Chicago, IL, 2004

Bhatia, Suresh, *The Mahabodhi Temple*, Pilgrims Publishing, Varanasi, 2007

Blomfield, Vishvapani, *Gautama Buddha*, Quercus, London, 2012

Brown, Mick, *The Dance of 17 Lives: The Incredible True Story of Tibet's 17th Karmapa*, Bloomsbury, London, 2004

Brunnholzl, Karl, *The Heart Attack Sutra: A New Commentary on the Heart Sutra*, Snow Lion Publications, New York, 2012

Coleman, Graham, *A Handbook of Tibetan Culture: A Guide to Tibetan Centres and Resources Throughout the World*, Random House, London, 1993

—— *Meditations on Living, Dying and Loss: Ancient Knowledge for a Modern World*, Penguin Books, London, 2008

Coleman, Graham, Jinpa, Thupten (eds) and Dorje, Gyurme (trans.), *The Tibetan Book of the Dead*, Penguin Books, London, 2005

Cook, Elizabeth, *The Stupa: Sacred Symbol of Enlightenment*, Dharma Publishing, Berkeley, CA, 1997

Crystal Mirror Series, *The Stupa: Sacred Symbol of Enlightenment*, Dharma Publishing, Berkeley, CA, 1977

—— *Holy Places of the Buddha*, Dharma Publishing, Berkeley, CA, 1995

Cummings, Joe (text) and Wassman, Bill (photos), *Buddhist Stupas in Asia: The Shape of Perfection*, Lonely Planet, Melbourne, 2001

David-Neel, Alexandra, *Initiations and Initiates in Tibet*, Rider & Company, London, 1931

Dorjee, Pema, *Stupa and Its Technology: A Tibeto-Buddhist Perspective*, Motilal Banarsidass Publishers, New Delhi, 1996

Dowman, Keith, *The Legend of the Great Stupa: Two Termas from the Nyingma Tradition*, Dharma Publishing, Berkeley, CA, 1973

——— *The Power-Places of Central Tibet: The Pilgrim's Guide*, Routledge, London, 1988

——— *The Divine Madman: The Sublime Life and Songs of Drukpa Kunley*, Pilgrims Publishing, Varanasi, 2000

Dudjum Rinpoche, *Counsels from My Heart*, Shechen Publications, New Delhi, 2004

——— *A Torch Lighting the Way to Freedom*, Shambala Publications, Boston, MA, 2011

Evans-Wentz, W. Y., *The Tibetan Book of the Great Liberation*, Oxford University Press, London, 1954

Fremantle, Francesca and Trungpa, Chogyam, *The Tibetan Book of the Dead*, Shambala Publications, London, 1975

French, Patrick, *Younghusband: The Last Great Imperial Adventurer*, HarperCollins, London, 1994

——— *Tibet, Tibet: A Personal History of a Lost Land*, HarperCollins, London, 2003

Gethin, R. M. L., *The Buddhist Path to Awakening*, Oneworld Publications, Oxford, 2001

Goldberg, Kory and Decary, Michelle, *Along the Path*, Pariyatti Press, Onalaska, WA, 2009

Govinda, Lama Anagarika, *The Way of the White Clouds*, Ebury, London, 1966

——— *Psycho-cosmic Symbolism of the Buddhist Stupa*, Dharma Publishing, Berkeley, CA, 1976

Govinda, Li Gotami, *Tibet in Pictures*, Dharma Publishing, Berkeley, CA, 1979

Gregson, Jonathan, *Kingdoms Beyond the Clouds: Journeys in Search of the Himalayan Kings*, Pan Books, London, 2001

Grunfeld, A. Tom, *The Making of Modern Tibet*, Zed Books, London, 1987

Harewood, George, Earl of, *The Tongs and the Bones: The Memoirs of Lord Harewood*, Weidenfeld & Nicolson, London, 1981

Harrer, Heinrich, *Seven Years in Tibet*, Rupert Hart-Davis, London, 1953

Harvey, Andrew, *A Journey in Ladakh*, Jonathan Cape, London, 1983

Hilton, Isabel, *The Search for the Panchen Lama*, Penguin Books, London, 1999

Hopkirk, Peter, *Foreign Devils on the Silk Road: The Search for the Lost Treasures of Central Asia*, Oxford University Press, Oxford, 1980

—— *Trespassers on the Roof of the World: The Race for Lhasa*, Oxford University Press, Oxford, 1983

Jinpa, Thupten, *A Fearless Heart: Why Compassion is the Key to Greater Wellbeing*, Piatkus, London, 2015

—— *Tsongkhapa: A Buddha in the Land of Snows*, Shambala, Boulder, CO, 2019

Khenchen Thrangu Rinpoche, *The Four Noble Truths*, Namo Buddha Publications, Boulder, CO, 1994

Kojima, Mitsuaki, *The Mystery over Lord Buddha's Roots: An Analysis of the Mystery of the Shakya Kingdom*, Nirala Publications, New Delhi, 2015

Lahiri, Nayanjot, *Ashoka in Ancient India*, Harvard University Press, Boston, MA, 2015

Lawlor, Robert, *Sacred Geometry: Philosophy & Practice*, Thames & Hudson, London, 1982

Lhalungpa, Lobsang P. (trans.), *The Life of Milarepa*, Paladin, London, 1979

Longhurst, A. H., *The Story of the Stupa*, Arvali Books International, New Delhi, 1997 (first published 1936)

Lopez, Donald S. (ed.), *Buddhist Scriptures*, Penguin Books, London, 2004

Losel, Khenpo, *Namo Buddha: The Radiant Light of a Solitary Retreat*, Dharmakara Publications, Kathmandu, 2008

Lundy, Miranda, *Sacred Geometry*, Wooden Books, Glastonbury, 2006

Macdonald, A. W. (ed.), *Mandala and Landscape*, D.K. Printworld, New Delhi, 1997

Mackenzie, Vicki, *Cave in the Snow*, Bloomsbury Publishing, London, 1998

Mauchline, Mary, *Harewood House*, Moorland Publishing, Ashbourne, 1992

Mitra, Swati (ed.), *Walking with the Buddha*, Goodearth Publications, New Delhi, 1999

Moran, Kerry (text) and Johnson, Russell (photos), *Kailas: On Pilgrimage to the Sacred Mountain of Tibet*, Thames & Hudson, London, 1989

Nairn, Rob, *Living, Dreaming, Dying*, Shambala Publications, Boston, MA, 2004

Nanamoli, Bhikku, *The Life of the Buddha*, Buddhist Publication Society, Kandy, Sri Lanka, 1972

Nathwani, Nilesh D., *Kailash Manasarova, Diary of a Pilgrim*, New Age Books, New Delhi, 2005

Norman, Alexander, *Holder of the White Lotus*, Abacus, London, 2009

Olivelle, Patrick (ed.), *Asoka in History and Historical Memory*, Motilal Banarsidass Publishers, New Delhi, 2009

Olschak, Blanche C. (text) and Gansser, Ursula and Augusto (photos), *Bhutan, Land of Hidden Treasures*, George Allen & Unwin, London, 1971

Pommaret, Françoise, *Bhutan*, The Guidebook Company, Hong Kong, 1990

Pritchard-Jones, Sian and Gibbons, Bob, *The Mount Kailash Trek*, Cicerone, Milnthorpe, 2007

Ray, Reginald A., *In the Presence of Masters*, Shambala Publications, Boston, MA, 2004

Shakspo, Nawang Tsering, *A Cultural History of Ladakh*, Centre for Research on Ladakh, Leh, Ladakh, 2010

Sharma, Veena, *Kailash Manasarova, a Sacred Journey*, Roli Books, New Delhi, 2004

Shrady, Nicholas, *Sacred Roads*, Viking, London, 1999

Singh, Rana P. B., *Where the Buddha Walked*, Indica Books, Varanasi, 2003

Snellgrove, David L. and Richardson, Hugh, *A Cultural History of Tibet*, Orchid Press, Bangkok, 2003 (first edition 1968)

Snelling, John, *The Sacred Mountain*, Motilal Banarsidass Publishers, New Delhi, 1990

Snodgrass, Adrian, *The Symbolism of the Stupa*, Motilal Banarsidass Publishers, New Delhi, 1992

Sucitto, Ajahn and Scott, Nick, *Rude Awakenings*, Wisdom Publications, Boston, MA, 2006

Tashi Tsering, Geshe, *The Four Noble Truths*, Wisdom Publications, Boston, MA, 2005

—— *Emptiness*, Wisdom Publications, Boston, MA, 2009

Tenzin Namdak, Lopon, *Bonpo Dzogchen Teachings*, Vajra Publications, Kathmandu, 2006

Thompson, Evan, *Waking, Dreaming, Being*, Columbia University Press, New York, 2015

Thubron, Colin, *To a Mountain in Tibet*, Chatto & Windus, London, 2011

Thurman, Robert and Wise, Tad, *Circling the Sacred Mountain*, Bantam Books, New York, 1999

Titmuss, Christopher, *The Buddha's Book of Daily Meditations*, Rider, London, 2001

Toomey, Christine, *The Saffron Road*, Portobello Books, London, 2015

Tree, Isabella, *The Living Goddess*, Penguin Books, London, 2014

Tsering, Lama, *Dharmakaya Stupa*, Thimphu, Bhutan, 1998

Tsering, Dr Nawang (text) and Arya, Ardita (photos), *Alchi, the Living Heritage of Ladakh*, Central Institute of Buddhist Studies, Leh, Ladakh, 2009

Tsongkhapa, *Lam Rim Chen Mo*, Snow Lion Publications, Ithaca, NY, 2002

Tucci, Giuseppe, *Stupa: Art, Architectonics and Symbolism*, Aditya Prakashan, New Delhi, 1983 (first published Rome 1932)

Van Schaik, Sam, *Tibet – A History*, Yale University Press, New Haven, CT, 2011

Various authors, *Kyichu Lhakhang, the Sacred Jewel of Bhutan*, Gatshel Publishing, Bangkok, 2015

Waddell, L. Austine, *Buddhism of Tibet or Lamaism*, W. H. Allen, London, 1895

White, J. Claude, *Sikkim and Bhutan, Twenty-One Years on the North-East Frontier 1887–1908*, Asian Educational Services, New Delhi, 1996 (first published London 1906)

Winkler, Ken, *A Thousand Journeys: The Biography of Lama Anagarika Govinda*, Element Books, Shaftesbury, 1990

Zangpo, Ngawang, *Guru Rinpoche: His Life and Times*, Snow Lion, New York, 2002

Zopa, Lama, *Benefits and Practices Related to Statues and Stupas*, FPMT Education Dept, Portland, OR, 2003

—— *How to Practice Dharma*, Lama Yeshe Wisdom Archive, Boston, MA, 2012

—— *How to Enjoy Death*, Wisdom Publications, Somerville, MA, 2016

Acknowledgements

This book has been a long time in the writing and a lot of people have played their part in helping me make it a reality. Quite a few of them appear in the book in person but I'm going to attempt to mention and thank those who didn't as well. For anyone I have inadvertently left out, humble apologies, but, as I said, it has been a long time.

The stupa builders: Lama Sonam Choepel, Cheku, Phub Dorji, Kesang Dorji.

The consecration team: Lama Baso Karpo, Rinchen, Lhap Tsering, Phub Dorji, Tsewang Dorji, Tshewang Namgay, Norbu Gyaltsen.

In Bhutan: Chen Chen Dorji, Tobgye Sonam Dorji, Genzing Dorji, Kandu Om Dorji, Chuki Om Dorji, Michael Rutland, Sangay Choden, Dechen Coleman, Emily Lascelles, Judy Alston, Andy Campbell, Pip Heywood, Ali Heywood, Mette Jacobsgaard, Ralph Day, Susy Kirk.

At Harewood: Terry Suthers, Trevor Nicholson, Patrick Graham, Christopher Ussher, Ian Copeland and the stupa building team (Darren Beard, Tony Brown, Ian Harrison, Ed Preston, Ken Wiseman, Jim Galt and Stonecraft), Brenda Grant, Simon Lay, Geetha Uphadyaya, Shree Uphadyaya, Udai Allay, Romilla Subba.

In India and Nepal: Namgyal Dorjee and all the Orient Foundation staff; Lisa Choegyal; James Hopkins; Tsering Dolkar and the staff of the Hotel Tibet International in Boudhanath; Marcus Cotton and the staff of Tiger Mountain Pokhara Lodge; Robert Chilton; Khenpo Rangdol; Dolpo Tulku Rinpoche; Minling Khenchen Rinpoche.

Kailash: Binod Rai and Insight Himalaya, Mike Allen and Ussher Tours, Paul Dolan, Charles Garrad, Ben Lascelles, Orly Lascelles, Eddy Lascelles.

Readers: Polly Feversham, Lynne Green, Rommi Smith, Sara Davies, Nima Poovaya-Smith, Bash Born, Zoe Ross at United Agents, the Unbound team.

I have been lucky enough to meet and in some cases receive teachings from many lamas, including some of the greatest practitioners of the late twentieth and early twenty-first century including: HH the Dalai Lama; HH Rangjung Rigpe Dorje the Karmapa; HH Ngawang Kunga the Sakya Trizin; HH Kyabje Dudjum Rinpoche; HH the Drikung Kyabgon Chetsang; HE the 7th Kyabje Yongzin Ling Rinpoche. And in the UK Geshe Tashi Tsering, the Venerable Mary Reavey and my friends at the Jamyang Buddhist Centres in Leeds and London.

There are three people to whom I am especially grateful.

Thupten Jinpa Langri was there at the very beginning when we identified the possible stupa site at Harewood. He has been a support and guide through the process, especially when I, slightly nervously, sent him an early draft of this book for his comments and to make sure I got all of the Buddhist stories and references right. His positive response and academic rigour mean that I really have no excuse for any errors in the text. Any that remain are entirely my fault.

Graham Coleman and I have been friends for more than fifty years. Without his encouragement and knowledge and without his connections in the Buddhist community worldwide as well as in Bhutan there would not have been a stupa at Harewood. I will never be able to thank him enough for cajoling me into turning what might have remained just a romantic idea into a reality.

And of course Diane Howse: reader, photographer, designer, literary critic. Also best friend and wife of more than thirty years. Without her . . .

A Note on the Author

David Lascelles is a producer of both documentaries and drama for television and the cinema. Several of his films have been nominated for awards, including *Inspector Morse*, *Wide-Eyed and Legless*, *The Fortunes and Misfortunes of Moll Flanders* and *Richard III*. He lives at Harewood in Yorkshire, which has been his family's home since the eighteenth century, and for many years has chaired Harewood House Trust, the educational charitable trust that looks after the house, gardens and collections for the public benefit. On the death of his father in 2011 he became the 8th Earl of Harewood. David has travelled widely in the Himalayas. *A Hare-Marked Moon* is his first book.

Index

343

Unbound is the world's first crowdfunding publisher, established in 2011.

We believe that wonderful things can happen when you clear a path for people who share a passion. That's why we've built a platform that brings together readers and authors to crowdfund books they believe in – and give fresh ideas that don't fit the traditional mould the chance they deserve.

This book is in your hands because readers made it possible. Everyone who pledged their support is listed below. Join them by visiting unbound.com and supporting a book today.

Owen Connor
Teo Connor
Jude Cook
Harry Cooke
Mark R Cordell
Allan Corduner
M Cotton
Jon Crompton
Julian Crowe
Robert Davies
Sara Davies
Ralph Day
Kathy Dean
Yvonne Deane
Richard Demarco
Roland Denning
Anna Dewsnap
Imtiaz Dharker
Diane Dickson
Cathy Dixon
Jamie Durham
Dave Eagle
Amanda Elder
Andrew Esson
Jonathan Eyre
Rachel Feldberg
Lisa Felix
Polly Feversham
Zara Fleming

Peter Foolen
Elizabeth Forbes
Paul Forth
Richard Fullerton
John Furse
Charles Garrad
Pauline Graham-King
Brenda Grant
James Gregory-Monk
Heather Griffiths
Jessica Hackett
Jen Hallam
Andrew Halley
Lavinia Hankinson
Jerry Hardman-Jones
John Hawley
Haworth Tompkins Ltd
Beverly Hetherington
Pip Heywood
Bruce Higham
Jeremy Hill
Julian Honer
James Hopkins
Richard Ingleby
Paul Jabore
Gemma Jackson
Mette Jacobsgaard
Jamyang Buddhist Centre
    Leeds

Marie Jenkins
Christine Johnson
Joshua Johnson
Chris Jones
Geoffrey Jukes
Ashley Karrell
Susan Kellett
Molly Kelly
Dan Kieran
Judy Klinpikuln
Felicity Lane
Ben Lascelles
Benjamin Lascelles
Catherine Lascelles
Eddy Lascelles
Ellen Lascelles
Frieda Lascelles
James Lascelles
Jeremy Lascelles
Julie Lascelles
Margaret Lascelles
Mark Lascelles
Orly Lascelles
Sylvie Lawrence
Peter Le Blond
Andy Leighton
Paul Levy
Virginia Lloyd
Jenny Macqueen

Rachel Mapplebeck
Deborah Marks
Jane Marriott
Peter Marshall
Paula Martin
Selina McGonagle
Ann Means
Scott Meek
Josie Merck
Janet Millar
Rehana Minhas
Umi Mistry
John Mitchinson
Linda Monckton
Christopher & Betsy
    Monger & Zajko
Eleanor Moreton
Anita Morris
Carlo Navato
Susie Needham
John Newby
Sally and Charles Nicholl
William Nicholl
Trevor Nicholson
Kitty North
Bernadette O'sullivan
Hannah Obee
Tim Pearce
Hugo Perks

Liz Phillips
Justin Pollard
Lindsey Porter
Kenneth Powell
Nicky Quint
Jane Rasch
Sofia Rebelo
Ken Reid
Nick Renton
Benjamin Rhodes
Hugh Roberts
Jane Roberts
Elizabeth Rowlands
Barrie Rutter
Fiona Sale
Susan Salierno
Sarah Sarhandi
Anna Scrine
Charles Sebag-Montefiore
Neil Sellers
Laurence Shapiro
Barbara Shard
Claire Shaw
Rebecca Shaw
Michael Shmith
Jay Simpson
Debbie Slater
Daniel Smith
Drew Smith

Wendy Staden
Seth Stein
Nicola Stephenson
Alan Stromberg
Amanda Sturman
Terry Suthers
Andrew Sutton
Sue Swingler
Philippa Taylor
Richard Taylor
Clare Thalmann
Rupert Thorpe
Delma Tomlin
Robert Tunmore
Shripati Upadhyaya
Richard Ussher
Stephanie Volk
Elsie Walker
Poppy Walker
Nigel Walsh
Simon Warner
Rae Williams
Deborah Wilson
Keeley Wilson
Gretchen Woelfle
Nigel Wong
Elijah & Isaiah Wray
Jo Wright